CHURCHILL AND STALIN'S SECRET AGENTS

OPERATION PICKAXE AT RAF TEMPSFORD

BERNARD O'CONNOR

FONTHILL

Fonthill Media Limited
www.fonthillmedia.com
office@fonthillmedia.com

This edition published in the United Kingdom 2012

British Library Cataloguing in Publication Data
A catalogue record for this book is available
from the British Library

ISBN 978-1-78155-002-1 (print)
ISBN 978-1-78155-132-5 (e-book)

Typeset in 9.5/13 pt Sabon
Printed and bound in England.

Connect with us
 facebook.com/fonthillmedia   twitter.com/fonthillmedia

CONTENTS

INTRODUCTION

While I was researching the history of RAF Tempsford, a remote Bedfordshire airfield about 50 miles north of London, I read a book written by one of the pilots who flew from there during the Second World War. In Freddie Clark's *Agents by Moonlight*, he used the Operations Record Books of 138 and 161 Special Duties Squadrons to provide a detailed chronological account of their top secret flights to help the resistance groups in occupied Europe between 1941 and 1945.

In his book, Clark mentioned that on 12 February 1942, the Soviet ship *SS Arcos* docked in a Scottish port and five passengers disembarked. Which port it was, who the passengers were, who they were met by, where they were taken, and what they did over the following few weeks was not stated, but he wrote that on 4 March, three of them arrived at Tempsford and were flown out and parachuted into the Mediterranean area of France.

He added that they were NKVD agents, one of them a woman, and that their mission was to set up a radio link between Lyon and Moscow. In Clark's glossary, I learned that NKVD (*Norodny Kommissariat Vnutrennich Dyel*) was the Soviet People's Commissariat for Internal Affairs – the forerunner of the KGB (*Komitet Gosudarstvennoi Besopastnosti*). I was intrigued.

Two attempts were made later in March to drop the other two agents but the pilots had to abort the missions due to bad weather. On the third attempt, on a night when Bomber Command had cancelled all flights, the station commander insisted that they should go; Wing Commander Farley piloted the flight, crashing a few hours later in dense fog in the Bavarian Alps, killing all on board.

As I'd researched the history of the airfield and the women involved directly and indirectly, and written a book on the American connection with the 'Tempsford Academy', I decided to investigate the story of the Soviet agents.

It has proved a challenge, but I've been able to access contemporary documents in the National Archives, and find published articles, books, and snippets of information on the subject on various websites to put together what I hope you will find to be a fascinating account of the Soviet Union's connection with Tempsford. Rather than a dry historic account, I have tried to provide the human story within a complex web of political intrigue and diplomacy.

I have to acknowledge the work already done by Freddie Clark, Igor Cornelissen, Bickham Sweet-Escott, M. R. D. Foot, Anatoli Granovsky, Martin Kitchen, Frans Kluiters, William Mackenzie, Barry McLoughlin, Gunter Nollau, Donal O'Sullivan, Hans Schafranek, Johannes Tuchel, Hugh Verity, Werner Warmbrunn, and Ludwig Zindel. The National Archives' online catalogue allowed me to identify relevant documents and the staff there very kindly provided access to recently released correspondence and mission papers related to the Soviet missions. Ron Basich helped me obtain copies of documents in the Hoover Institute in California. Sandy Library staff have also been very helpful in locating out-of-county books and articles from academic journals. Steven Kippax and members of the Special Operations Executive user group on yahoo.com have provided answers to my queries and stimulated further research. I am also deeply indebted to Jasper Hadman at Fonthill Media whose editorial insight helped polish what I hope you will find to be a thrilling read.

THE HISTORICAL BACKGROUND

The Molotov-Ribbentrop Pact and the Outbreak of the Second World War

In August 1939, Adolf Hitler, the leader of the ruling National Socialist German Workers (NAZI) party in Germany, having ordered his troops to annex Austria and the Sudetenland in Czechoslovakia the previous year, sent Joachim von Ribbentrop, his foreign minister, to Moscow to liaise with Vyacheslav Molotov, his Soviet counterpart.

Von Ribbentrop offered the Union of Soviet Socialist Republics (USSR) a Nazi-Soviet alliance whereby both parties agreed not to go to war. On 23 August, a 'Non-aggression Pact' was signed which included a 'secret protocol' that only came to light after the downfall of the USSR in 1989. They agreed that each country should be allowed to have their own 'spheres of influence' in Finland, Estonia, Latvia, Lithuania, Romania, and Poland. It amounted to an agreement to invade the countries of Northern and Eastern Europe and divide the land between them. An economic agreement was also reached, which committed the Soviet Union to provide Germany with raw materials and food products in exchange for German manufactured goods.

When Hitler's armed forces attacked Poland on the morning of 1 September 1939, the Soviet army did nothing. Neville Chamberlain, the leader of the British government, stated that if Germany did not withdraw from Poland, one of Britain's allies, then Britain would declare itself at war with Germany. Two days later, as Hitler had not ordered his troops to retreat, the Second World War had begun. On 17 September, Soviet army divisions rolled into eastern Poland to occupy their 'sphere of influence', designated in the secret protocol.

It took only six hours for the Germans to overcome Denmark and a month to force Norway to surrender in April 1940. On 10 May, the Whitsun weekend when most of Western Europe's population was on holiday, Hitler ordered the *Sichelschnitt* – sickle-cut – a surprise military attack through the Low Countries of Holland, Belgium, and Luxembourg, and into France, avoiding the heavily defended Maginot Line along the Franco-German border.

Within weeks, Hitler's forces had reached the coastline and secured ports, airfields, towns, and cities, imposing German rule on a shocked population. The speed and ferocity of armed parachutists and the German Panzer divisions in their push to the North Sea and the English Channel caught the British off-guard. General John Gort, the head of the British Expeditionary Force, ordered a retreat, blowing up bridges as they left. During this *Blitzkrieg* – lightning war – many people fled. Most went south into France, while others managed to catch ships and boats and sailed to Britain, America, or Canada.

Hitler's plans for the domination of Western Europe included utilising airfields in France and the Low Countries for attacks on Britain, and factories to support the Third Reich's war effort. He intended to transport able-bodied men from these countries to supplement the German workforce in lieu of German men called up to fight. Also vital to Hitler's plans was the need to secure transport routes across Northwest Europe, particularly the Atlantic and North Sea ports. The next step, Operation Sea Lion, the seaborne invasion of Great Britain, was soon ready to commence.

Holland surrendered on 15 May, two days after their royal family and government were shipped to safety in England. The Germans pushed through to the coast within days. The Belgian artillery managed to hold off the full force of the *Blitzkrieg* until 28 May, enough time to allow the start of a major evacuation of 338,226 British, Canadian, Belgian, and French soldiers and civilians from the beaches at Dunkirk in northern France. A huge quantity of Allied military equipment and supplies had to be abandoned. Despite approximately 850 boats crossing the English Channel over the few days between 26 May and 4 June 1940, something like 40,000 Allied troops were left behind. They were either defending the main body of troops on the beach or were too sick or wounded to move. Nearly 10,000 surrendered in June 1940 at St Valery-en-Caux; for some, it was the end of the war. Those who were able followed the military directive to escape by any means and make their way back to Britain to rejoin their units.

Britain's Secret Intelligence Service (SIS), the undercover wing of the Foreign Office, known after the war as MI6, needed to rescue key personnel from behind enemy lines. Using their existing contacts, a section known as MI9 helped to establish and fund undercover escape lines in the occupied countries.

Operation Barbarossa

Operation Barbarossa was the Nazi's codename for their invasion of the Soviet Union. When Hitler broke the existing treaty between Germany and the USSR it is said to have come as a complete surprise to the Soviets. It was the largest military offensive in history.

In the early morning of 22 June 1941, over 4.5 million troops of the Axis powers invaded along a 1,800-mile front with about 600,000 motor vehicles and 750,000 horses.[1] When the news reached the War Office in London, Churchill made a number of decisions about how Great Britain would respond. That evening he made a memorable radio broadcast on the Soviet-German War:

> At 4 o'clock this morning Hitler attacked and invaded Russia. All his usual formalities of perfidy were observed with scrupulous technique. A non-aggression treaty had been solemnly signed and was in force between the two countries. No complaint had been made by Germany of its non-fulfilment. Under its cloak of false confidence the German armies drew up in immense strength along a line which stretched from the White Sea to the Black Sea and their air fleets and armoured divisions slowly and methodically took up their stations.
>
> Then, suddenly, without declaration of war, without even an ultimatum, the German bombs rained down from the sky upon the Russian cities; the German troops violated the Russian frontiers and an hour later the German Ambassador, who till the night before was lavishing his assurances of friendship, almost of alliance, upon the Russians, called upon the Russian Foreign Minister to tell him that a state of war existed between Germany and Russia.
>
> ... It follows, therefore, that we shall give whatever help we can to Russia and to the Russian people. We shall appeal to all our friends and Allies in every part of the world to take the same course and pursue it as we shall, faithfully and steadfastly to the end.
>
> We have offered to the Government of Soviet Russia any technical or economic assistance which is in our power and which is likely to be of service to them.[2]

What he did not tell the listeners was that he was prepared to offer assistance to the NKVD in infiltrating their agents into Western Europe. After the fall of France and the Dunkirk evacuation, the German forces prepared to invade Britain. Churchill realised that the only way to defeat the enemy was to invade France and force them back. When Dr Hugh Dalton, the Minister for Economic Warfare, was approached by the Foreign Office about setting up an agreement with the Soviets, the reaction was said to have been one of alarm. Charles de Gaulle's Free French section vetoed it. Despite this, M. R. D. Foot comments that, 'agile as a seasoned Marxist hard-liner,' SOE (Special Operations Executive) reversed its line overnight to conform to the Prime Minister's wishes. From now on, anyone the Nazis attacked was SOE's friend as well as Churchill's.[3]

THE SOE AND THE NKVD

The Creation of the Special Operations Executive

Before the war, the British government relied on the Secret Intelligence Service (SIS), spies working for the Foreign Office, as well as Military Intelligence. In 1938, Lord Halifax, Lord Hankey, Colonel Jo Holland, and others formed what became known as Section D. The D was said to stand for destruction. With the country facing the imminent threat of invasion, these men presented Winston Churchill, the British Home Secretary and First Lord of the Admiralty, with their plans for an intelligence agency which was independent of the SIS. Churchill was enthusiastic about the idea and asked Neville Chamberlain, the Prime Minister, to draft a charter for such an organisation. In May 1940, the Special Operations Executive was formed. Its official mission was 'to co-ordinate all action by way of subversion and sabotage against the enemy overseas'.[1] The chances of landing Allied agents on closely guarded coasts or passing them through the strict border controls of neutral countries were negligible. The best way in was by plane.

By early summer 1940, there was growing demand from resistance movements in occupied Europe and North Africa for weapons, ammunition, explosives and supplies of every kind. Efforts to locate these groups, and to encourage, finance, and co-ordinate their activities were continually blighted by a shortage of information.

In mid-summer 1940, Sir Stewart Menzies, the head of SIS, approached the Air Ministry with the suggestion that they parachute agents into occupied territory and attempt to land aircraft to pick up VIPs who could be useful for the war effort. Many people of great value to Britain and her allies had been left behind when the Germans overran France and the Low Countries. Some stayed on deliberately to train local populations to oppose the German assimilation of the conquered territories. These secret operatives occasionally needed to be brought back to England for debriefing and additional training before, if they were willing and able, they were sent back on new missions.

The urgency of the situation was taken on board and the SOE was formed. Its first head was conservative MP Sir Frank Nelson, who was in office until 1942. He was followed by Sir Charles Hambro, his former deputy, who at 30 had been the youngest ever director of the Bank of England. According to Graham Smith, the author of several books about Second World War airfields, the SOE 'had largely been the brainchild of Dr Hugh Dalton, the Minister for Economic Warfare, who intended that it would be used as a "Fourth Arm" or "Secret Army". The Executive's intention was to undertake irregular warfare in all forms.... Winston Churchill thought that this Fourth Arm would "Set Europe Ablaze!"'[2]

As we shall see, the kindling and matches were mostly supplied from RAF Tempsford, a remote Bedfordshire airfield, as were many of the people who would start the fires or train others how to. Irregular warfare involved teaching both men and women to kidnap, steal, cheat, or kill by the quickest, most ungentlemanly means possible. It also included propaganda. Hugh Davies, an SOE historian, told me that Churchill's idea, until the USA joined the war, was 'to rot the buggers from within'.

Dalton had been one of the officers in Military Intelligence (Research), a secret War Office department whose job had been to investigate irregular ways of causing problems for the German forces occupying Europe. He had written handbooks on guerrilla warfare and in 1939 had been working in Poland for Section D, a department of the SIS with headquarters in Broadway Buildings, near St James Park in London. Dalton was concerned with organising covert action in countries likely to come under Axis control; his plans were outlined in a memorandum he wrote to Lord Halifax, the Foreign Secretary, on 3 July 1940:

> We have got to organise movements in enemy-occupied territory comparable to the Sinn Fein movement in Ireland, to the Chinese Guerrillas now operating against Japan, to the Spanish Irregulars who played a notable part in Wellington's campaign or – one might as well admit it – to the organisations which the Nazis themselves had developed so remarkably in almost every country in the world. This 'democratic international' must use many different methods, including industrial and military sabotage, labour agitation and strikes, continuous propaganda, terrorist acts against traitors and German leaders, boycotts and riots.
>
> It is clear to me that an organisation on this scale and of this character is not something which can be handled by the ordinary department machinery of either the British Civil Service or the British military machine. What is needed is a new organisation to co-ordinate, inspire, control and assist the nationals of the oppressed countries who must themselves be the direct participants. We need absolute secrecy, a certain fanatical enthusiasm, willingness to work with people of different nationalities, complete political reliability. Some of these qualities are certainly to be found in some military officers and, if such men are available, they should undoubtedly be used. But the organisation should, in my view, be entirely independent of the War Office machine.[3]

There were difficulties initially in persuading Lord Harris, the Marshal of the Royal Air Force, to divert aircraft engaged in the country's defence to the Special Duties Squadrons, set up specifically to carry out missions for the SOE and SIS. Harris was loath to supply aircraft 'to carry ragamuffins to distant spots, in pursuit of objects no one seems anxious to explain.' Lord Portal, Chief of the Air Staff is quoted in Andre Hue and Ewen Southby-Tailyour's *The Next Moon* as saying to one of the SOE officers, 'Your work is a gamble which may give us a valuable dividend or may produce nothing.... My bombing offensive is not a gamble. Its dividend is certain; it is a gilt-edged investment. I cannot divert aircraft from a certainty to a gamble.'[4] As we shall see, the successes of some of the SOE operations helped those in the upper echelons of the SOE to persuade their critics in the Air Ministry to change their minds.

These 'Special Operations' were to be an 'invisible front', acts of 'unattributable' industrial sabotage, the raising and supplying of secret armies and the collecting of intelligence, all done under what M. R. D. Foot, the SOE historian, describes as 'the dense fog of secrecy'. The people employed by the SOE were termed by some as 'The Baker Street Irregulars'. Those in the know called the organisation 'The Firm', 'The Outfit', or 'The Racket'; for everyone else it was the Inter-Services Research Bureau. Its five-floor office block at 64 Baker Street in the Marylebone district of Westminster needed War Department cover, so the name MOI (SP) was coined and its telephone number was added to the War Office directory. Captain Peter Lee, an officer in MOI's security section, called it 'terribly clever. We said it stood for "Mysterious Operations in Special Places". We reckoned the Germans, with their lack of sense of humour, would never be able to unravel that one.'[5] Major Len Manderstam, an SOE officer who was later transferred to their Russian Section, commented:

> The organisation took over a role that had previously been the responsibility of several departments. It made up the rules as it went along and was loathed in the upper echelons of the Foreign Office, who looked upon SOE as beyond the pale, rather as a maiden aunt might regard a niece who had become a successful call girl.
>
> The Foreign Office, rulers of Britain's secret services for generations, preferred to operate in less direct ways. I called them 'the spooky boys'. But we were spooky boys, too. We had to bury our identities and live the roles we had been given.[6]

While all this planning was going on, Britain was under air attack. Virtually every night, Hermann Göring, the head of the Luftwaffe, ordered German heavy bombers, protected by Messerschmitt fighter planes, to attack Britain's shipping convoys, its naval shipyards and port facilities, RAF airfields, aircraft factories, transport infrastructure, and by autumn 1940, the country's heavy industrial and commercial centres.

The NKVD

The Soviet Union's equivalent of SIS and SOE was the *Norodny Kommissariat Vnutrennich Dyel* (NKVD), the People's Commissariat for Internal Affairs, which replaced the Russian Tsar's police force after the communist revolution in 1917. Its multifarious role included policing traffic, guarding the borders, looking after the country's archives, conducting mass executions, running the gulags (the penal labour camps responsible for building roads and canals), suppressing underground resistance, conducting mass deportations to unpopulated parts of the country, undertaking espionage and political assassinations abroad, influencing foreign governments, and enforcing Josef Stalin's policies in communist countries elsewhere.

In William Mackenzie's *The Secret History of the SOE*, he considered the NKVD organisation to be

> the only one among the Allies (or among the enemy for that matter) which approached the theoretical conception of an all-embracing service dealing with all subversion and also with all 'black' activities of whatever kind. It embraced within itself all the activities dispersed among various secret or semi-secret organisations in Great Britain – M.I.5, the 'Special branch', S.O.E., S.I.S., P.W.E. [Political Warfare Executive]; it also had pretty large general responsibility for propaganda, internal and external; and (like Himmler's organisation) it tended in some cases to become a State within a State. In relation to this body S.O.E. was a junior organisation dealing with one which had great power and endless ramifications outside S.O.E.'s sphere; the direct contacts which S.O.E. possessed were only with one corner of N.K.V.D. – the internal reactions of that organisation as a whole remained mysterious to the end.[7]

The NKVD operated under Stalin's close supervision as, since the 1930s, he had shaped this Commissariat as his most valuable tool. Historian Donal O'Sullivan claims that Stalin effectively ran the Commissariat, selected its mid-rank officials, supervised interrogation procedures, sometimes participating in the questioning of prominent victims, and edited 'confessions' obtained during the show trials.[8]

When the NKVD was taken over by 30-year-old Pavel Fitin in 1939, he dispatched about 200 officers with diplomatic cover to forty stations abroad, as well as an unspecified number of 'illegals', agents working for the Soviet Union. In the United States, China, Italy, Germany, France, and Great Britain, Soviet intelligence was said to able to count on more than 600 'sources'.[9]

Alexander Korotkov was responsible for the selection and training of the NKVD's agents in Red Army camps at Pushkino and Pionerskaya near Moscow. He had worked for the NKVD in Vienna, Copenhagen, and Berlin in the 1930s. Major Maria Polyakova was an instructor at one of the camps. In March 1942,

George Hill, SOE's man in Moscow, was taken by General Alexander 'Ossipov' (real name Gaik Ovakimyan) to visit a partisan camp south of the capital. Unknown to Hill or the SOE, Ossipov had just returned to Moscow having been expelled from the United States on espionage charges. Out in the woods, Hill was introduced to a man called Batka.

> ... we compared SOE and NKVD training methods, aims, arms, equipment and particularly wireless equipment and technique. I didn't think much of their equipment. Rather poor battery sets with a short range. These partisans had nothing like the speed of sending and receiving that we train our men to. However, they have a simple, quite brilliant method of coding which we could copy. None of these men had ever parachuted, nor had they been in an aeroplane. Their general training seems to be rather similar to SOE's, perhaps a bit more thorough on physical training. They are equipped with a knife, rather like ours, for stabbing, only theirs is rather like that of the Gurkas with a double purpose blade for hacking and stabbing. Instead of carrying the knife on the edge of a coat, theirs is fitted into a slot made in the top of their jackboots. I did not think very much of their compasses, small, no night sights, and rather unsteady in comparison with our issue. I formed a poor opinion of four of these partisans. By my standards they would have been out. None of them would have passed our wireless standards in sending or receiving.
>
> ...While we encourage resistance in every form; train agents and saboteurs, supply arms, munitions, money, but we urge Partisan leaders in the field to take no action until instructed to do so. We do not want waste and unco-ordinated action. We shun useless sacrifice, waste of life and liberty. Soviet policy chooses just the opposite policy. They demand action all the time. The more partisans that are killed, the greater will be reaction in the masses to the invader. Reprisals by the enemy for sabotage and partisan activities in towns and villages by executing men, women and children, and leaving corpses exposed to public gaze, serves to anger the population and drive them to fresh activities. Not alone does the Red Army work on the principle that man power is expendable, for the NKVD does the same. Sabotage is a nasty, mean business, dirtier I hold than Secret Services. Both have to be ruthless to get results, whether it be by our SOE methods or the NKVD.[10]

All prospective agents being sent to Britain were said to have had lessons in conspiracy, radio communication and ciphers. As Korotkov had returned to Moscow in 1941 after operating in Berlin, he knew which papers and documents agents needed. At one training school the 'students' lived outside during both summer and winter, only using the buildings for classes and housing their instructors.[11]

Further details about the Soviet agents' preparation come from Johann Sanitzer, a Gestapo officer and member of the German Intelligence Service who was captured and interrogated after the war. He said that his interrogations of captured agents had revealed that there was also an NKVD/Comintern training school at Kushnarenko, near Moscow.

> Five or six agents lived there together in one bungalow. Each had been given a cover name and was under strict orders not to reveal anything about their backgrounds to each other. They were trained in handling explosives, guns and conditions in their target country. The agents dropped in Austria told the Gestapo that they had been instructed by a female NKVD major, approximately 35 years old, medium height, dark hair [the British files included a handwritten remark 'Polyakova GRU' – Glavnoye Razvedyvatel'noye Upravleniye – the foreign military intelligence directorate of the Red Army]. She was married to an Austrian Schutzbund member called Dobritzberger.

On the eve of their departure, the agents were given their orders which they had to read, sign and return. A clause stipulated that they were cognizant to suffer 'any punishment' should they fail in their mission or betray any secrets.[12]

Military Detachment 113 – NKVD's Espionage School

Whether any of the Soviet agents destined for Britain attended the Bykovo espionage school has not been documented in their SOE files, but Anatoli Granovsky's account of his training by the NKVD provides fascinating insight into the preparations that were made for Soviet agents destined to be sent abroad. After a short course in basic military training, Granovsky was sent to Bykovo on the banks of the River Verekya, about 30 miles south of Moscow, partly to improve his shooting and practice jumping and landing skills, but mostly to master espionage skills. The three-storey granite building with green slated turrets dated back to Tsarist times, in a style reminiscent of a fifteenth-century *schloss*. The count had been dispossessed and the property, surrounded by high walls, was guarded day and night by plain-clothes NKVD men. Inside, the great hall was covered in mahogany parquet flooring and the walls were painted with murals above the oak panelling. Although it was known as 'Military Detachment 113', students were not allowed to send correspondence with that address or let anyone know where they were.

The commandant was Major General Sudoplatov, described as vastly experienced in the field of espionage, mathematically efficient, strong, energetic, with a tremendous memory for detail and a cool, incisive mind. There were about a hundred students for each course, divided into groups of fifteen, each with a commander and radio telegraphist.

Granovsky was given individual tuition. He described being taken into a private room, given a sheet of paper on which five fictitious situations had been typed and told to study and develop them as convincingly as he could. This, he explained, was the NKVD terminology for writing a legend, or in SOE parlance, a cover story. In the first he had to imagine he was a Red Army officer captured in combat by the Germans. In the second he was a wounded soldier, unnoticed by the Russian medical staff and captured by the Germans. In the third he was a Red Army deserter, throwing himself on the mercy of German front-line troops. In the fourth he was a Red paratrooper dropped behind enemy lines and giving himself up. And in the last he was a civilian who presents himself as a refugee to the Germans, either having crossed the frontier or having found his hometown overrun.

Granovsky was given pen, paper, and ink and proceeded to write how he would convince the Germans that they could trust him. Knowing his stories would be scrutinised by his superiors, Granovsky had to make them as realistic as possible. He told of how he had given himself up to the Germans of his own free will, was glad to find himself in their hands, and that he hated the Soviet regime. In reality, he was being sent to make contact in order to gain freedom of movement for espionage purposes.

After breakfast they had lessons in map-reading, sketch-map drawing, pathfinding, and 'woodmanship' (fieldcraft), and after lunch there was practical work in the grounds of the estate. It was always practice and theory. Everything they did was carefully criticised until they no longer made mistakes.

All the time the students were being closely observed; their habits, mannerisms, even their language was sedulously watched until the NKVD officers knew them better than they knew themselves. The pitch of their voice, hesitations in answering, the way they ate, the way they smoked a cigarette, even the way they moved their hands in different situations was commented on and criticised. The officers tolerated no excuses. Inconvenient habits had to be removed and substituted with proper, reliable and controlled reactions.

Although physically and mentally exhausting, there was no alternative. Granovsky admitted that he had to endure it as the alternative would have meant years in Siberia. He was trained to be accepted by the Germans, to win their trust and be of service when the time was ripe. To ensure he kept to his legends, every few days he had to rewrite them from memory. Initially, there were the inevitable slight differences or omissions which were minutely criticised until he made no mistakes. 'Memory had to be developed', he said, 'there is no limit to its possibilities.' It had to be as reliable as a photographic archive. It was drummed into him that memory was the key.

He was given sketch maps and told to memorise them within certain amounts of time and then reproduce them perfectly, sometimes over a week later, sometimes after vigorous exercises. Sometimes he would be woken in the middle of the night and expected to reproduce the layout of some factory building.

He was also given lessons in love-making. He was told that the directors of some important organisations in the West were women. As they were able to direct national affairs, agents or counter-agents needed to learn how to influence them. These women would not succumb to offers of money, invitations to parties or gifts of jewellery, but a young, ardent and skilled lover was an extraordinary gift.

It was explained that men had an ingrained habit of asking women for advice and that consequently, wives had an indirect influence over a nation's affairs, out of all proportion to their qualifications. Women could be an invaluable help to an agent in bringing a subject round to a desired way of thinking. Should the agent fail to commit himself and fail sexually, all his efforts could be nullified.

NKVD agents were expected to seduce married women and get them to encourage their husbands to have a more sympathetic attitude towards communism. It was drummed into them that they had to let the woman know that they loved them, that she excited them; if they were successful in love-making, she would love them. Granovsky remembered being told that a woman's love is more passionate and less selfish than a man's in all its manifestations, except the sexual one. Not being able to satisfy a woman's sexual urges arouses her contempt and boredom. Men become tedious, even hated. Students were shown charts showing various parts of a woman's anatomy. It was purely academic, with nothing about emotional involvement.

There were also practical lessons with local girls, sometimes more than one, and often with an instructor present. The point was made very strongly that emotions and weakness of the flesh had to be mastered. The mind of the true *tchekist* had to be concentrated on the objective and how to achieve it. There had to be no preconceptions, no absolute truths, no principles and no values other than efficiency. He was expected to be the perfect servant and guardian of the State, to train incessantly until he became a 'one hundred per cent efficient human machine'.[13]

The Soviet agents, termed Pickaxes, were either émigrés from Germany, Austria, Holland, and France, or Soviet citizens who had earlier experience in working for the NKVD. All had to have foreign language skills. Most were ardent communist supporters; some had held high positions in their country's communist parties or trade unions. In Barry McLoughlin's article, *Proletarian Cadres en Route*, he claims that the NKVD based political considerations over age, enthusiasm, physical fitness, and sound military training. While some were 'good proletarians', motivated by a desire to return to their homeland, there was a common desire to defeat the Nazis and reinstate Social Democracy. To be dropped by parachute or landed by boat or submarine behind enemy lines demanded a degree of courage, but unlike the agents sent in by the SOE, SIS and the American Office of Strategic Services (OSS), the Soviet agents have been largely forgotten or rebranded as 'traitors', 'wreckers', and 'enemies of the people'. There appeared to be no attempt to criticise bad planning or faulty decision making on behalf of the NKVD.[14]

As NKVD personnel and operational files have not been released, one needs to understand that what follows is based largely on the evidence found in British documents and therefore cannot be considered impartial.

SOE's Russian Section

SOE had sections for all the countries it dealt with. In Barry McLoughlin's article, 'Proletarian Cadres en Route', he states that the Russian Section, D/P, originally consisted of a Country and a Liaison Section which were later merged under the command of Major A. D. Seddon. Like Major General Colin Gubbins, then head of SOE, Seddon had served with British interventionist forces during the Russian Civil War. Assisting him in the Country Section were Captain A. L. McLaughlin (ex-Territorial Army), Captain W. Wild, Captain J. G. Darton, women from the FANY (First Aid Nursing Yeomanry) and White Russian émigrés of NCO rank. [15]

The Liaison Section was run jointly by George Wiskeman, who had been in the Scandinavian Section, and 48-year-old Major George Hill, who was working in SOE's 'D' Section. Hill had worked as an SIS agent for and against Russia during the First World War. He worked alongside 'Sidney Reilly', another SIS agent who, according to M. R. D. Foot, almost toppled Lenin's shaky original regime altogether. They were both awarded the Military Cross.[16]

Hill claimed to have won the confidence of Trotsky and to have helped develop both the Cheka, the precursor of the NKVD and KGB, and the military intelligence organisation for the Bolshevik army, later the GRU. Among his adventures was a sabotage mission in Russia. He had also been a source handler there, but many of them were tracked down by the Russians and shot. After the First World War, Hill continued to work for SIS. He transported the Romanian crown jewels through five battlefronts, worked as Trotsky's air adviser and wrote a number of amusing books about his experiences. Fluent in Russian, almost so in German, and with a fair knowledge of Bulgarian, he was keen to join the Secret Service but he believed that Menzies vetoed his application. Menzies argued that he had 'blown' his cover by publishing two books about his SIS exploits in the 1930s.[17]

Hill contacted his literary agent who commissioned him to write three articles on sabotage for *The War,* a new magazine, at 30 guineas each.

> The first article dealt simply with the fundamentals of sabotage, the unarmed combat weapon of a civilian population under enemy occupation. The dropping of lumps of sugar in a petrol tank, a handful of fine sand in the hot box of a railway truck, a sharp knife to puncture a tyre, the cutting of telegraph wires, and the changing of destination labels on railway trucks to cause confusion on congested railways, tricks that I had practised in Russia and occupied Ukrania in 1917 and 1918.[18]

Hill was invited for lunch at St Ermin's Hotel, SIS's offices off Victoria Street, and was asked by Major Laurence Grand to join SOE's 'D' Section (Sabotage) on the fourth floor. As his 'parish' was Northern Europe, he set about making a study of each country, the leading personalities in politics, the press, British and

French diplomatic and Consular representatives, the strength of the police, and the German influence and menace. Making contact with France's Secret Service based in offices on Duke Street, London, was also a high priority, as was updating his knowledge of high explosives and codes. After attending a course at Aston House, outside Stevenage, he spent time liaising with his French counterparts in Paris. When his attempt to supply the Belgian resistance with explosives and detonators, what he called 'sweets' and 'toys', was thwarted by the German advance, he drove a modified Rolls Royce to Bordeaux and caught the last cruiser back to England in June 1940.[19]

He was then sent by Grand to run his newly established explosives training school at Brickendonbury Manor, outside Hertford. While there, with 'D's agreement, he set up a separate skeleton section to deal with developments in the USSR.

> I held, and 'D' agreed with me, that the USSR would either in the course of the war, come in with Hitler against us, or Hitler would turn on the USSR. In either case it would be wise to have a nucleus section to hand. A room was put aside for this purpose in one of the buildings in Baker Street, S.O.E.'s new headquarters, for the embryo Russian section, with maps and card indexes, which I kept with the assistance of my secretary, Miss Angela Hatfield.[20]

Between Baker Street and Brickendonbury, setting up SOE's Russian section in May 1941, Hill also spent time helping train agents at Group B's 'Finishing School' at Beaulieu. SOE had requisitioned eleven large country houses in the grounds of Lord Montagu's estate in the New Forest where agents were trained in clandestine operations. This included physical exercise, choosing and describing suitable dropping zones, setting up and training reception committees, learning correct procedures for parachute drops and landings, codes and ciphers, map reading, microphotography, disguises, how to use and arrange messages on the BBC, ways of recognising and making forgeries, use of new weapons, burglary, safe and lock breaking, withstanding interrogation and torture. There was also spycraft: constant vigilance, organising safe letter boxes and safe houses, using 'cut-outs', recognising enemy counter-intelligence uniforms, memorising a cover story, and finally, two- or three-day missions to different towns or cities to practise clandestine activities.

Hill's fellow instructor, Kim Philby, described him as immensely paunchy and referred to him as 'Jolly George Hill'. He once said that he was the only man he had ever met who had sabotaged trains by putting sand in their axle boxes. Others referred to him as 'Uncle' or 'Pop' as he was so much older than them.[21]

The Russian-speaking personnel Hill recruited for the Russian Section included Major A. D. Seddon, Major Charles Milnes-Gaskell, Second Lieutenant R. F. Hingley, Second Lieutenant M. O. Walshe, Captain W. S. Morgan, Lieutenant

R. Schlee, Lieutenant L. Knoop (later known as Connop), and Lieutenant M. R. Chaplin. All were sent to observe the agents' training programme at Beaulieu. From there they were sent to Special Training School (STS) 26, Arisaig, in desolate and windswept Inverness-shire, north-west Scotland, where they observed agents being taught what was termed 'ungentlemanly warfare'. This included outdoor survival, weapons training, sabotage, unarmed combat, and silent killing. Afterwards, they went to Oxford for a refresher course in the Russian language. This provided them with intimate knowledge of what the Pickaxe agents would need for their overseas missions.

RAF TEMPSFORD

In response to SIS's enquiry, the Special Duties Squadrons were created to carry out missions into Europe, North Africa, and later in the war, the Far East. What was known as 419 Flight was initially based on the heath at Newmarket Racecourse, about 12 miles east of Cambridge, but the planes were eventually allocated a proper airfield with concrete runways. As shall be seen, RAF Tempsford was chosen to be 419's base and it went on to play a vital role in Churchill's plan 'to set Europe ablaze'.

Everton Heath, on top of the 200-foot-high Greensand Ridge in north-east Bedfordshire, was a large area of relatively flat, well-drained, light, sandy soil. As early as 1936, it had been pinpointed as a potential site for an airfield. When the landowner, Leslie Pym MP, was approached by the Air Ministry, he expressed opposition to the proposal. He claimed that it would interfere with the shooting parties that he hosted on his estate.

After war broke out, Britain's merchant navy, which was bringing in imported food supplies, was under constant threat by the German navy while the country was under threat of invasion. More airfields were needed. The top of the Greensand Ridge was now thought to be too exposed for an airfield engaged in top secret missions. It would be easily visible to any enemy planes that broke through the defences approaching from the east. Also, the market gardening land was now considered invaluable for food production. Mr Pym therefore volunteered an alternative site on the poorly drained clay land skirting the west facing slopes of the Greensand Ridge. This was land on Gibraltar, Port Mahon and Waterloo Farms, named following his ancestors' military successes during the Napoleonic Wars.

During the Great Depression of the 1930s, many of the tenant farmers on the Pym Estate had given up farming. It was uneconomic and they couldn't afford to pay the rents. Some farms went untenanted. Many of the farm buildings were empty and the fields had become overgrown.

The site eventually chosen by the Air Ministry was on what was called 'Tempsford Flats', an area with a number of natural advantages. The plan was for a Class A standard airfield to act as a satellite to RAF Bassingbourn, a small

Cambridgeshire village about 11 miles to the south-east, which was being used by Bomber Command. Apart from being at the foot of the Greensand Ridge, the new airfield was about as far from the coast as any could be. It was also almost completely flat and largely overgrown with hawthorn bushes, which attracted colonies of blackbirds and flocks of nightingales. William Flint, the then tenant on Waterloo Farm (now Fernbury Farm), was said to have paid his rent from shooting rabbits.

The area designated for the airfield was on the eastern banks of the River Ivel, about a mile and a half wide and about 10 miles long – easily enough room to build three concrete runways, a perimeter track, hangars, and administration and accommodation buildings. As it was aligned roughly south-west–north-east, the site was ideal for a main runway to allow planes to take advantage of the prevailing south-westerly winds.

The soil was heavy, yellow Oxford clay, and rock and boulder free so it could easily be worked. To the west was the main London to Edinburgh railway line of the London and North-Eastern Railway (LNER), which usefully limited access to the site to Everton level crossing and Tempsford railway station, just over a mile to the north-west. To the east ran the old Roman Road, a public bridleway running roughly north–south along the base of the west-facing Greensand Ridge. Bisecting it on an east–west line was the road down the hill from Everton to Tempsford.

There were no built-up areas nearby and the population density within a 10-mile radius was very low. The nearest villages of Everton and Tempsford were small agricultural communities where no major interest might be expected to arise from an isolated airfield. The only drawback was that this low-lying area of the Great Ouse and Ivel Valleys often experienced heavy mist and dense fogs that rolled inland from the Wash.

By October 1940, work had started on the drainage. Draining the heavy clay soil meant miles of ditches had to be dug, almost 10 feet deep in places. The footings for the three runways consisted of bricks and building rubble brought in by trucks from the bombed out parts of London and Peterborough. One section was reported to be 9 feet thick.

A line of ancient elm trees on top of the ridge to the east between St Mary's Church and Storey Farm on the Woodbury Estate was cut down to facilitate an easier landing for returning pilots.

Because of the top secret nature of the Special Duties Squadrons, the airfield was said to have been designed by an illusionist. Jasper Maskelyne, described by David Fisher, his biographer, as 'The War Magician', had entertained audiences in London theatres in the 1930s; when war was declared, he volunteered his services to the War Department.

Maskelyne and his 'Magic Gang' were involved in numerous deceptions against the Germans, Tempsford Airfield was just one example. It was built to resemble a disused airfield. Some of the farm labourers' cottages and farm buildings were demolished. A local man told me that his first job when he was 16 was working for Laings, the construction firm that had won the building contract. He recalled sitting on the roof of Gibraltar Farm, on the north side of the road between Everton and Tempsford, taking its slate tiles off and throwing them into the farmyard below. A contemporary photograph showed one of the double gable end roofs had been dismantled. To make the building look even more derelict, the glass in the widows was deliberately broken. Sacks were draped across the inside of the window frames in front of the black-out curtains. Some of the doors were left rickety, hanging from only one hinge. Much of the black Bedfordshire weather-boarding was removed. The adjacent farm buildings got the same treatment and visitors reported seeing them mildewed, cobwebbed, and covered in mouldering thatch.

Inside Gibraltar Farm it was a different matter. The walls were reinforced to withstand bomb damage. It was said that the stairs, ceiling, and first floor were removed to create a large control room and office. A large table stood in the middle of the room on which several maps of Europe and aerial photographs of the proposed dropzones could be spread out. One wall had a huge blackboard on which details of the night's missions were chalked up, and another had an enormous map attached which stretched from the Arctic Circle in the north to North Africa in the south, and from Ireland in the west to Poland and the Soviet Union in the east. One of those step ladders usually used in libraries to reach the books on the upper shelves was used to allow one of the WAAFs (Women's Auxiliary Air Force) to stick different coloured little flags in to pinpoint the destinations of the planes flying each night.

This was to become the airfield's nerve centre where only authorised personnel were allowed entry. All the hangars and domestic buildings were camouflaged to blend in with the surrounding farmland and some new ones were said to have been thatched – to give the impression that they were farm buildings. Nissen huts resembled pig sties or cow sheds. Some locals say that tarpaulins were draped over hangars and some of the administration buildings on which dilapidated buildings had been painted. The roofs of the nearby Cardington hangars, in which kite balloons were made, were painted to resemble the rooftops of the adjacent rows of Victorian terraced housing.

Outside Gibraltar Farm, the pond was left with a few odd ducks. Genuine tractors were left, and driven occasionally in the fields and yards. The runways were painted grey and green in places to look like they were overgrown. At one point a thick black line was painted across the runway, to give overflying pilots the impression that it was the continuation of a hedge. Cattle were deliberately grazed on some of the fields when the runways were not in use to fool any overflying German pilots into thinking that it was an old airfield now used for agriculture. The disguises succeeded. Even though over 2,000 personnel were eventually based at RAF Tempsford, it is thought that German intelligence decided that the site was a disused airfield.

The local people knew there was an airfield, but they were not allowed access during the fourteen nights between the waxing and waning of the full moon. It was on these nights, weather permitting, that the planes took off. Chains were padlocked around the telephone boxes to ensure no one made any out-going calls. Signs saying 'Road closed to the public' were erected at each end of the minor road between Everton and Tempsford, and armed guards manned the barriers. For security reasons, many of those who had some involvement with the airfield called it 'Gibraltar Farm' or 'Tempsford Station'. Locals never knew what went on there. They were not supposed to.

The First Arrivals at Tempsford

When the Special Duties Squadron was offered 'Gibraltar Farm' they took it. Reassigned 1419 Flight, they arrived on 1 March 1941, bringing four Wellington IIIs to trial TR 1335 or 'GEE', top secret radio navigation equipment. On the airfield it was known as 'A' Flight and was joined by members of the Free Fighting Forces, mostly French and Polish pilots and crews who had arrived in England after their countries were overrun by invading German forces. Regarding security at 'Tempsford Station', Hugh Verity, author of *We Landed by Moonlight* and one of the Special Duties Squadron pilots, comments:

> The Squadron Record Book in the early days was deliberately vague. In 419 Flight ... the security blanket was really tight – no base airfield names, nor target names were allowed in log books. The intelligence officer at Newmarket did not know the real function, although he knew the area of each operation. There were a number of different clients, none of whom wanted any of the others to know about their operations. In fact SIS forbade any written matter. Their operations were 'officially inadmissible'.[1]

As the SOE was a military organisation, it decided on what and who was to be sent where and when, and then gave the job to 1419 Squadron. This squadron was renamed 138 Squadron on 25 August 1940, and became the air arm for the SOE, the SIS, and the SAS (Special Air Service).

Once established at 'Tempsford Station', the 'Moon Squadrons', as they became known, were allocated other planes including the much larger Short Stirling and the Handley Page Halifax bomber for parachute drops, and Hudsons and Lysanders for landing and pick-up operations. On Valentine's Day 1942, 161 Squadron was formed. Although based at Tempsford, during the nights of the full moon they changed camp to RAF Tangmere, near Christchurch on the south coast. From here their STOL (Short Take Off and Landing) Lysanders could reach deeper into France and the Whitleys and Hudsons could go further into Europe.

The larger planes had to be modified to carry containers, packages, and parachutists, while the smaller Lysander was adapted to carry secret agents to areas within a 500-mile radius of the English coast, limiting its field of operations to France. Once the passengers got out with their luggage, the England-bound passengers climbed in. These VIPs included military personnel, politicians, industrialists, resistance leaders, and secret agents who had been in the field for some time and needed bringing back. Occasionally, downed aircrew and escaped prisoners-of-war were returned this way, but they usually made their way back via escape lines over the Alps into Switzerland or the Pyrenees into Spain, and from there, via Portugal or Gibraltar back to Britain.

Missions to nineteen countries flown from RAF Tempsford show the airfield's importance. Major Robert Fish, the operations officer of the American 'Carpetbaggers' missions, which assisted SOE in its special operations from Tempsford initially and then later from RAF Harrington, recalled seeing huge wall maps in the operations rooms at Gibraltar Farm. There was a tiny flag for each drop reception ground and landing field in Europe. There were thousands of flags, from the tip of Norway to the remotest corner of Austria. Hundreds clustered around Paris, Oslo, Copenhagen, Brest, and Brussels. There were even drop areas outside Berlin and Hamburg and in the Bavarian mountains.[2]

THE SOE AND NKVD AGREEMENT

As early as December 1940, Sir Stewart Menzies, codenamed 'C', had suggested that the SOE should send a representative to Moscow. His suggestion, however, was not acted upon. Another suggestion was made in March 1941, but again, it was declined. The following month, Sir Stafford Cripps, the openly pro-Soviet British Ambassador in Moscow, suggested indirect contact with the Czechs 'who were always careful to maintain intimate relations with Moscow'. When this was not pursued, Stafford Cripps approached Stalin about the possibility of an SOE officer being attached to the Embassy. The Soviet leader proposed that the British and Soviet subversive warfare organisations should work together in Germany, the Balkans, and in other areas.[1]

Stalin's far-reaching and enthusiastic response took London by surprise. They encouraged Stafford Cripps to secure Soviet agreement to a formal, five-point agenda for discussion. The ambassador regarded 'such pussyfooting as otiose', and demanded a senior SOE representative to be sent immediately to enter into direct negotiations with the NKVD.[2]

The Foreign Office agreed to send Lieutenant Colonel D. R. 'Bobby' Guinness, a professional sapper and non-Russian speaker. He arrived by plane in Moscow in August 1941 and rented rooms in the National Hotel with a mission to exchange information with the NKVD about subverting the Nazi war effort. To be on the safe side, the Russians opened all his mail. In *Dealing With the Devil*, Donal O'Sullivan claims that the Soviets knew from their agents inside 'the British organisation' that their counterpart was called 'Special Operations Executive', an off-shoot of SIS. Hence, the Soviet codename for SOE was 'the sect'.[3]

From November 1940, most of Stafford Cripp's correspondence with the Foreign Office was forwarded to the Soviet leadership who also received details of communications between London and British embassies in the USSR, USA, Canada, Turkey, Iran, Japan, and other countries. They also received the SIS's weekly digest, the War Cabinet's protocols, as well as counter-intelligence material on the Soviet embassy.[4]

Having been promoted to full Colonel, Guinness began negotiations with Vyacheslav Molotov, the Soviet Foreign Commissar, Lavrentie Beria, the

Commissar of the NKVD, and Pavel Fitin, the 'Direktor' of NKVD's Fifth Department who was supervising the USSR's foreign intelligence (the Soviet Union's equivalent of MI6). Discussions about security issues with General 'Nikolaev' (real name Vassili Zarubin) lasted for three to four hours a day, until 'Nikolaev' was posted to Washington. Guinness then continued discussions with General Alexander 'Ossipov' (real name Gaik Ovakimyan).[5]

After a fortnight's negotiations, Guinness, an expert signaller, cabled the proposals to Menzies and Sir Orme Sargent, the Deputy Under-Secretary of State. Gladwyn Jebb, previously Private Secretary to the Permanent Under-Secretary of State at the Foreign Office and appointed by Dalton as his Assistant Under-Secretary, decided not to register Guinness's reports.

> Even a rumour that we were negotiating with the Russians on such subjects would, I imagine, be likely to have the most unfortunate effects in certain countries; and Guinness says the Russians themselves are just as nervous about a rumour getting round that they are negotiating on matters not affecting the Comintern with representatives of British Imperialism![6]

In Martin Kitchen's article 'SOE's Man in Moscow', he mentions that part of the agreement signed between Guinness and General B. Nicolaev on 30 September 1941 included an assertion that the Soviet Union would co-operate with Britain by delivering propaganda to inspire the local population in occupied territories to co-ordinate sabotage activities and subversion. What would have surprised the SOE in Baker Street was the agreement that both parties would help each other to introduce agents into occupied territory. They would also provide whatever documents and cover stories as necessary, exchange information, provide wireless equipment and 'any devices that might be useful'.[7]

Pressure from the Foreign Office led to liaison missions being exchanged between the SOE and NKVD with each country giving 'all possible assistance in introducing each other's agents into occupied territory'. They also 'could consider the possibility of permitting the establishment in their own territories of the other party's W/T terminals'.[8] In the 'Agreed Record of Discussions between British and Soviet Representatives on the Question of Subversive Activities against Germany and her Allies' it was added:

> In co-operating with and assisting each other the British and Soviet authorities do not wish to do anything that might endanger their organisations or unduly compromise their agents. The secret British and Soviet organisations will not be revealed to each other, nor will there normally be any contacts in the field, unless the heads of their respective organisations are assured that such contact would be advantageous.[9]

In September 1941, His Majesty's Government, represented by the SOE, agreed to assist the NKVD by supplying intelligence, training facilities, documents, and logistics for infiltrating Soviet agents into Nazi occupied Europe. In return the Soviet Government agreed, amongst other things, to assist the Allies by mobilising longshoremen around the world to help sabotage German shipping.

It was further agreed that, following general military strategy, they would conduct subversive activities together, but would not operate in each others 'sphere of responsibility'. Workers in occupied countries were to be provided with propaganda aimed at hampering German trade. This was particularly appreciated by the British as they recognised that many shipyard and railway workers were communist members or sympathisers. Britain's sphere was from Norway to Spain, Yugoslavia, and Greece. The Soviet's included Finland, Bulgaria, and Romania. Germany, Austria, Poland, and Hungary were not mentioned.

At the time, the Soviets were desperately short of transport airplanes of any sort, even to support their own front-line forces. As the Nazis controlled virtually all the territory between Moscow and the English Channel, the prospect of Soviet planes parachuting their agents with their wireless transmitters was considered unrealistic. It was about a 2,200-mile return flight from Moscow to Berlin, but only about a 1,200-mile return flight from RAF Tempsford. To give one an idea of the airtime, the Special Duties Squadron return flights to Poland were up to 14 hours. Also, to reduce the chances of being spotted and brought down by enemy planes, they only flew during the long dark nights of autumn and winter.

A formal arrangement called the 'Preliminary Survey' was signed whereby SOE would arrange the infiltration of NKVD agents into German-controlled territory. According to O'Sullivan, their general targets were believed to include oil fields, electricity generating stations, chemical industries, armament factories and transport infrastructure of rail, road, canal and shipping.[10]

> The British and Soviet organisations will give each other every possible assistance in making contact with their respective agents, especially when one party has no means of communication. One of the methods by which such communications could be arranged is through accommodation addresses. The agents of the party which has no communication could then pass messages, already enciphered in their own code through these addresses. The other party would then send these messages which would be passed on to the liaison sections concerned.[11]

The SAM Mission in Moscow

In October 1941, only a month after the Russian Section was formed, George Wiskeman's services were required exclusively for Scandinavia and George Hill was sent to head SOE's mission in Moscow. Major Milnes-Gaskell was left in charge of the Russian Section. The Admiralty was prevailed upon to provide Hill, his team, and another British delegation, spaces on board HMS *Leda*, a mine-sweeper, travelling in convoy to Archangel.

> I lost no time in getting ready, selecting winter kit, codes for communication, samples of our 'sweets and toys' and finally a safe, one of Mr. Chubb's very best. Chubb's fire-resisting, burglar-proof safes are famed throughout the world. This was a combination one. These activities were fitted in with long consultation with 'D' [Sir Frank Nelson], the Foreign Office and Dr. Dalton ... Finally, I was fully briefed and had my instructions in writing.[12]

On hearing on the ship's radio that an Anglo-American mission headed by Lord Beaverbrook, the Minister of Aircraft Production, and Averell Harriman, the US Ambassador to the USSR, had already reached Moscow, Hill commented in his diary:

> Beaverbrook, brilliant though I know him to be and a go-getter, has not the least idea of modern Russia – or should I say Bolshevik mentality. I know nothing of Harriman, except that he has been wandering about as one of Roosevelt's representatives. I do not believe they will be any more successful in negotiating with the Soviets in favour of our interests and will prove as futile as the wretched Strong-Drax mission in 1939, on the eve of the Ribbentrop-Molotov coup d'etat. This Anglo-American Mission I fear will approach the task on the lines used by Americans and British when negotiating tricky matters, vis., give and take, fair dealing, in fact on 'the old boy' basis. That's not the way to get results from the Bolshevik. Will the West never learn that the Bolsheviks have never worked or will work on an old boy basis! Might is all they understand, although to give them their due, they do at times keep to written agreements and stand to their bond. The Soviets are up against it (reaping what they have sown) and, while I absolutely agree with Churchill that anyone who fights against Hitler will have our aid, it should be aid on our terms. Now is the time to impose our terms and to get in writing on what conditions we are prepared to give aid.[13]

As the Soviets had a great respect for military authority, Hill was awarded the rank of Lieutenant Colonel. Assisting him in the mission was Captain Graham from the Intelligence Corps and Major Truskowski, the liaison officer with the Polish Forces in the Soviet Union. Hill was unhappy at the choice of Truskowski, whom he described as a 'fanatical hater of Russia', as he thought he would cause the NKVD to doubt his bona fides. When he landed after a three-week trip, Hill noted: 'Would to God he was in hell and not on the banks of the river Dvina, which to my mind at the moment, is the same thing.'[14]

The mission was codenamed 'SAM', but the other diplomats called them 'The Guinea Pigs'. They were accommodated at the Metropole Hotel, and as well as being provided with fitted fur coats and fur hats, the NKVD, who the British and the Americans in Moscow affectionately termed the 'YMCA', supplied Hill and his team with female company, alcohol, and luxuries that most Soviet citizens never saw. Acknowledged by the NKVD as an 'expert', Hill was described as having a valuable skill: being able to drink large quantities of alcohol. His cover was that he was part of the 'British Liaison Mission to the Russian Defence Department'. According to Kim Philby, Hill's arrival was welcomed by Soviet Intelligence chiefs as 'he was a source of unprecedented security leaks.'[15] An American Naval attaché described him as an easygoing, cherubic oldster who played the British hand with remarkable finesse. 'I enjoyed nothing more than an evening in "Pop" Hill's beautifully appointed mess, along with his half-dozen or so wholly unaffected fellow spooks, a fascinating slice of time, totally out of the ordinary.'[16]

Hill, Guinness, and Truskowski were entertained one evening by General Ossipov, who was described as about 40, stockily built, strong-limbed, quite well-dressed and of a pleasant appearance. An accomplished parachutist, he had made over sixty jumps. He spoke excellent English and was very quick on the uptake. The menu consisted of 'pressed caviar, butter and warm soft rolls and soused herrings, then a cabbage soup, very hot and good, followed by roast spring chicken and a dressed green salad, vanilla ice, a round of vodka, a glass of fair red Caucasian wine. With coffee a Russian brandy – horrid, and a really gorgeous dry Apricot liqueur. The meal lasted a full two hours.'[17]

Hill's first memorandum to London suggested there were already strategies in place to sabotage the German invasion plans for the Soviet Union. It appears that he thought the Soviet agents sent to Britain would participate in such activities.

> The Directive is out to fight the Huns and to collaborate with the U.S.S.R. towards a common end. It may be assumed that the policy of the Soviet Gov … will be actively or positively to tantalize, goad, threaten, infuriate [illegible], hurt, wound the Hun by every method, however base and however bloody, to attack individually and collectively Germans on U.S.S.R. territory. This in theory is a very fair assumption. But the Russian character may intervene … It will be the primary duty of the British S.O.2 [Special Operations] Mission to keep the Russians up to their job. Not an impossible task at all. The Russians want a bit of leading. The Germans know that, so do the Georgians (viz. Stalin) and the Letts (viz. Devinsky) [sic] [German technicians who know Russia] must be liquidated. The people to do the liquidating – under S.O.2 direction – are the Russian OGPU [secret police]. And it will not be difficult. Therefore we must resort to and encourage every kind of terror.[18]

When the German armies advanced on Moscow, just before Christmas 1941, the Russians evacuated the foreign contingent on the 'diplomatic train' to Kuibyshev, about 1,700 miles further south-east, near the border with Kazakhstan. The SAM mission invited other members of the diplomatic corps to their compartment for a dinner consisting of cold pork, pickled mushrooms and cucumbers and black bread bought at exorbitant prices from peasants at the railway stations. Dessert included Gaborne biscuits and a small square of chocolate. Drinks includes a swig of Crimean red wine, a tot of Scotch, a mug of tea and a tot of brandy. 'It was great fun; shortage of knives, forks, plates, made finger-eating essential.'[19]

Other diplomatic and military missions were housed in Kuibyshev, alongside various Soviet ministries, the Moscow Ballet, the Opera and the State Circus. The locals had been evacuated to Siberia to provide the newcomers with furnished accommodation. Faced with rationed goods in the 'Dip Shop', where the diplomats could make purchases on showing their credentials, they had to make do with the little on offer. Provided with a maid and a woodcutter who informed the NKVD of their comings and goings, the SAM mission managed on a meagre diet until Ossipov sent them a hamper. Inside his 'little present' were 'loaves of white bread, butter, a large tin of Astrakan caviar, Portuguese sardines, Riga sprouts, Italian-like sausages, salami etc., also some dried smoked fish – a great Russian delicacy – a few slabs of chocolate and about a dozen bottles of mixed spirits and wine! All packed à la Fortnum and Mason.' They were especially pleased to have been given a brand new 1941 Phillips Wireless, with which they were able to pick up BBC London as clear as a bell. Hill commented on how Ossipov was behaving as a Westerner, not a Communist, 'with the simple purpose of softening us up. Between our and their policies and aims there is already conflict of principles and interests.' Outside their room, someone had pinned a notice which read: 'The Hutch. The animals may not be fed, but may freely be offered liquor.'[20]

Following the Japanese attack on Pearl Harbor, the NKVD provided armed guards for the SAM mission. As they were changed every two hours, it meant the residents got little sleep. All three rooms of their flat were believed to have been bugged, and having noticed that their woodcutter had a camera, they had to be extra careful about leaving documents around. As the Chubb safe had been left in Moscow, they kept their papers in a suitcase nailed to the floor.[21]

At a meeting with Ossipov, Hill was told that the USSR had no intention of opening a 'Second Front' in the east as they already had their hands full with Germany, Austria, Italy, and the Spanish. Hill immediately contacted Ambassador Stafford Cripps. He had received no such information from Molotov or anyone in the Russian Foreign Office. Hill commented:

> Oh, the Soviet mind is indeed a strange hemmed-in one! How different the reactions of Churchill and Roosevelt to each other and to the world problems affecting our respective countries. The Russians infuriate me with their narrow-minded, suspicious and cynical outlook. They are, in part, very pleased that Capitalist America is in deadly conflict with Imperialist Japan.[22]

While in Kuibyshev, Hill established contact with various foreign diplomats and correspondents and encoded details of what he learned back to the SOE. He was allocated an international sleeping car for his train journey back to Moscow in February 1942, with a rucksack, one suitcase and a string bag containing rations, drinks, and a thermos of coffee. In his attaché case he had his passport, maps, compass, code, cypher pads, gold sovereigns, US dollars, and Russian roubles.[23] On Hill's return, the SAM mission was provided with accommodation overlooking the Kremlin with a female cook, two female servants, a female woodcutter, washerwoman, and three male chauffeurs to drive their four cars.[24]

Living in the villa next door, protected by a barbed wire cage, was the Peoples' Commissar of the Interior, Lavrentie Beria, the head of the NKVD. Described as a plump, small, dark, bespectacled creature, with a sallow complexion and sullen countenance, he was driven round in an armour-plated limousine with bullet-proof, blacked-out windows, accompanied by twelve guards armed with machine guns. Although Hill did not have a permanent armed guard, he was followed everywhere he went by a car.[25]

According to Kitchen, the SAM mission cost £1,500 a month; their office was bugged and every move they made was watched. Philby claimed that 'a very belated check of his conference room in Moscow revealed a fearsome number of sources of leakages.'[26]

Before Guinness was evacuated from Moscow, he had taken quite a shine to Luba Polik, a widow, who was disappointed when she was told that he'd returned to London. Hill described her as 'a pleasant trim woman of about thirty or perhaps a year or two more. She is the manageress of the National Hotel, and sits at the desk watching all who come in and out.' He set out to win her over.

What good was my liaison with NKVD doing for the war effort? If the Germans entered Moscow, as they would have to do if they wanted to win the war, it would be well worth while watching them and reporting home on their doings and dispositions. Even if the Red Army was beaten back to the Volga, or to the foot of the Urals, I had no doubt whatever in my mind that Stalin and Co. would hold out until we and the United States beat Hitler. What then? We had gone to war inter-alia to support Poland. Would Stalin have other than a Communist Poland on his post-war frontier? Would Stalin have other than a Communist Rumania, Bulgaria, or Yugoslavia? No, he would not. If one stayed in Moscow, at the breakthrough one might be able to help in forming Anti-Communist organisations, that with Allied help might form a more suitable Government than a Communist one to sit at the Council tables of Europe! One might! A dream? No one might. With Luba Polik I might be able to form an underground headquarters from which to operate. 'Might' was certainly the operative word to my thought. I would have to try and gain the affection of Luba – a pleasant philandering – but did I want that? I was happily married. My third wife in

England. Did I want to jeopardise our happiness? No, certainly not. But I do not mean to go back to Kuibyshev, that was now certain. I must think the whole matter carefully over, weigh the 'pros and cons' dispassionately. Find out more about Luba. I heard myself saying, 'Guinness, don't be a ruddy fool, try to be your age. NKVD agent that's what she is and make no mistake about it!' Yes, that's precisely what I had said.[27]

Whether it was SOE policy or not is unknown, but Hill cabled Joan Dodd, at Baker Street asking her to direct Wing Commander John D. Venner, SOE's paymaster, to read pages 212 to 230 of his book *Go Spy the Land*. It must have justified him needing money to win over Luba's attention as 'it will be an expensive business'. He took her to the opera, the ballet, the theatre, the circus, and top restaurants.[28]

It was Foot's opinion that Hill had been 'quietly nobbled' by the NKVD as his Russian mistress was in their pay. He gave the NKVD no trouble and they did not trouble him. 'They gave him no advice either; no fragment of the experiences of the party-dominated partisan groups was ever passed officially to SOE.'[29] Hill admitted being wary of NKVD's intentions as early as summer 1942.

Ossipov now seems to want SOE to co-operate with NKVD in Turkey, Persia, the Balkans and Central Europe. Such co-operation is full of dangers and at best would be very tricky. I feel SOE is rightly being sceptical about its practicality, and right in instructing me to stall for the time being, for other negotiations are taking place on the highest level between the UK and the USSR. The Soviet Government has probably worked out a long-term policy for when Hitler is defeated (which our Government has certainly not). What they – Narkomindel (Soviet F.O.) and NKVD want, is with our help, to infiltrate their agents into Central Europe, the Balkans, and in fact where ever they have difficulties in communications, and for such agents to create Communist cells in order to establish Communist domination when the time becomes ripe. We must steer clear of such a trap. This is not going to be easy, as we have already agreed in principle to drop Soviet agents into enemy territory, but that is, of course, quite different to co-operating on an inter-organisation basis.[30]

When Hill first met Beria in Lubianka, the NKVD headquarters, he found him badly briefed. He knew little about the SOE and did not know the names of the Soviet mission in London. He was more interested in silent weapons and poisons. When asked whether SOE would carry out its promise to drop NKVD agents as agreed in principle, Hill's response was that SOE kept its promises 'within the limits of possibilities'.

In July 1942, Major Truskowski returned to London, owing to the worsening of Russo-Polish relations, and was replaced as second-in-command by Milnes-Gaskell, who was joined by Captain J. H. Darton in October.

The DPR Mission in London

The NKVD's reciprocal mission, attached to the SOE in London, had the aim, according to Bickham Sweet-Escott, an SOE officer codenamed G/M 150, of facilitating the parachuting of Soviet agents into France for onward travel into Germany and Austria. Soviet agents already in place in France, Belgium, Holland, and Germany had been cut off following the German military occupation. When the Vichy government broke off diplomatic ties with the USSR, the NKVD lost contact with their existing agents. Moscow was therefore very keen to provide them with badly needed finance, support, and new instructions. There were other reasons too. Even though the USSR had made great efforts to prepare undercover networks abroad for the anticipated war, the German assault caught them unprepared. The most able men and women had been executed during purges, suspected of being double agents in the pay of Japan, Germany, France, or Britain. Often agents' well-organised networks collapsed because the NKVD representative was recalled to Moscow and killed. 'During 1937-38, out of 450 foreign intelligence officers, 275 were "repressed" – led off, arrested, executed. Several committed suicide or decided not to return to the USSR.'[31]

In mid-September 1941, the SOE was informed by the Foreign Office that there would be a small Russian mission, headed by 46-year-old Colonel Ivan Chichaev (sometimes written Tchitchaeff), attached to them in London. Its codename was DPR. Chichaev arrived in London on 30 September 1941, followed a fortnight later by his wife, child, and two assistants, Captain Nikolai Toropchenko and Lieutenant Vasiliy Suvorov, the wireless operator. Temporary accommodation was provided in the Soviet Embassy until Chichaev and his family moved to 3 Addison Road, W.1. His wife, Ksenia Mitrofanovna, worked as secretary and cipher clerk to the DPR mission.

Two months later, they moved to 54 Campden Hill Court, Notting Hill Gate, a salubrious quarter of Kensington where many foreign embassies were located. Toropchenko and Suvorov also moved in with their wireless set. Chichaev stayed there until his family were bombed out in September 1944 and they moved to Flat 4, 10 Palace Gardens, a grade II-listed, eight-bedroomed property near Notting Hill Gate tube station in Kensington. The mission was complete with the arrival of Major Andrei Graur, who had been promoted from deputy to head of the NKVD's Anglo-American section.[32]

Chichaev, known as 'Tchitch' by some of the British, occasionally visited the Soviet agents at SOE's Special Training Schools, holding establishments in the English countryside, and 'safe' houses and flats rented by the SOE in London. More often, however, it was Captain Toropchenko.

Over the years of the SOE/NKVD agreement, a character assessment was built up of each member of the Russian mission. The anonymously written 'Notes on the Russian Section of S.O.E.' provided details of General Nikolaev, Lieutenant-General Fitin, and General Ossipov. Details about the men in the London mission are included to give one a better understanding of who the SOE and SIS had to deal with.

Colonel Ivan CHICHAEV

This officer was a subordinate of General Nikolaev in the Soviet subversive organisation. He is a colonel in the Red Army and subsequently became their liaison officer in England.

He is a man of about 42, probably of Siberian stock. He is inclined to be affectionate, with a passion for roses, one of which he usually carries in his pocket. He drinks little and has a dislike for vodka.

He was born in the Volga basin where he lived and worked in the river trade all during the war of 1914-18. He became a revolutionary and later a guerrilla in Siberia and was wounded through the palm of his left hand which has weakened several fingers. He rose to be a colonel in the Red Army and then joined the O.G.P.U. He is married and has a son of nine. His wife is believed to be of good family, and she and the child were both in this country with him.

Short (5'4'), well-built, clean-shaven, with dark brown hair and of Jewish appearance; a distinguishing mark is a bullet scar on the back of the left hand.

Unlike most of the members of the Russian Mission, he was a very mild mannered man and at any rate gave the impression of wanting to behave in a 'western way'. To what extent he had real authority or not will probably never be known, but we are inclined to think that he was little more than the echo of his bosses in Moscow. His English was good and was learnt, according to himself, in the U.S.A., but according to a member of the Polish Forces in this country, he had learnt it at the Polytechnic in London in 1935/6. It is possible that this last suggestion was true, as unlike all other Russians who had learnt English in America, he had no nasal accent.

Colonel GRAUR

He was by far the strongest personality in the Russian Liaison Mission, of about 35 years of age, dark and swarthy and according to his own statement, a Ukrainian from Nikolaev on the Black Sea. When he first came to England in February, 1942, he was extremely uncultured, even in the Russian sense of the word. He was married and had one child which died in England.

On all qualities, official and otherwise, was inclined to call a spade a spade, and his spades were always excessively one-sided ones. This did nothing to improve his relationship with our section and indeed on one occasion he very nearly had a stand-up fight with Major Milnes Gaskell. However, as time went on, he began to mellow and even to develop a warped sense of humour. During Colonel Chichaev's visit to Russia during the spring and summer of 1943, he was in control of affairs. Graur's main subjects of conversation were, firstly, the delay in the opening of the Second Front, and secondly, the role of General Mihajlovic [sic] in Yugoslavia; these two topics he never failed to bring up in any talks with us.

He returned to the Soviet Union in the autumn of 1943, where he became Colonel (later General) Ossipov's second-in-command. Since the beginning of

1945, he appears to have been our senior opposite number in place of General Ossipov who was latterly only very rarely available.

Although very blunt and naturally of a sarcastic disposition, he gives the impression of being perhaps rather more honest than any of his colleagues, and on more than one occasion, especially in Moscow, he gave us direct proof of his willingness to help. His rugged appearance may well hide a genuine admiration for this country and indeed once, when very drunk, he became most complimentary about Britain and the British. We suspected him of being the 'political supervisor' of the Russian Liaison Mission.

Captain TOROPCHENKO

Aged about 30, he was the complete opposite in character of Suvorov (with whom he came to England) and he was inclined to order the latter about. Short, heavily-built, with black close-cropped hair and a rather bull-dog jaw. He gave the impression of being rather suspicious of his surroundings and conscious of the fact that as a good Soviet citizen, he must be critical of the 'home of capitalism'. He therefore assumed a slightly disparaging air about everything he saw, and while admitting rather grudgingly that the trees in London were very beautiful, implied in the same breath that most things are rather second-rate compared with Moscow. Not an attractive person, but he definitely gave the impression of being a somewhat weak character and put on a bluff exterior to hide a very strong inferiority complex. He possessed little real intelligence – apart from being quite a creditable chess player, as various members of our section found out at training schools and while waiting for aircraft.

Although he possessed a smattering of English when he arrived, he learnt practically nothing while he was here and to every remark or question he would always answer 'All right' very quickly and with a very guttural 'r' – a fact which led to many complications.

Lieut. SUVOROV

A technician, small, slight and fair, aged about 26. Arrived in England in October 1941. He had never been out of Russia before and rather tended to show it. He displayed an almost childlike interest in his surroundings, wanted to finger everything he saw in shops and evidently intended to make the most of his first trip outside his own country. Rather shy and sensitive, he was very conscious of the fact that he was a stranger in a strange land. A pleasant personality, but not a strong one. He learnt an astonishing amount of English in the time that he was here. His wife and child were also in England. His job was to operate the W/T set, of which he appeared to have a fair knowledge, though we were told by a British W/T expert that his procedure was very clumsy and old-fashioned. He was occasionally given [?] with Pickaxes, but this only happened when none of his colleagues was available. He left the country in the autumn of 1943.[33]

OPERATIONS PICKAXE I
AND PICKAXE II

According to Barry McLoughlin, the Soviet agents were forwarded to Britain by the Fourth Directorate for Special Tasks and Guerrilla Warfare, headed by Pavel Sudoplatov. One of his section chiefs was Yakov Serebryansky, who had founded the organisation. It is probable that they came up with the term 'Pickaxe' to describe these missions as both had been involved in the planning and execution of what were called 'wet jobs' overseas, including the assassination of Stalin's opponents.

In August 1940, 'having murdered or driven to suicide many members of Leon Trotsky's family, scores of his closest friends and collaborators, and countless numbers of the leaders and supporters of the International Left Opposition,' one of the NKVD's team killed Trotsky in Mexico with an ice pick blow to the skull.[1] One wonders whether the irony was appreciated by those in the British secret services.

In a letter dated 12 November 1941, T. G. N. Bardwell, on behalf of Lieutenant-Colonel J. H. Adam, informed the Senior Commanding Officers at Leith, Aberdeen, Glasgow, Newcastle, and Hull of the imminent arrival of SS *Ijhora* from Archangel, one of the Soviet Union's Arctic ports.

Three Soviets on board – Anna Ouspenskaya, Petyr Kousnetsov, and Pavel Koubitsky – were to be kept in port until an officer arrived to collect them. It was instructed that 'this should be done as unobtrusively as possible so that other passengers will not realise that different treatment is being meted out to these three.'[2]

Advance notice was also given of the arrival of Grigory Rodinov, Ivan Danilov, Anna Frovola, Ernst Horman, Karl Schwarz, Kurt Traub, Peter Staritsky, Vasselod Troussevitch, and Maria Dicksen. They too had to be held until their escort arrived. A report on their arrival, addressed to A.D., the codename of George Taylor, director of SOE's overseas groups and missions, stated:

D/P.1 [Milnes-Gaskell] travelled up to Edinburgh on the night of the 18 November, having obtained information from D/NAVY that the Soviet ship 'IJHORA' was due in Methil [north-east of Edinburgh] on or about 20 November.

D/P.1 reported to MI5 at Edinburgh where he learnt that this ship had broken down and would remain at Scapa [Orkneys] for some days. Arrangements were consequently made for the Pickaxe Party to come down to Thurso by train on Friday 21st. D/P.1 met the party at Inverness and brought them back to London, arriving on the Sunday, 23 November. D/P.2 [Conducting Officer Captain Darton] conducted the party, which consisted of two males for Germany and one woman for France, to a house in the Beaulieu estate chosen by MT [SOE's accommodation section].

Two complications are at present holding up the program:

Those for Germany left behind on the boat a suitcase containing wireless set, as they were frightened to show these to any customs officials. Every effort is now being made to get hold of the case.

The female has now declared that she is unable to jump and, furthermore, has arrived without any papers. Her future plans are now being discussed.

The two males are leaving for STS No. 51 [Ringway aerodrome, near Manchester, where agents were provided with parachute training] on Wednesday, 26 November, escorted by D/P.2.[3]

Although the two men had been well equipped with papers, they all needed appropriate clothing for the British winter. L. Mine & Co. provided suits but other clothing came from SOE's stores. Milnes-Gaskell and Darton then accompanied them to 'The Drokes', one of the houses on the Beaulieu Estate. Which course, if any, the Pickaxes attended, was not documented in their files. There were no reports from the commanding officer as to how successful a Pickaxe agent was thought to be, as was the routine for SOE agents.

STS 51 was Ringway aerodrome, now Manchester Airport, where agents were provided with parachute training. Many stayed at nearby Dunham House, an eighteenth-century Georgian mansion. Usually, after an introduction to jumps, harnesses, and parachutes, agents had three jumps from an air balloon and two from a converted Whitley bomber, one taking place at night. They landed in the grounds of the adjoining Tatton Park. Once they had 'won their wings', the Pickaxes were returned to London, where they were accommodated at 40 Porchester Gate, Bayswater.

On 9 December, a report stated that the second Pickaxe party of nine persons would be arriving shortly, consisting of three bound for France who required documents and clothes, and six for Austria, all needing clothes. Four of them required documents and wireless sets that were capable of reaching Moscow from Vienna. As it was a distance of 1,050 miles over mountains, it was suggested that a Mark III set was needed. A document sent from Major Milnes-Gaskell (D/P.1) to Sir George Moss (O/X), an adviser in Intelligence section covering India, Burma and China, stated:

As far as possible, arrangements have been made to deal with these requests; but in some directions, extreme difficulty is being experienced, and the position is as follows:

1. Clothes. It is evident that we shall be expected to equip all agents, masculine and feminine, with everything from clothes down to razors, lip-stick and cigarettes. One had hoped that 'C' [Sir Stewart Menzies, head of SIS] would have amassed a large stock of all these things before the war, but it appears that this is not the case and they are unable to help at all. The first Pickaxe party was therefore equipped with oddments gleaned from M.E.W. [Ministry of Economic Warfare], M.I.5. and a number of things had to be bought. In order to be prepared for the next, and any future parties, it is intended to collect a stock of suitable clothes, etc. from P/W [Prisoner-of-war] and internment camps throughout the country, and this is in the process of being done.[4]

The most vital and pressing question was the quality of their documents. The SOE acknowledged that they could not get hold of German documents and so a request was made to the NKVD to supply these. It was expected that the SOE's forgery section would take up to three months to produce documents needed for agents going to Austria. The urgency of the situation prompted the Russian Section to suggest:

The support of Lisbon, Berne and Stockholm be enlisted in collecting any papers, notepapers, rubber stamps, etc.

'C' should be asked as soon as possible for their permission for us to approach a big printing firm such as Waterlow's or de la Rue's. With the resources and experience of one of these big firms, who are moreover accustomed to printing foreign banknotes, etc. there is some hope that the job will be completed in the time. And the expense would be mitigated by the fact that, apart from satisfying our immediate needs, we should be assured of a large stock for future use.

The demands of the Russians are often as unpredictable as their reasoning is obscure, and it is not beyond the bounds of possibility that they are thrusting these sudden responsibilities upon us, in order to test what we can do. D.P.R.1. [Chichaev] always shows a most healthy interest in our methods and capabilities (in so far as he knows them), and one tries to give the impression that everything works on oiled wheels. But the requests both of himself and his agents are seldom made until the last possible moment, and it is difficult to carry out one's promises, unless everything down to the smallest detail is prepared and ready. And for this it seems essential to have a stock of everything which these agents are likely to find useful.[5]

The Bank of England was asked to supply any papers related to Germany and Austria containing letter headings, signatures and dates. The forgery section was interested in size, shape, and texture of the paper of documents used by banks, government offices, private firms, and hotels. When Captain Hackett was approached at his 'forgery school' at Wall Hall (STS 39) in Aldenham, his response was that the SOE might get into trouble with foreign governments when they discover Britain was sending in communist agents supplied with their forged documents. Their role was largely manufacturing subversive propaganda. The Russian Section had to tread carefully as, following their request through SAM, they were being supplied with German, Austrian and Hungarian documents.[6] Prior to the arrival of what was codenamed the Coffee party, the following note was added to their file:

> The original understanding was that these Russians would arrive fully equipped. If, as seems probable, they are not fully equipped, D/P [Russian] Section cannot be held responsible for any delay which may occur. As regards documents, X [German] Section can probably, within a reasonable time, produce: Wehrpass [a military call-up card with biographical details], Kennkarte [Identity Card], Arbeitsbuch [Employment history], Ausweis de Arbeitfront [Trade Union Card], N.S.D.A.P. (or Frauenverein) card [Nazi Party card], Abmeldungs forms [Registration forms for residences and changes of residence], Headed note-paper and Rubber stamps.
>
> X Section will find it impossible to produce German ration cards, which are changed monthly.
>
> In any case, papers cannot be supplied for these nine Russians until after they have arrived because papers have to be 'built up' around the 'story' of the individuals and the 'stories' are not known.
>
> I report the above in anticipation of delay on account of these Russians for which the Russians, and not we, will be responsible.[7]

The SIS informed the Russian Section that they were unable to reproduce the identity cards because they were not able to procure suitable cloth for the outside cover. Requests had to be made to Canada to supply the material. They also claimed not to have the material or facilities to produce the other papers. In the circumstances, a telegram was sent to SAM setting out SOE's limits and urging that no more agents be sent unless they were provided with papers by the NKVD themselves. It was estimated that it would take four to five months to forge Austrian paperwork, so it was intended to supply them with Czech documents forged by MX, SOE's forgery section at Briggens (STS 14), a seventeenth-century country house in Roydon, near Harlow in Essex.

Anna Ouspenskaya

Known to the British as 'Anna Harcourt', 26-year-old Anna Ouspenskaya became extremely nervous when faced with the prospect of being taken to Ringway for parachute training. As she absolutely refused to jump, she was examined by a doctor who identified her as suffering from an over-active thyroid with 'threatenings of Basedow's Disease'. On 24 November, a note in her file stated that her position was both difficult and unsatisfactory. Having explored every possibility, the Russian Section 'had no alternative but to say that ANNA must either learn immediately how to jump or else she should return.'[8]

The response from Moscow took seventeen days. The NKVD's attitude to her problem was that she should be forbidden to jump and that, instead, she should be landed anywhere in occupied or unoccupied France, either by sea or air. The Russian Section's comment in response was, 'If he [the NKVD] orders her to go, she must go. It would be an impossible situation if we were to revise Russian orders to Russians.'[9]

Thought therefore was given as how to get her into France. Special Duties Squadron Leader Jack Benham, then based at Newmarket, considered giving her drugs or putting her through a course of treatment. He contacted the RAF Psychological Laboratory at South Farnborough in Hampshire who replied on 2 December with advice for any potential airsick parachutist.

Dear Jack,

In case I can't get down to see the airsick lamb I am enclosing some capsules for you. I think the best thing to do would be to give him a trial flight approximating to the length of the duty flight. I suggest that to start with he is given two capsules half an hour before flying and another in the air if he feels queasy. If this is of no avail it is permissible to give one capsule at half hourly intervals up to a maximum of six. There is no risk attached to a jump done after taking the dope, as I have made a couple myself and the landing was no worse than usual.

I do think it very important to stress the accessory factors which are responsible for airsickness and in his case particular attention should be paid to these.

1. Clothing. It is of the utmost importance that he should have a reasonable body temperature and be neither too hot nor too cold, while at the same time his clothing should be loose and not constricted at any point. If he is wearing a collar I should get him to take it off for the flight and get him to loose his fly buttons.

2. Diet. I think I should see that he gets a good plain meal as near to take-off as possible, making sure that it is not greasy and little fat is included. Your chicken sandwich specials should prove adequate for the flight.

3. Alcohol. While this is not generally recommended, some people do seem to obtain relief from a sip of brandy while in the air. I should, however, reserve this until such time as he feels he really is just about to vomit.

4. General comfort. I know that you pay particular attention to this and I suggest that he lies down for the trip. As mentioned above in connection with looseness of clothing, I think it is important that he should put on the harness at the very last possible moment.

5. Noise. The problem of noise is another point worth paying attention to. I suggest that he plugs his ears with cotton wool or uses ear plugs.

    Yours sincerely,
     Ronald Winfield

PS. Since these capsules contain Benzedrine he should not be provided with your blue pellets.[10]

Benzedrine was an amphetamine issued to agents to help keep them awake, particularly useful for wireless operators whose transmission period might be in the early hours of the morning. What the blue pellets contained was not mentioned, but they were probably sleeping pills.

A note in Anna's report stated that 'A Lysander landing is definitely not possible since no arrangements could be made at the other end [the dropzone in France] and it is upon these that a Lysander operation depends.'[11] If what they called 'the body' was a good sailor, the Naval authorities could provide a fast craft and land them on a deserted beach on the north coast of Normandy. If 'the body' was a poor sailor they could go by fishing boat and land on the west coast of Brittany, west of Brest. Concern was expressed about bodies being dropped in a 'zone interdite' in the occupied part of France, and 'there would be many difficulties for the body to overcome before it arrives at its destination.'[12]

The decision was made to take her by a fast craft with a dinghy for landing. On 22 December, she was sent a cover story, which will be referred to later, and on Christmas Eve, arrangements were made for her to visit rooms under the police station in Savile Row to meet 'Kenmore'. He was the tailor in charge of providing agents with appropriate clothing for the country they were to be sent to. There she was provided with a complete wardrobe of appropriate French clothing. SOE's agents were taken to a specialist dentist who ensured their fillings were identical to those used in the country they were going to. If they weren't, they were replaced. No mention of Pickaxes being taken to see a dentist appeared in their files.

Prior to her departure, Anna would have been shown aerial photographs and maps of the proposed landing site, and the alternative beach if the first was considered too dangerous. She was also provided with details of known German watch posts and 25-mm gun emplacements along this section of the 'Atlantik Wall', the German's coastal defence system. Careful study of the local geographical features would have helped her decide which route she had to take to the nearest railway station.

On 31 December 1941, Lance Corporal Kratzoff, one of the Russian Section's conducting officers, escorted her from Beaulieu to catch the first train from

Brockenhurst station to Waterloo. However, there was a delay over getting her appropriate French papers from the Foreign Office, who had requested that they be consulted before permission was given for any Soviet agent to be sent to France. Misgivings were expressed in the Russian section about Anna. In a note dated 3 January 1942, L/PS.1, an officer in SOE's planning section, wrote to Milnes-Gaskell:

I cannot help commenting on the fact that this poor girl struck me as most inadequately prepared for her mission. Apart from what you have told me of her physical disabilities, it was very patent that her nerve was not what one expects in an agent on the point of leaving for the field. I am quite certain that if she is once accosted by the Feldgendarmerie or the French police she will be incapable of acting normally. I agree with you that her nondescript appearance is to some extent in her favour, but I fear that this is offset by the fact that she is to land in a Forbidden Zone in which the controls are becoming more and more strict.

In addition, surely her knowledge of current conditions in France is little more than rudimentary, since it has been imparted in something like a couple of hours.

In the matter of her French accent I was obliged to speak somewhat optimistically in her presence. In Brittany she should have little difficulty in passing for French, but I fear that in Paris it would have been better for her to have posed as Flemish or Alsatian speaking, for I think it inevitable that her accent will be noticed.

On the whole I feel that the question of her morale is the most serious; the presence of her ultra-Oppenheim mentor, producing in her presence ideas such as carrying a revolver in case she should meet a German sentry on the shore, carrying Ovaltine tablets and meat extracts, hiding bank notes in shoes, and then capping it by enquiring whether there are any serious climatic variations between this country and Brittany, all this can scarcely be conclusive to building up confidence.

Please do not believe that I am suggesting that you are not aware of these difficulties. On the other hand, I feel it may not be out of place for you to have a quite independent and unbiased opinion to corroborate your own views.[13]

In another note, L/PS.1 suggested that her chances of ever reaching Paris were remote, 'failing the most extraordinary good luck'. The response of Major A. D. Seddon (AD/W) at 64 Baker Street was that, in the short time available, all that was possible was done 'to fill the lacunae in this agent's training, and responsibility for her ultimate fate can in no way rest on the D/P Section.'[14]

The Navy's 'Operation Overcloud' in early 1942 delayed Anna's trip, but on 10 January 1942, having successfully obtained all the necessary documents and papers and memorised her cover story, Major Milnes-Gaskell, her conducting officer, took her by car to the Radcliffe Hotel in Paignton. On the evening of the following day, motor gunboat 314 slipped out of Dartmouth harbour and made its way south across the English Channel to Lannion Bay, in Brittany. The journey of about 125 miles took about ten hours, but she was provided with warm clothing and sea sickness pills.

When the boat approached the French coast, the engines were silenced to avoid the attention of enemy sentries, and despite the bad weather, Anna landed on an isolated beach shortly before 0500 hours with snow falling. The report said she was very seasick on the way but behaved very courageously. As it turned out, the file stated that she had left a vital part of her equipment behind in the hotel. What she had left behind was not stated.

Using a new identity as 'Jeannette Dupont', her mission was to make contact with the Soviet network at 118 Boulevard Raspail in Paris, whose people had been cut off following the German invasion. She had to deliver instructions and provide them with funds and new codes.[15]

In her cover story, she was born on 14 May 1915 at Carnac les Mines in the Tarn, and worked as a waitress at Hotel de la Gare, Place de l'Embarcadére, Montpellier.

Mlle. Jeannette DUPONT left her job towards the end of November, and decided to make her way to Occupied France in order to find her fiancé, Robert DELACROIX. He is a mechanic and employed at an aircraft factory in NANTES. In his last letter, written early in August, he said he was hoping to obtain a better job in a factory at ST. BRIEUC. She took a train from MONTPELLIER at CHATEROUS [sic] on 30 November. Here she spent a night with a gendarme friend of hers, a M. Jean LEY, rue de Marché. The next day she set out on foot and went north to a friend's farm near LA CHAPELLE MONMARTIN. The farmer's name was BARBOU. She was taken across the line early in December by another farmer, name unknown, and spent the next night at ROMORANTIN, with friends of the farmer. She then took the train to NANTES. There was a control on the train, but she was allowed to pass, after she had explained her position and shed many tears.

At NANTES she stayed with a friend, a M. DUMAS, who keeps a restaurant du Chalet, in the rue de la Prairie. She asked at several of the NANTES factories, but no one could help her and she was advised to enquire at a factory near ST. BRIEUC, Acieries de Sambre et Meuse. She then went to NANTES and made her way via VANNES to PONTIVY. Here she spent the night at the station, and on the following day, she took the wrong train to MORLAIX and she is now on her way to ST. BRIEUC. If she finds her fiancé, she will settle down at ST. BRIEUC, but if he is not there, she intends to make her way to Paris and find work there. Her money is now running low.[16]

How many French francs she was given was not stated. Her report described her as between 28 and 30 years of age, of small stature, auburn haired and singularly unattractive.

> Both the Russians who travelled with her and the English who met her, failed to find any signs of charm. She was highly nervous and ought never to have been sent to this country, for medical reasons. While in England, she suffered from excess thyroid, and, on more than one occasion, visited a doctor. Her condition was far too gone for treatment and an operation would have necessitated several months in England. Doctor Jones' opinion was that if subjected to any great physical strain, her heart might give out.
>
> She had not been in France for some years and already her accent was far from perfect. She had studied in Paris and had definitely worked for the Soviet Government as an agent on some previous occasion. She related that on one occasion she had been passed across the frontier and left by her guides without the necessary information; in consequence, she was more than anxious that we should avoid any repetition of such a performance. There can be no doubt that she was a genuine whole-hearted uncompromising Communist. In spite of several years in Russia, she believed that France could only survive as a national entity if the Communist party came to power.
>
> It was her duty to reach Paris at all costs and there she had to visit certain Soviet agents, with one object – re-establishing the wireless communication between Occupied France and the U.S.S.R. If she achieved this purpose, it appeared that there were no further plans for her future.
>
> She had, on the whole, a reasonable chance of success; she was completely insignificant. She was not a type you would normally select for such duties but, thanks to her cover story provided by us, she was assured a reasonable chance of success. If she succeeded in avoiding capture during the first twenty-four hours, it was felt that she should achieve her object. Unfortunately, there has been no trace of her since her departure and the Soviet authorities, in June, had given up hopes of her safe arrival in Paris.
>
> We supplied her with a revolver and food for twenty-four hours. She carried on her two effective 'L' tablets hidden in lipstick. She was entirely clothed by this organisation.[17]

'L' pills contained lethal potassium cyanide crystals in a biteable, thin rubber coating. They were often hidden in a specially hollowed out cavity in a wisdom tooth, the top inside part of a jacket, in hollowed-out wine bottle corks or tubes of lipstick. Once chewed, 'L' pills would kill a man in 15 seconds. SOE agents reported being told that the Catholic Church had given them a special dispensation to use the pill 'in extremis'. Other agents were issued 'E' pills, a quick-working anaesthetic that would knock a person out in 30 seconds, and 'K' pills, which would induce sleep for up to 24 hours.

Some were given 'M & B 693' (May and Baker's sulfapyridine) pills which were used before penicillin to counter wound infections and reduce the risk of pneumonia and gangrene. There were also 'Q' and 'U' poison pills and halibut liver oil capsules. One deadly poison SOE issued left no trace except those of endemic syphilis.[18]

Following confirmation that Anna Ouspenskaya had been dropped safely, the SOE responded to a query about her from the Foreign Office. After summarising the problems they had experienced, someone in the Russian Section replied that the expression Pickaxe would never be used again for an operation, and that they would apply to them for a codename whenever a party was ready. [19] As shall be seen, subsequent agents had their own codenames but the term 'Pickaxes' continued to be used to describe the Soviet agents.

In a note in Anna's file, it was agreed that the four other NKVD agents destined for France should not be sent until the matter of delivering communists had been taken up with Charles de Gaulle's Fighting French. It also included the comment:

> You may have noted in the *Evening Standard* three days ago a German announcement from Paris that a Communist woman spy of Polish nationality, who had reached France through England in 1941 or 1942, had been arrested and was to be shot. This looks perilously like one of the PICKAXE party whom we landed by boat early this year. I only hope that the Fighting French will not believe the report in the Press.[20]

A copy of the *Gringoire*, a Marseilles newspaper dated 18 December 1942, was sent in the diplomatic bag from Lisbon. At the end of an article entitled 'Repetez-Le', there were the following paragraphs:

> The most singular finding is that the chief terrorist leaders from Moscow's school of civil war always manage to escape. The truth is that they have a complex network with links overseas and interchangeable identities. In addition, they don't act until they have carefully prepared the ground.
>
> The case of the Polish Jew, Szyllra Lapszye, is typical. She had been sent to France in 1933. She moved to Caen, then to Toulouse, and then was a mouthpiece of Communist propaganda in Spain. She returned to Poland, via Sweden and Latvia where the Comintern gives her a more important mission.
>
> In December 1940 she was in Russia. In August 1941, she went to France via England. Arriving in Paris she made contact with a group made up of Poles and Russians, all Jews. She took command, and under her leadership, started making clandestine radio broadcasts and organising the methodical destruction of grain reserves by setting them alight.
>
> One is amazed at how easy displaced these representatives of the Comintern are. It is true that they have considerable numbers. As Basilio in 'The Barber' says, 'these devilish characters always have a pocket full of irresistible arguments.'[21]

The final note in Anna's file, dated 14 January 1943, suggested that there were too many differences in the story for this to have been the agent they dropped the previous year. O'Sullivan's research into Soviet papers showed that Anna reached Paris, made contact with leading Soviet agents 'Rom' and 'Gustav' and re-established radio communication with Moscow. Reports were sent on the names and location of French and German troops and what sabotage activity had taken place. However, she did not last long in the field.

While she was trying to set fire to a grain depot, she was caught, presumably without her lipstick, as she was arrested by the gendarmes and handed over to the Abwehr, the German secret police. According to files referred to in the Russian account, she collaborated willingly with her interrogators, which led to the arrest of more than ten Soviet agents. Torture or the offer of financial reward was commonly used by the Gestapo to extract intelligence from foreign agents. Maybe they captured her wireless set and got the codes needed to transmit not only back to London, but also to the Soviet Union. No mention was made of 'Gustav', but according to O'Sullivan, Anna and 'Rom' were subsequently executed.[22] Confirmation of Anna's demise came in a letter in SOE's Russian folder, dated 30 May 1956 and signed F. M. Teall. Addressed to a blanked out recipient, it expresses extreme interest in there still being an alleged independent network of Soviet agents in France.

We have no previous trace of the name Szyfra LIPSZYC and agree with you that on the information given she must be identified with Anna Ouspenskaya.... I should be most interested to receive any further information you may obtain regarding this alleged network and also anything to show whether its activities are confined to France or might possibly be used against this country.[23]

Another letter with the addressee and recipient blanked out, dated 23 May 1958, added:

The scarce details of the BECK case [Robert Beck was a Soviet agent shot by the Germans at end of 1942] show that the Germans rounded up a considerable Soviet network, and as a result, a number of Soviet agents were shot. Amongst them was a certain Szyfra LIPSZYC (Czech), born 14.5.15 in WARSAW, a pre-war militant member of the P.C.F. [?Polish Communist Force]. During the Spanish War she served with the International Brigade, and subsequently went to the USSR. In 1941 she was apparently sent by the R.I.S. [?Russian Intelligence Service] to the U.K., from where she landed in France, near LANNION (Cotes du Nord) from a British vessel. She was arrested by the Germans in 1942, confessed to everything she knew about the réseau [network] and was finally shot.[24]

Operation Pickaxe II

Petyr Kousnetsov and Pavel Koubitsky arrived with Anna Ouspenskaya at Scapa in the Orkneys aboard SS *Ijhora* on 20 November 1941. From there they were transferred to the mainland and proceeded by train to Inverness where they were met by conducting officer Lance Corporal Kratzoff. He escorted them to London on 23 November, where they became known as Pickaxe Party II. After being provided with second-hand British clothes and briefed by the DPR mission, they were driven down to The Drokes at Beaulieu.

An SOE meeting held on the day they arrived in London decreed that the two agents should have their wireless set and all other equipment ready for packing and delivery to Major Douglas Dodds-Parker (MO/B), SOE's mission planner in charge of infiltrating and exfiltrating agents into Europe, by 30 November and to be ready to fly from 3 December. At this stage of the war, agents' luggage and other supplies for their mission were being packed in different sized containers at Audley End (STS 43), an eighteenth-century mansion outside Saffron Walden, in Essex. The designated airfield for the flight was Newmarket. The proposed 'DZ', dropzone, was in the Belgian Ardennes, an area north of Elsenborn, south of the woods. Their file included a list of items they were to be provided with:

Appendix 'A'

4 .32 Automatic (Mauser or Colt)

2 Spare Magazines for Colt

150 rounds .32 ammunition

2 knives, locking

2 compasses, pocket. Normal marching type, unless otherwise specified. Marks to be carefully removed.

2 First Aid dressing

2 Pocket torch with spare battery and bulb

4 Tins Horlicks tablets

8 Tins meat lozenges

2 Emergency rations (concentrated chocolate)

2 pair anklets

4 Crepe bandages

2 Tablets 'L' (Lethal)

2 pair gloves, gauntlets

2 Flying suits (overall cover with pockets)

60 Tablets B (Benzedrine)

2 full tubes Tablet K (Sleeping)

2 Spine pads

4 Heel pads

2 Bakelite Grenades
2 Mills Bombs

Appendix 'B'
2 Spades in web carrier
2 Helmets, padded
2 Parachutes (W/T set attached)
2 Spirit flasks, full

For use in aircraft
2 Sleeping bags, heated
2 Thermos flasks
Sandwiches[25]

In the meantime they were taken to Ringway for parachute training, where they stayed at Dunham House. The commandant's report stated that, 'Both these men trained and jumped well. The taller of the two was still suffering from the effects of the sea voyage and felt dizzy on the trapeze, but he completed his jump successfully. Owing to bad visibility the descent was made from the balloon and had to be done with ordinary chutes, there being no fitting for large or small A's on the balloon.' Although bad weather prevented them from making a drop from a Whitley Bomber, 'they had a good idea of our equipment given to them'.[26]

Back at The Drokes, their cover stories were created and learned off by heart while they waited for their papers to be forged. Koubitsky was recorded as being 'in possession of secret code, together with wave-length and time of transmission. No messages to be sent back to this country.'[27]

In David Stafford's *Churchill and the Secret Service,* he relates how Douglas Dodds-Parker, reported two Soviet agents being taken to visit Churchill at Number 10, Downing Street.[28] According to O'Sullivan, Dodds-Parker arranged the meeting with Colonel Chichaev and it was the only time a British Prime Minister knowingly met Soviet operatives on duty.[29] There is no official record of any meeting between Churchill and the Pickaxes, or between Churchill and Dodds-Parker. However, as O'Sullivan put it, as Churchill was the Pickaxes' chief champion, it seems likely that he would have wanted to have been informed about the progress of the co-operation. Should Chichaev's correspondence be in an NKVD file somewhere, it would shed interesting light onto the incident.

On Saturday 27 December, when informed that their flight was on, the two men were driven up the A1 to Gaynes Hall, a thirteen-bedroom Georgian mansion set in 23 acres of the Cambridgeshire countryside in Perry, near St Neots. About half an hour's drive from Tempsford, it was one of SOE's holding stations where agents were provided with rest and recreation prior to their flight.

After a hot meal, the agents' stores and clothing were checked and they left for what was called 'S' aerodrome. This was Stradishall, about 8 miles south-east of Newmarket. Whether there were no planes available at Tempsford that night is not known. What followed was a series of incidents leading ultimately to the death of Koubitsky. Major Milnes-Gaskell made the following report:

> No sooner were they fully ready than an airman informed us that a two-hour delay was inevitable as certain instruments on the Whitley Bomber were not in working order. This meant that the departure was postponed from 1800 to 2000 hours. The agents were taken to the aeroplane so as to practice the procedure for the jump and then we all waited in the Wing Commander's sitting room.
>
> At 19.45, we drove down to the aeroplane and after a further delay of 45 minutes, the agents boarded the aeroplane. The engines were started up and at the appropriate time to leave, the party was held up by another 'plane which had crashed and it was necessary to move the flare path. When this had been accomplished, the aeroplane taxied forward to the run-way but unfortunately in the process, the pilot left the concrete road and the near-side wheel stuck in the mud. A tractor was sent for but this broke down and some time elapsed before another arrived on the scene. At 2150, the aeroplane left and the pilot intended to fly direct to the appointed place. I returned to S.T.S. 61 and I decided to wait here until Wing Commander Benham had reported on the operation. It was essential for me to have all the details of the flight before my return so that I could explain to DPR.1 [Chichaev] the full history of the operation.
>
> In the morning I was told that Wing Commander Benham had not returned but was likely to come back at any moment. I did not gain the impression that this had any special significance. I was then rung up by MO section and informed of the tragedy. I asked the office to inform D/CE [Major-General J. H. Lakin, Security Section] and DPR.1 without delay.
>
> In company with Major Rees I drove over to the aerodrome, arriving there at 10.30 hours. We spoke to Wing Commander Benham and Major Perkins who had both taken part in the rescue work and were given further particulars of the accident. Subsequently I had an interview with the Doctor who arranged for me to see the wounded man. I was particularly anxious to speak to him before making any further plans, for the doctor told me that the shock had been great and that he might not survive. I thought that the man might have some messages to give.
>
> The doctor had to make certain arrangements first of all for the injured personnel of the crew and it was after eleven when he took me to see the man. I conversed with him and I was able to put his mind at rest on certain points. After this I went through all his clothes and placed the documents and personal property in an envelope which is now in the possession of Major Rose. When this was completed, Wing Commander Benham and I went to the Mortuary as I felt

that DPR.1 would require first-hand evidence. This was an unpleasant ordeal, as the body had been severely burnt. I was not able to rescue any papers owing to the state of the clothing. At about 1210 hours we put through a call to London since the question of settling where the wounded man was to be sent was urgent. The doctor declared plainly that the case must be moved without delay.

At 12.45 I spoke again with D/CE and made certain arrangements as ordered. I was not at first able to locate Group Captain Weston, and, in general, officers, even those of a senior rank, are extremely difficult to find at an aerodrome. When finally I was told that he was lunching at a neighbouring Mess (Newmarket) I was unable to speak to him as the receiver on the Officers' mess telephone had not been replaced. I put a call through to London to report progress and to give Wing Commander Farley the opportunity to speak to Colonel Perry.

Meanwhile I contacted Group Captain Weston who stated that he was coming immediately to our aerodrome. At 1400 hours I spoke to Colonel Berry and on further instructions I prepared immediately to drive to London. Major Rose undertook to look after all arrangements there and to see that the wounded man was admitted to Ely Military Hospital in a suitable way from the security point of view. I did not arrive in London until 1750 hours as we had a puncture and a minor collision on the road.

After reporting to D/CR [an officer in SOE's security section] I drove round to see DPR.1. He was in a highly nervous condition and while I conversed with him he paced backward and forward across the small room. I felt that out of fairness to him he should have the opportunity to converse with someone above me. The fact that he was threatening to report the incident in an unfavourable light to his government was not as alarming as the prospect of a complete loss of confidence in our organisation. DPR.1. spoke to D/CE.1 [Lieutenant-Colonel J. Senter, Security Section] by telephone and expressed his wish to leave immediately for the aerodrome. In spite of argument he could not see why he should not go. Before leaving I gave D/CE's message and I pointed out that the enquiry must take place first and that the security aspect was of great importance.

I fear that the effects of this incident will be grievous as DPR.1 and his government had great confidence in these agents and considered their work of the utmost importance. Those who had met these men will readily confirm that they were the very best type of agents.

I should like to say how helpful were the officers at S.T.S. 61 and at the aerodrome. No effort was spared.[30]

The letter sent to Chichaev stated that Pavel's death was instantaneous and that he had suffered severe injuries to his head and skull, including a multiple fracture of the frontal bones. Both arms had been broken in several places. The face was totally burned, as were the arms, neck and chest and there were minor injuries on his legs and body. Major Seddon wrote to Chichaev, saying, 'The incident is regretted by all, particularly as your friend had made such a great impression upon us. It is a calamity which we all regret.'[31] The cause of the accident and the 'certain arrangements' referred to were included in the pilot's report:

> 21.50 Plane obliged to turn back owing to snowstorms over Belgium. Crashed on landing at Stradishall. Koubitski [sic] together with a number of the crew were killed. His body has been dropped by container into the sea. His papers and personal belongings were burnt in the accident, as also was his W/T set.[32]

Although Freddie Clark made no specific mention in his book, *Agents By Moonlight*, of NKVD agents being flown on 27 December 1941, he mentioned two missions flown by 138 Squadron that night. One of them, a Whitley bomber Z9385, piloted by Flight Sergeant A. W. Rimmer, crashed on the airfield killing Sergeant J. R. Petts, Sergeant G. R. S. Gordon and Corporal H. A. Pickering. Rimmer died two weeks later. Unusually for Clark, he did not provide more details apart from mentioning that Wireless Operator 'AG' and 'RG' baled out.[33]

On 28 December, J. Wallston (MO/D.1), one of SOE's operations section officers, wrote to A.D./4, an unidentified officer in George Taylor's overseas groups and missions section:

> MO/BL telephoned to me from Stradishall at about 4.30 a.m. to inform me that the aeroplane which was sent out on the MUSJID/PICKAXE operations had returned to Stradishall, having failed to carry out either operation and had crashed on landing. He said that one of the two Pickaxes had been killed and that the other was seriously injured and was in hospital. He also said that one of the crew had been killed and all the others had been injured … with the exception of one who was unhurt. Almost immediately he rang off, the MO [Medical Orderly] arrived and we decided that there was nothing we could do until about 8 a.m. when we would have to try to get in touch with Major Milnes-Gaskell. I succeeded in getting in touch with Major Milnes-Gaskell who was at S.T.S. 61 [Gaynes Hall] about 8.30 a.m. and informed him of what had happened. He asked me to inform 'the Colonel' without saying who I myself was. Major Milnes-Gaskell said that he would go over to Stradishall immediately and try to find out what the situation was. I then got in touch with Commander Senter and informed him of the situation. During the course of the morning, we had conflicting reports as to the state of health of the second Pickaxe. It now appears that he is alive and is likely to recover. I understand that Major Milnes-Gaskell is now on his way to London from Stradishall and he will doubtless make a full report to you on arrival.[34]

The pilot's report shed further light on the incident. The delays before take-off had meant that the reception committee at MUSJID's dropzone had left. Although the target was then set to drop the Pickaxe II agents, the plan was abandoned.

The area around Lac de Gilleppe was very difficult to pin-point owing to low cloud and snow showers. The aircraft returned to base and after a circuit of the aerodrome came in as if to land, but when about 50 feet off the ground the engines opened up and it appeared to be about to make another circuit when it spun into the ground and burst into flames. One of the Pickaxes was pinned underneath the wreckage and no doubt killed instantly, as also a member of the crew. The remainder of the crew and the other Pickaxe were either dragged from the wreckage or thrown clear. Two further members of the crew died after admission to Station Sick Quarters. The injured Pickaxe, although seriously hurt, is understood to stand an excellent chance of recovery.[35]

Petyr Kousnetsov was admitted into Ely hospital under the name of Corporal Ivan Robert, but he was not expected to walk for three months. While he was recuperating, plans were put in place for another mission.

OPERATION COFFEE

The second group of Pickaxes to arrive from the USSR was codenamed the Coffee party; it consisted of Willi Wagner and his wife Hilde Uxa, Anton Barak, Leopold Stancl and Alvin Mayr. Mayr joined them later under the names of Georg Martens and Jaan Runo. All were Austrian communists who had fled from Vienna to Czechoslovakia in the 1930s and then sought exile in the Soviet Union. Barak, Stancl and Mayr had all volunteered to fight for the International Brigade in the Spanish Civil War.

Mayr took part in the defence of Madrid in late 1936 when he was serving with the XIth (German) International Brigade. After completing an officer's training course, he was promoted to captain, and the following year he led a company in most of the major battles. Despite being described as 'a good comrade, extremely brave, but soft' by the Cadres Department in Albacete, he was appointed Chief of Signals, but was then sent to France following a car crash in which he was badly injured.

Barak served in the multinational XIIIth (Chapayev) Brigade, but he was wounded during his first engagement at Teruel in Christmas 1936. After recovering in hospital he was promoted to lieutenant, but the following year, in the attack on Romanillos, he was shot several times in the abdomen and was forced to spend a year in hospital and rest homes before being evacuated to France.

Stancl was Barak's company chief in the XIIIth Brigade and later commanded the XIth Brigade's Austrian '12 Feber' Battalion. He was also wounded and evacuated to France where he suffered from recurrent bouts of typhus.

The French communist party provided the three men with cover stories and accommodation until the KPÖ, the Austrian communist party, arranged for their transport back to the Soviet Union in March/April 1939. The Comintern considered them to be valuable party cadres.[1]

Willi Wagner worked in Elektrozavod before enrolling in the International Lenin School where, using the cover name of Arnold Schmidt, he met and later married the Viennese Hilde Uxa, who went by the name Hilde Hassler. Wagner's attempt to join the International Brigade was opposed by Hilde, so instead he worked as an interpreter on a Soviet steamer carrying arms to Spain.

Following Operation Barbarossa, the NKVD organised the most trustworthy of the Austrian communist party, including Wagner, Barak, Mayr, and Stancl, into a so-called 'Destruction Battalion'. They were transferred to a camp on the Kursk railway, south of Moscow. Following a course in basic military training, Wagner, Stancl, and Barak were sent back to an espionage school in Moscow to practice parachute jumping and improve their shooting skills. On completion of their training, they had to sign a statement that they were prepared to carry out a mission behind German lines for the NKVD. Wagner must have discussed his plans with Hilde as she also signed the pledge, volunteering to go with them.

As the German army approached Kursk, the espionage school was evacuated to Kuibyshev. Then, in November 1941, Barak, Stancl, Wagner and his wife went by train to Archangel where they boarded the SS *Hartlebury* for Britain. The member of the SAM staff who accompanied the Coffee agents to Archangel was said to have been shocked by their appearance: 'shabbily dressed, without winter clothing, their luggage wrapped in a few paper parcels.' Insisting that they ought to arrive in Britain 'complete with fingers and toes', the SAM officer managed to persuade his NKVD counterpart to issue the agents with suitable footwear, gloves, and caps.

Alvin Mayr, meanwhile, was allocated a different mission. He was sent on an intensive wireless operator's course and did not arrive in Britain until ten months later.[2]

When they arrived in London in December 1941, the Soviet-trained agents claimed to be natives of Engels in the Volga mountains, but they had no documents, no wireless set, and according to their SOE file, they were totally untrained. New identities and cover stories had to be created for them. According to a list of Pickaxe agents drawn up after the war, the names of the Coffee party included Maria Dicksen, alias Hilde Windern, whose real name was Hilde Uxa; Kurt Traub, alias Wilhelm Krauze, real name Willi Wagner; Karl Schwarz, alias Leopold Huntze, real name Leopold Stancl; and Gustav Hoffman, alias Anton Bolen, real name Anton Barak.[3] According to the SOE, none of them were said to have known why they were sent to Britain until they met Chichaev.

On 5 January 1942, having been issued with identity cards claiming them as Swiss nationals to avoid scrutiny from Scotland Yard, they were taken by train to Ringway, where they stayed at Dunham House. They were shown parachutes being packed and witnessed some practice drops from air balloons and specially adapted Whitley bombers. However, a medical inspection found them unfit to jump and the station commander refused to take responsibility for what might happen during their training.

They were returned to London to be seen by Dr Jones, who found that Hilde Uxa (Maria Dicksen) suffered dizzy spells due to a thyroid gland operation in the Soviet Union, while Barak (Hoffman) and Stancl (Schwarz) still suffered from wounds received in Spain, and Stancl's typhus and dysentery had so damaged his liver that he needed hospitalisation.[4]

Although it was determined that they would never be fit for severe physical training, Chichaev insisted they jump, regardless of their medical condition. They were sent back to Ringway three weeks later where, perhaps understandably, they were said to have shown alarming signs of low morale.

> Barak [Hoffman], who performed his jump with coolness, was considered 'very unpunctual' and of a 'resigned fatalistic nature'. According to his training staff, Willi Wagner was equally unenthusiastic and had to be ordered three times before he jumped from a barrage balloon, and afterwards from an aircraft. His wife showed little interest in the preliminaries and became so ill above ground that she did not jump at all.[5]

A flight was scheduled for 20 January. However, it had to be postponed when Stancl was rushed to St Thomas's Hospital for observation. After Dr Jones examined him, he was declared medically unfit for the task. With Chichaev's aquiesence, arrangements were made for him to be returned to the Soviet Union, leaving from Sunderland on 19 February on the SS *Sevzaples*.[6]

While Stancl's fate was being decided, preparations went ahead for his three comrades. Discussions were held on the choice of dropzone, with the agents, Chichaev, and the Air Ministry each proposing different pinpoints. Eventually, the Air Ministry's choice of a spot on the banks of Neusiedler Lake, based on road communications and its susceptibility to night fog, was decided on. Orders were placed for a .32 Mauser or Luger, a spare magazine, and 100 rounds of ammunition to be issued to each agent. No explosives or sabotage equipment were issued. As well as the necessary parachuting attire, each person's medication included six 'B' pills, six 'K' pills, and one 'L' pill.

Once again, a lack of documents was causing delay. At the end of January 1943, Captain Darton (D/P.2) noted:

> Unless the papers do arrive from Russia I still do not see how the party can be made ready for the February moon. After exhaustive enquiries, we are only now beginning to collect German documents and papers, reproduction of which will take weeks, and in some cases, months.[7]

Unaware of these developments, Captain Tice, the air liaison officer at Tempsford, offered the party a new date, 28 February. It had to be cancelled as they could not go without a radio operator. Stancl's replacement, Alvin Mayr (alias Georg Martens), who was supposed to bring their documents with him, had not left the Soviet Union. While they waited, they were accommodated at Little Hansteads, a secluded fourteen-roomed Georgian-style country mansion in Bricket Wood, near St Albans, an hour's drive from London.[8] There they lived in boredom, with no money or freedom, and only the odd excursion to the local pub or a restaurant in London to divert them.[9]

As the hours of daylight increased, the chances of the Coffee party being able to undertake their mission diminished. Once the March/April moons had passed, all flights to Austria were cancelled until the autumn. Knowing that they had a long wait, SOE transferred them to The Drokes, and then, to create a change, they were taken to stay at Inchmery, a large mansion overlooking the Solent to the Isle of Wight, then to Gumley Hall, near Market Harborough in Northamptonshire, and Chicheley Hall, near Newport Pagnell in Buckinghamshire.

While at Chicheley in the summer, they received two hours of signalling a day. It seemed their morale had improved. Captain Darton, their SOE officer, commented in his report:

> The three students are enjoying life and are grateful for the excellent treatment they receive. I was duly impressed by the artistic work of the eldest member, while I understand that another is fisherman with plenty of enthusiasm, but not great skill.[10]

Hilde informed him that she needed a new trousseau – four sets of underwear, a frock or blouse, a skirt, three pairs of stockings, an overcoat and some wool and other items. Captain Darton arranged for a Miss Hatfield, presumably one of the FANYs, to take her from Wolverton by train to London for two days' shopping. Sixty clothing coupons were needed to cover the bill for £22 5s.0d.[11]

As the summer progressed, arrangements were made for Hilde to retake her parachute training. Captain Thornton was given the task of helping her. Back in Dunham House, she was provided with a separate mess room so as not to mix with the other agents. But it being the height of summer, she disobeyed her instructions and went through the French windows into the gardens. Whether she had conversed with other trainees was not mentioned, but it was an incident deemed worthy of informing SOE about. Her breach of security was noted as having 'completely defeated the object of having a separate room at their disposal'. The commandant's report stated:

> [She is] A very frightened type of person who had a weak heart and a weak ankle. After each descent she cried, and showed no interest at all in parachuting. Her two jumps however were done quite well, but in both her landings she landed backwards and slightly bruised herself. Morale Bad. TWO DESCENTS. 3rd CLASS.[12]

She complained of having hurt herself badly. An X-ray revealed no internal injuries or fractures of the spine. Dr Jones suggested it was nervous shock and the pain would eventually go. However, as she was still suffering on her return to London, she was seen by Dr Finlayson who recommended her to see a gynaecologist for diathermy treatment. Arrangements were made for her to have an operation at

University College Hospital under the name of Hedy Wendern. However, Chichaev refused to allow the operation at the last moment, a decision Hilde was not to forget.[13]

Stancl's replacement, Alvin Mayr and four new Pickaxe agents (the Tonic and Sodawater parties, see Chapter 13) sailed from Archangel through the frigid Arctic waters to Scotland in late September 1942. They were lucky to survive a German U-boat attack that sank the ship and sent their luggage, wireless codes, and their vital documents – including Mayr's Soviet-made documents for the Coffee party – to the sea bed. The passengers were rescued by the liner *Queen Mary* and taken via Iceland to Scotland.

When Mayr eventually joined the Coffee party on 5 October under the name of Jaan Runo, they learnt that he had not brought their documents. However, to focus their attention on the mission, the agents were informed of a new dropzone, about 12 miles north-west of Wiener Heustadt, 5 miles south-west of Berndorf in Austria, and told that the flight would take place during the December moon period.[14]

The replacement documents for the Coffee party contained identical photographs for documents purporting to have been issued over a ten-year period, and omitted the medical reasons for the men being excused military training. Expressing their dissatisfaction with the inadequate and poorly forged papers, the Coffee party demanded the right to ask advice from the English. This request was refused and they were told that, if they did not obey orders, they would be returned to Moscow. They had all decided that they were being sent on a suicide mission. They felt that the mission had been badly planned by the NKVD in the Soviet Union, and they had been badly treated by Chichaev and Toropchenko who rarely visited them and gave them very little money and inadequate clothing.[15]

In the meantime, in an attempt to soothe Anglo-Soviet relations, someone in the Russian Section drafted a letter, praising the first-class help provided by Captain Thornton. It was commented that his student, Maria Dickson (Hilde Uxa),

> ... was delighted and expressed her great admiration for the manner with which she was treated and has formed a very good impression of the work there.
>
> This in itself may be a small matter but when one realises that all of these things are passed on to our local Russian colleague [Chichaev] and thence almost certainly to Moscow, I think a word of thanks to the Commandant and especially to Thornton would not be amiss, and I should be grateful if you will tell them how much we appreciate their assistance.
>
> These good impressions make our relations with our foreign friends much easier.[16]

In November, Lieutenant-Colonel Wild escorted the Coffee party to London for a meeting with Chichaev. While waiting in an adjacent room he overheard 'a good old bobbery and loud altercation going on'.[17] On questioning them on what happened afterwards, only Alvin Mayr was prepared to talk. Chichaev had insisted on the three men going alone to a dropzone, 40 miles from Vienna. They refused to go without Hilde, and objected to being dropped in December when temperatures might be as low as -30°. They suggested postponing the mission until March or April 1943.

Further details of what transpired during the meeting were revealed in a report drawn up by one of their conducting officers.

> At the end of November, a new set of documents arrived for the whole party. Although this section was never permitted to see these documents, it is understood that they consisted of three incorrect Wehrpässe, and a faulty identity card. They were dissatisfied with these documents. Kurt [Willi Wagner) and Maria [Hilde Uxa] protested vehemently to DPR.1 [Chichaev] and demanded that, either they should have a complete set of proper documents sent from Russia, or that they be allowed to confer with this section, who, they felt, might be able to make up some kind of cover story for them. DPR.1 after a suitable pause informed them that they would either travel with the documents as they were or that they would have to return to Russia. Under no circumstances were they to communicate with the English.[18]

It was the final breach of trust between the Coffee party and their masters. Major E. K. Saunders, codename D/P.5, SOE's man in charge of country houses, commented on Hilde Uxa's attitude:

> ... [her] sole ambition seems to be to remain here and spend money and grumble from morning to night at everything, upsetting the others in the process. She never evinces a spark of gratitude for all that is done for her.
>
> Gustav [Barak] seems in the depths of despondency since his papers came back from Moscow all wrong. [19]

When Hill was informed, he laid part of the blame on the SOE. The ration cards they issued to the Coffee party, although valid for several months, had already expired because of the delay. They were seemingly unaware that the Germans issued new ones every month.[20]

Chichaev refused to wait for new documents to be created or to allow the British to create new cover stories for the Coffee party. As they refused to go, he cancelled their mission and instructed what he called the 'Hoffman Group' to return to the Soviet Union. He commented that, from a moral and physical viewpoint, they had been badly chosen.[21]

An anonymous, undated memo in their file admitted:

There is no doubt that COFFEE were the most peculiar people that this section has had to deal with up to the present. They appeared always to have been split up into two groups of which Maria [Uxa] and Kurt [Wagner] formed one and Gustav [Barak] (later to be joined by Runo [Mayr]) the other. The former confided in us more than it was safe for them to do. Hence probably their ultimate fate. The latter, though their feelings were the same, behaved more circumspect and in fact did not completely break down until the last day.

They all disliked DPR.1 and company intensely and were frightened of them. Their history was (according to Maria, and there appears little need to doubt their story) that they arrived in this country full of hope and anti-Fascism, with implicit faith in the Russian documents and wanting nothing better than to return to Vienna. During the inevitable early delays, they came into conversation with members of this section and gradually the germs of, firstly, doubt and, secondly, democratic principle, began to rear their ugly heads. They started to mistrust DPR section. A further delay was caused by the return of Schwarz [Stancl] and by the end of the summer they were in almost open revolt. Runo [Mayr] became infected with the same ideas soon after he had joined them.[22]

Despite the Coffee party's entreaties for the SOE to arrange their naturalisation as British subjects or allow them to join the British armed forces, they were told that as the British Government was bound by the terms of the treaty, they could do nothing. False papers were issued for the voyage, identifying them as Wilhelm Krauze (Kurt Traub/Wilhelm Wagner), Anton Bolen (Gustav Hoffman/ Anton Barak), Jaan Runo (Georg Martens/Alvin Mayr), and Hilde Windern (Maria Dicksen/Hilde Uxa). At the end of January 1943, Major Saunders was given the task of escorting them to the port. Having made sure that anything that could possibly link them with Britain had been removed from their person, he saw them onto a Russian ship bound for Murmansk.

That was not the end of their story. After over two months on board, heavy storms in the North Atlantic forced the convoy to disperse and the ship had to return to shelter in Western Scotland to await another convoy. Having reached port, the ship's medical officer arranged for Hilde to be taken to Royal Northern Hospital in Inverness as she was suffering from severe stomach pains. While convalescing in hospital, Hilde wrote an emotional letter to Captain A. L. McLaughlin (D/P.4), one of the Russian Section officers she had come into close contact with, appealing for help.

Dear Mr. McLaughlin,

You will certainly be surprised to hear from me after such a long time but it is true; but I cannot tell you whether it is a good thing or a bad thing that we are back in England again. You will be wondering how it is that I can write you an ordinary open letter. The position is this; for nearly a week I have been very ill and yesterday

I was landed and brought to a hospital. You can imagine, Captain, how difficult it is for me; doctors and patients all speak Scotch, plus some English, but as you know, I understand the latter badly and the former not at all. By means of gesticulations I have more or less arrived at getting paper and pencil – the important things, however, either I cannot tell them, or I cannot understand what they answer. My dear Captain, we have been seventy days on the ship and God alone knows when we shall get out of this – believe me, we cannot stand it much longer. The ship's Captain would be only too pleased to get rid of us. We are suspect to all those on board because of our foreign accent and they believe us to be anything but what our passports say we are. This feeling pervades everything. 'Our people' would not worry themselves about us, even were we to be another two months living under the same conditions. The prospects of any change in the immediate future are not apparent. Oh dear Captain, cannot you really help us to get out of this? The people in charge of the business must know how long we are supposed to stay here. Could we not live in some house – after all we are passengers – and could leave the ship. Here in hospital the people are very good, in some things even too good. They are trying their hardest to patch me up as quickly as possible for the voyage and to get me back to the ship.

Captain, Gustav will already have told you where we are at the moment.

Please excuse my bad writing but I cannot get up and I am not used to writing in bed.

Please give our very kindest regards to Major Seddon and Miss Hatfield – oh, we would love to be with you all again, even if only for a short time.

Again, with very best wishes and please, please, don't forget us.

Please think the matter over; I am sure you will find some way out. We are convinced that you, and you alone, can help us.

Maria.[22]

If McLaughlin responded, his letter was not in the Coffee party's file. The SOE's response was to discuss it with the upper echelons of the security services.

Barak, Wagner, and Mayr had been taken to the Albert Hotel in Inverness where they were 'cared for' by SOE staff. However, on 20 March, two weeks before Hilde wrote her letter to Captain McLaughlin, Toropchenko telephoned Captain McLaughlin to say that Barak was seriously ill at Loch Ewe. Although the Russians made arrangements for him to travel to London where he had to report to 13 Kensington Palace Gardens, the SOE refused responsibility for him. Chichaev wanted him put on the next convoy but this was impossible as his passport had expired on 8 February 1942. Then, on 26 March, Toropchenko rang to say the trip was cancelled and asked that a doctor be sent to see Barak at the Inverness Court Hotel in Bayswater.[24]

Complaining about being very fatigued and grossly constipated, it was decided to send Barak to St Thomas's Hospital for investigations. A few days later, Dr Jones reported that X-rays revealed nothing structurally abnormal but that he had many adhesions from the gun shot wounds he received in the Spanish Civil War. As he was described as being comfortable and peaceful, the SOE decided that his armed guard could be removed. He was in 'one of the bricked-in wards' and as he was 'so grossly debilitated' and not fit enough to take full care of himself for a week to ten days, he was sent to a country hospital in Godalming for observation and convalescence.[25]

Although Toropchenko was accommodated in the same hotel, MI5 arranged for a 'Captain Brown' to visit them, pretending to be an SOE officer. Major Seddon and Major G. P. Wethered also went to speak to the Coffee party.[26] MI5's involvement was to determine whether the Coffee party's defection was genuine, or whether they were double agents and part of a plot to infiltrate the SOE or to be allowed to stay in Britain under deep cover, continuing to work secretly for the Soviets. Their interrogators identified that all were terrified of what would happen should they be returned to Moscow. It was suggested that

... as they were going via America, it would be possible for them to be arrested in the Panama Canal and taken off the ship by arrangement with American police on some charge or other. They hope that help may come from the British through the Americans. After the hue and cry has died down, they might come back to England, or go on to Austria to carry on the fight.

They would like to work at their respective trades in America, thereby becoming independent and recovering their self-respect. They would be more than willing to work for the British to help their own country.

They are very careful in their dealings with Toropchenko who will 'accompany' them to Moscow. This man does not know what will happen to them when they arrive in Moscow (for that matter, neither do the agents themselves, officially), but all have a fairly good idea. Toropchenko has no suspicion whatsoever that the British are helping in any way; on the contrary, he was grateful for the help we gave him. He is travelling on the ship in the capacity of an officer; this will enable him to keep a better watch on the others, all of whom are to work below decks – Traub [Wagner] as a machinist, Hoffman [Barak] as 5th electrician, Martens [Mayr] as 3rd mechanic and Dicksen [Uxa] as stewardess.

...they have decided that if no help is forthcoming at the last American port (San Francisco) they will make a break anyway. Martens has a very good friend (German) in New York. They have asked if anything could be arranged to find them work there. They do not want to stay long, but wish to help the Allies as best they can. They mentioned that, had it only been possible to remain in England, they would have liked to have helped open the Second Front. All stressed the importance of Austria, and how much they could help.[27]

A report on the NKVD/SOE agreement addressed to Sir Charles Hambro (CD), the head of SOE, presupposed that their mission included sabotage. Captain

McLaughlin claimed that it also included assassination assignments in Vienna, but there was no mention of that in their file. However, there was an admission:

> ... one of the section's aims [has been] to penetrate the veil of Soviet intentions in an endeavour to ascertain the exact role of the agents. A loyal adherence to the terms of secrecy enjoined has prevented them from approaching the problem frontally and such information as has been obtained has come to them fortuitously, either as the result of confidence instilled by SOE into the agents themselves, or by reason of the fact that most of the NKVD agents have accepted their task as a means of escape from Russia.
>
> For some considerable time it has been clear that the directives to agents have given no impression of being concerned with active subversion and the suspicion that these agents were part of a post-war political plan has been more than once intensified by odd remarks in casual conversation and from every party.
>
> The section is now in possession of more detailed information as the result of the 'volte face' on the part of the COFFEE agents. Their treatment by the NKVD has been of such a nature that they are now prepared to go to any lengths to escape from Soviet clutches, even, so they have stated, to a demand for Police protection in exchange for a full exposure of the Soviet instructions to them. They have in fact communicated to the section a certain amount of data about their training and orders from NKVD and their general treatment in Russia, and this can be furnished if of interest.
>
> ...The aim of the Soviet was to prepare the ground for an anti-British and anti-American campaign in which Germany was not to be included, but was to be treated as a possible ally.
>
> They were to obtain access to the already existing communist cells and furnish them with further means of communication with Moscow and the Soviet authorities.
>
> ...The importance of these statements, which naturally cannot be verified, lies in the fact that we may, by our action in introducing the agents, [be] unwittingly building up an enemy organisation under our very noses and that far from collaborating in attack on the Axis, we may be subscribing to the doctrine of hari-kari.[28]

In an attempt to inform the rest of the intelligence community, a letter outlining the SOE's plans was sent to Sir Alexander Cadogan of the Foreign Office and was circulated to the other sections. It acknowledged that as the SOE were unsure of the Coffee party's bona fides, the Austrians could not be given any indication that the SOE was trying to help them avoid returning to the Soviet Union. The final paragraph stated: 'I feel you should be informed personally of this plan so that in case there should be any repercussions you are informed of our intentions.'[29] Cadogan's response suggested caution:

The memo enclosed in your letter rather suggests that your people accept the party's story that the purpose of their mission was to prepare the ground for an anti-British and anti-American campaign looking forward to the post-war period, and I see that the story will probably be passed to M.I.5. I think we should guard against any assumption that the party's story is undoubtedly true. If they do not want to go back to the Soviet Union they may well have invented the story in order to avoid this; or they may even be 'agents provocateurs' intended to test S.O.E's feelings. I think this point should be brought out in passing your information to M.I.5.

For this reason, I am all the more in favour of your present plan, under which S.O.E. is absolved of all responsibility vis-à-vis the N.K.V.D., although I imagine that it is not all that certain that the Americans will be ready to take the party off a Russian ship in Panama and let them escape, since this involves an obvious risk of creating bad blood between the American and Soviet Authorities.[30]

As it was Cadogan's opinion that Britain had to be seen to be complying with the terms of the treaty, the SOE was instructed to see the four agents aboard and then inform the Americans.

May Day celebrations were very quiet for the Coffee party. Uxa and Barak had returned to Loch Ewe, and Toropchenko suggested that their conducting officer, Sergeant Kratzoff, should spend 'a few pounds' on a party. He noted that the four were 'rather disgusted with his meanness on their national holiday, knowing that he had a considerable sum of money in his possession, but for safety's sake did not say very much about it.'[31]

Two days later, Colonel Graur arrived with instructions for their departure. That night, they were taken by train to Middlesbrough where arrangements were made for their passage aboard a 6,000-ton Dutch-built cargo ship bound for Vladivostok via the Panama Canal. In his diary, Kratzoff noted:

10.5.43

I took the party down to Immigration Office. Their baggage was searched, but not thoroughly. Passed by Immigration Officer. Each member of party declared about £8 and $4, except for Toropchenko who declared £3 and $20....

I put the party aboard and inspected their quarters. They were very cramped, although Toropchenko was fairly comfortable. All had dinner in Captain's saloon.

I made my farewells, the party asked me to convey their thanks etc., and hoped that they would not be forgotten.[32]

A telegram to SAM was drafted which attempted to explain the situation, but its contents and style were not approved by Hambro. Part of it read:

A return match is being played at B where the team is in training before their transfer to C via D.

Although hopes do not run high they have put in some good practice and have started to heel the ball cleanly in their determination to make a quick getaway.

Conditions are pretty heavy and a muddy ball in the hands of our scrum-half may lead to a change of team tactics.

Will let you know result of match immediately it comes through.[33]

Because of the politically sensitive nature of the incident, careful discussions took place between the SOE and the Foreign Office. A proposed plane crash was dismissed in favour of asking the Americans to help. A carefully worded telegram and photographs of the four passengers were forwarded to William Stephenson, codenamed 'G', SOE's man in New York, for the attention of the FBI. But in the end, despite SOE officers being sympathetic and generally sceptical about the Soviet Union, the authority to decide the fate of the Coffee party lay with Whitehall. Exactly what was decided is still shrouded in mystery.

Whether or not an arrangement was finally agreed with the FBI via Stephenson, for the Austrians to jump ship in Panama and seek asylum in the US, the plan failed. However, they did manage to escape in San Francisco and make it over the border to Vancouver in Canada. Attempts to find British Security Coordination (BSC) files that would shed light on whether they managed to get assistance from the FBI have come to nothing.

The Coffee party's appeals for political asylum in Canada were turned down. One can only surmise that either Whitehall or the echelons of the SOE (possibly both) put pressure on the Canadian Government to deport the Austrians for fear that they would tell their story and reveal to the Canadians (and possibly the Americans) the 'debriefing' they were given in the UK, confirming that Britain was involved in infiltrating communists into occupied Europe. As Soviet foreign ministry officials remonstrated with the Canadian Government, the 'Hoffman Group' was deported aboard the Soviet vessel SS *Mayakovsky* to Vladivostok. The British authorities made no attempt to enquire what happened to them.

O'Sullivan mentions that the official Soviet record shows that the SOE recruited Wagner in 1942 to work against the Soviet Union. In return for £10, he gave the the SOE details on the instructions the group had been given in Moscow and operational information about their plans once they arrived in Austria. The SOE also asked Wagner to provide them with his codes and ciphers. There is no evidence of this in the SOE files and the SIS neither confirm nor deny their involvement. While this scenario cannot be ruled out, it seems far more likely that the group simply defected because of declining morale.

When the news of their claiming asylum in Canada reached London, it was agreed to delay the result of their appeal until the Soviet ship had left. Sir Charles Hambro sent an urgent telegram to Stephenson in New York.

Most important that S.O.E. connection with this affair should be confined to barest minimum information necessary to help external affairs.

You may say that I was informed about them and that I consider their case a genuine one for sympathetic treatment.

It is of vital urgency that no repeat no Soviet representative should become aware of any conversations between S.O.E. representatives and agents concerning this escape. All statements by agents which may suggest our connivance must be suppressed.[34]

In McLoughlin's opinion, the differences between NKVD and SOE agents were that the Soviets' controllers were more concerned with the political convictions of their agents, rather than their age, enthusiasm, physical fitness, and military training. Bickham Sweet Escott, in his autobiographical account of his war years with SOE, commented that, in contrast to what they had heard of the NKVD, they were surprised to discover that the training of their agents was 'lamentably poor'. Sweet-Escott adds that, as the Coffee party had disobeyed their seniors and refused to be parachuted into occupied Europe, no doubt a 'singularly unpleasant fate awaited them' on their return to Russia.[35]

In May 1944, six months after their return to Moscow, the four Coffee agents were tried. Mayr received twenty-five years for 'espionage' and the others received ten years. Barak committed suicide in Lubianka Prison in Moscow, but Wagner, Uxa, and Mayr survived twelve years in forced labour camps (gulags). They were released in 1956.[36]

OPERATION RUM

SOE's first attempts to drop the Pickaxes were criticised as being 'hardly encouraging'.[1] In a note dated 19 December 1941, Hill informed Seddon that the ship meant to be carrying two men destined for Holland and Belgium had already sailed from Archangel. Apparently the men disappeared into thin air before the ship left harbour. Who they were and whether they were sent later is not known. There was also mention of a man and woman due to arrive in March 1942 to be dropped into Belgium.[2] Who they were has not come to light, but it is possible that they were not sent as, at that time, SIS was against dropping agents into Belgium without the express agreement of the government-in-exile. When the SIS learned that SOE had already delivered Soviet agents into France, concern was expressed to Hambro, resulting in the following note:

> I can assure you that we do not and will not allow operations for infiltrating NKVD agents to prejudice our own operations in point of priority. Nor would we be a party to prejudicing your operations by this means.
>
> I note that General de Gaulle does not like the idea of introducing NKVD agents into France. Although I am in sympathy, this is somewhat surprising considering his avowed deep friendship with Moscow![3]

On 19 February 1942, concerns were being expressed in the Russian Section about the Pickaxe operations. The Swiss, Yugoslav, and Spanish governments had refused to allow Soviet missions into their countries. Maybe this explains why some of the other Pickaxes were returned to Moscow. Although the Foreign Office was demanding to be consulted over all the Soviet agents to be dropped into Europe, the SOE was determined to oppose this vetting. Milnes-Gaskell advised:

> If the Foreign Office are going to argue, and we are going to accept the argument, that because the contacts of SOE, a Secret Government Agency, with certain foreign elements would, if discovered, possibly embarrass HMG [His Majesty's Government], the Foreign Office must therefore have a veto on such contacts, then SOE had better shut up shop.

If we are to be of any use at all, we must be allowed to proceed as a secret organisation, to make contacts and establish machinery off our own bat, on the understanding that if anything leaks out, we will simply be disowned.

... The immediate practical problem, is, as you know, what to do with the party of three men [sic] and one woman which is scheduled to go to France on 28th February [Operation RUM]. We may be able to persuade Sir A. Cadogan to accept our view before this date. Alternatively, we may send the party whilst still arguing with the Foreign Office. We could, I suppose, ask the agreement of the Foreign Office for this particular party without prejudice to the principle which is now under discussion (though this I certainly would not like as it would undoubtedly compromise our position). The one thing that is clear, is that the party should go as arranged since otherwise there will be the most frightful row with Chichaeff, and a complete loss of confidence in the honesty of our intentions.[4]

Milnes-Gaskell made enquiries with higher quarters, and in early March 1942, he reported to Sir Alexander Cadogan from the Ministry of Economic Warfare in Berkeley Square House. Sending Rum, a team of two men and a woman, into unoccupied France would avoid an impossible breakdown with the NKVD and the potential withdrawal of 'our Mission in Moscow'. He hoped the decision would bring tangible results in the long run.

Operation Rum (original name Brandy) included three agents with French passports: 31-year-old Ivan Danilov, alias Pierre Dandin, 39-year-old Grigory Rodionov, alias Georges Robigot, and 25-year-old Anna Frolova, alias Annette Fauberge. Having sailed from Archangel via Reykjavik aboard SS *Arcos*, they arrived at Loch Ewe, Scotland, on 8 February 1942. They were accompanied by four other Soviet agents who had also left Russia aboard *Arcos*. Two of these – both men – were bound for Vienna in Operation Whiskey, but the fate of the other two remains a mystery. They were perhaps the two whose mission to Belgium was aborted and were then returned to Russia. They all travelled as a group as far as Edinburgh, but were then separated. From Edinburgh, Danilov, Rodionov, and Frolova were transported to London and the Rhodesia Court Hotel, 29 Harrington Gardens, where they arrived on 12 February. They were briefed by the NKVD, presumably Chichaev, at this address, and promptly complained to the SOE that their accomodation was too open to the public. Accordingly, SOE arranged for them to be transferred to The Drokes, where they stayed between 16 and 22 February. While there, the SOE was informed that their operation's name had been changed to Rum as there was already an agent in Holland called Brandy.

From the New Forest, Second Lieutenant Walshe, their conducting officer, and Captain Toropchenko, their accompanying officer, escorted the three agents by train for their parachute training at Ringway. Like the other Pickaxe parties, they stayed at Dunham House in a separate mess to keep the other students from discovering that Britain was training Soviet agents.

Major Edwards, commanding officer at Ringway, summed them up as 'a very mixed party, whose chief faults were indecision and unpunctuality. They got through their program of drops with fair success.' On Captain Toropchenko, Edwards commented, 'did not jump, very determined and forceful. Very stern over his party's jumping.' Danilov was described as 'rather a nervous type. Very poor on ground training. He made a poor descent from the balloon, but improved greatly, and made a good aircraft drop.'[5] Rodionov was considered 'quiet and determined', the best of the party, while Frolova 'showed good spirit', if little skill in her balloon drop. Comparing them to previous Pickaxe parties, the commandant declared they were 'certainly ... better material.'[6]

The agents returned to London on 26 February and stayed at 40 Porchester Court. This had been rented to house Pickaxes and used as a meeting place for SOE's Russian Section and the NKVD. While residing here, the Rum agents were provided with cover stories, forged identity cards, demobilisation forms and personal letters. Exact copies of the appropriate French police commissioner's signature and accurate official stamps had to be added to ensure that the documents looked authentic. The 500 dollars and 85 Swedish crowns they had each been given was converted to francs, and they were all supplied with appropriate clothing.[7] Their mission was thought to be to assist the isolated Soviet agents in Lyon and provide communication with Moscow.

Anna Frolova (Annette Fauberge) was given a new identity as 'Jeanne Claude Garnier'. Her SOE report described her as

a good-looking French woman; extremely hard, and it was impossible to find out from her any facts about her former history. Her luggage was carefully examined and from the enclosed photograph, we deduced that she had been 'married' and had produced a small son during the autumn of 1939.

She was a stenographer by trade and had lived in Paris. For some reason which we do not know she left France for Copenhagen in 1940, whence she proceeded to Russia. From her clothes it would appear that she had been well-off and belonged to the bourgeois class.

She would make a good agent and should successfully pass any normal police examination.[8]

Ivan Danilov's (Pierre Dandin) new identity was as 'Louis Pierre Dupré'.

[A] small insignificant man who belonged to the working class. He was in every way a typical Frenchman and could best be described as the ordinary 'man in the street'.

He is not intelligent and did not possess sufficient confidence for a good agent. He had worked until 1939, in the centre of Paris as a librarian until he was called up. He deserted from the Army and found his way to Russia.

He was anxious to return to France but it is doubtful whether he will fulfil any useful role as an agent. He was plausible but of a nervous disposition. We gained the impression that once he has established himself in France, he would not take seriously his duties as a Soviet agent.[9]

Grigory Rodionov's (Georges Robigot) new identity was as 'Marcel Jacques Ménard'.

[He] belonged to the middle-class and was a typical Frenchman of the bourgeois type. He had lived for the most part in the Paris district, and, on the outbreak of war, was called up for his regiment. He served for some months in the Army, but deserted and made his way to Russia, presumably through Denmark and Scandinavia. He was in every way typically French, shrewd, intelligent, and with a penchant for good cuisine.

As an agent, he would clearly fit easily into the French background. He was very reticent about his past history, also about the work which he was undertaking in France. His first objective was to reach Lyons where his duty was to deliver a wireless set and open up communications between Occupied France and USSR. He was not himself a wireless operator. His secondary task was to cross the frontier and proceed to Paris.

I do not believe that Menard would be able to undergo a severe police examination. It struck me that his nerve was not good and he was inclined to tell too many lies. Incidentally, he did not give the impression of being a good Communist; on several occasions, he recounted his experiences in Russia and repeated 'Que c'est dur, que c'est dur, la bas.' He was most impressed by his treatment in England, and was firmly convinced that we would win the war.[10]

The original plan was for three accompanying officers and Miss Jackson, a FANY officer, to take the Rum agents to Gaynes Hall to wait for their flight from Tempsford, but circumstances must have changed. On 3 March 1942, the agents, accompanied by Toropchenko, Dodds-Parker, and Milnes-Gaskell, left London at 1530 hours and proceeded to Tangmere Airfield. The original time of departure was scheduled for 1930, but at 1900 hours it was cancelled. Later, at 1945 hours this decision was reversed; the agents were dressed and ready by 2015 hours.

Having been given their farewell drinks, their general morale was described as 'excellent'. The SOE had provided them with a wireless set camouflaged as a suitcase. It was considered a tactful gesture as a Soviet wireless set had been destroyed when Pickaxe II crashed.[11]

The agents had requested to be dropped west of Montpellier so the RAF pinpointed a dropzone east of the River Herault and north of the railway line between Paulhan and Montpellier. On the night of 3/4 March, Czech pilot, Pilot Officer L. M. Anderle, flying Whitley Z9158 on Operation Rum, reported in the squadron log book that, having climbed to 6,500 feet to cross the mountains in central France, he descended to 600 feet to drop three men and two packages at 600 feet having. All five parachutes were seen to open. They returned to Tempsford, landing at 0536.[12]

The final note in the Rum agents' SOE file reads:

> ... three months after Rodionov was parachuted into France, the N.K.V.D. displayed considerable anxiety as they had heard nothing of him or his two colleagues.[13]

In 1945, MI5 discovered that French police had in their care a woman who called herself Marie-Claude Vallant-Couturier who had been rescued from Auschwitz Concentration Camp and who had excellent command of English. Upon being shown a photograph of Anna Frolova, the police did not think it was the same woman, unless her experiences had considerably altered her appearance.[14]

According to O'Sullivan, French investigations revealed that 'Dandin' was not Ivan Danilov, but Daniel Georges, a political commissar in the Spanish Civil War, and 'Robigot' was not Grigory Rodionov, but Raymond Guyot, a senior official of the Communist Youth International and a well-known French Communist. Guyot was married to Francine Fromont, who was executed by the Germans for espionage in August 1944. After the war, communist-controlled city councils honoured Francine Fromont by naming streets and schools after her.[15]

On 21 March 1942, SOE was informed that the NKVD had sixteen trained agents ready to be despatched to Europe, including six for France. Questions were sent back to SAM asking whether the six were destined for occupied or unoccupied France. It was stressed that certain destinations were now impracticable due to the shortening hours of darkness. A telegram from SAM suggested a ban on such agents would not only create problems between the SOE and NKVD, but also have far reaching consequences between the two governments. It was followed by an NKVD request to drop a further fifteen agents in Europe, including three in occupied France.[16]

After the successful despatch of the Rum agents into France without the permission of de Gaulle's 'Fighting French', Chichaev asked the SOE to arrange the rapid delivery of the other four agents that Danilov, Rodionov and Frolova arrived with on 8 February.

In a meeting held in late March 1942 by senior Intelligence Services and Foreign Office officials, including Sir Stewart Menzies, the head of the SIS, and Lord Cadogan, Under-Secretary for Foreign Affairs, further Pickaxe operations were strongly opposed.

The Foreign Office argued that the French, Belgian and Dutch Governments-in-exile might be 'seriously prejudiced' if they learned that Britain was dropping Communist agents into their countries without their knowledge.

Menzies complained that all his contacts were 'men of the right' and 'violently anti-communist' and might be tempted to 'throw in their hand' if they knew Britain was interfering with France's internal affairs. It could poison the contacts they were making with Marshall Petain's regime.[17]

Chichaev accused the SOE of not fulfilling its part of the treaty, of following an anti-Soviet policy and supporting General Draza Mihailovic, the Yugoslav Nationalist leader. The Soviets wanted SOE to supply the partisans with arms and ammunition as they were fighting the Germans and Italians, but Britain was supplying Mihailovic, who supported the monarchy, the Church and the landowners. After threatening to recommend that his government end co-operation with the SOE and withdraw the London mission, Chichaev returned to Moscow.

However, at the meeting held by senior Intelligence Services and Foreign Office officials, it was agreed to drop three Soviet agents in occupied France, two into Holland and one into Belgium, but they refused to parachute any into Vichy-controlled France.

By agreeing to the drops, the Foreign Office had hoped to bargain with Moscow to get them to support Mihailovic, the Yugoslav Nationalist leader, and to get permission to station the SOE representatives in Soviet-controlled Northern Iran and Vladivostok. When the NKVD insisted on sending its agents to Vichy France, the debate continued.[18]

SAM was told to cut back on the number of NKVD agents being sent to France, Belgium and Holland, and to use operational difficulties as an excuse.

Menzies was adamant that the SOE should not provide documentation for Soviet agents as it would be disastrous if the United States and other allied countries discovered that Britain was enabling Soviet agents to infiltrate occupied Europe. In July, Frank Roberts of the Foreign Office sent a memo to the SOE asking them not to drop any Soviet agents in Switzerland as it would harm Anglo-Swiss relations.[19]

Switzerland was considered 'violently anti-Russian' and SOE was trying to instil in them a more 'generous understanding of our relations with the Soviet'. When the NKVD inquired whether it would be possible to drop agents into Switzerland, SOE refused.[20]

When Chichaev returned to London in summer 1943, General Sir James Marshall Cornwall, at the request of Colonel Leslie Sheridan, one of the SOE officers at Baker Street, went to personally inform him of their decision not to infiltrate any Pickaxes into Switzerland.

When Major General Colin Gubbins, Sir Charles Hambro's deputy, told René Massigli, de Gaulle's Foreign Minister, of the plans to infiltrate Communists into France 'he nearly fell off his chair' and begged SOE not to let it happen.[21] It is highly unlikely that Gubbins told him about the two men and two women who had already been sent without permission.

OPERATION WHISKEY

The other two agents who arrived on SS *Arcos* with the three Rum agents, excluding the pair that nothing is known about, were Peter Staritsky, known in Britain as Peter Schulenburg, and Vsevelod Troussevitch, known as Johann Traun. They were destined for Vienna in an operation codenamed Whiskey. Having arrived in London on 12 February, they stayed at the Rhodesia Court Hotel, where they were briefed by Chichaev or others from the DPR mission.

Between 16 and 22 February, they were at The Drokes, the country house in Beaulieu. Corporal Spencer, their conducting officer, then took them via London to Ringway for parachute training, returning to London on 25 February. Major Edwards, the commanding officer at Ringway, commented that they 'had jumped in their own country and merely needed a refresher. Took quite quickly to the training, and took their jumps as a matter of course. Made one successful drop from A/C [aircraft].'[1]

Following Chichaev's protests about the security at Porchester Court, saying it 'housed part of the Czech Intelligence Service and sundry Poles', SOE put the Whiskey agents in rooms at 79 Bryanston Court.[2] It took the SOE two months to create necessary forged forms with stamps and letters supplied by the NKVD. The SIS provided them with relevant dates on the *Wehrpass* and 'altered' their letters, while the SOE provided fresh letters and *Bezugsscheine* for railway travel, a complete set of appropriate clothing, and food rations for Austria. In addition to the normal weapons, they were supplied with four Mills grenades and an extra revolver. The NKVD gave them £125, $400, and an undisclosed number of Swiss francs. The wireless set they had brought with them from Russia was given a good overhaul by the SOE. They were instructed to use it to send a message to Moscow to indicate their safe arrival.

Special Duties Squadrons had little intelligence about flak positions across Germany to Austria, where Soviet cells needed support. It was a long flight and there was also no access to reliable information on weather conditions. The winter of 1941/42 had been unusually bad and throughout the entire January moon period there were no nights when the weather was considered suitable enough for a flight to Austria or Czechoslovakia. The Whiskey operation was therefore planned for the end of February, the last moon period in which the nights would be long enough to allow enough time for a sortie into Eastern Europe.

As early as 19 February, Air Commodore Archie Boyle, who was posing as head of the SOE to Chichaev, expressed his doubts to Seddon and Walshe about the flight going ahead:

> ...owing to the special form of aeroplane required. You will, I know, appreciate the urgent necessity for the despatch of this party, particularly in view of the difficulties we have with regard to COFFEE. I should be grateful, therefore, if you could take this matter up on the highest level in any way you may think fit. MO/8 [an officer in the Air Ministry's planning section] foresees no difficulty in the despatch of RUM (late BRANDY).[3]

Perhaps there were no Halifaxes available at Tempsford for the next moon period as it was decided that the flight was to be from Stradishall airfield between 28 February and 5 March. It was to leave at 1800 hours and was estimated to reach the dropzone at 2230. To create a 'raison d'être' for the trip, a supply of leaflets was requested for the despatcher to drop near Vienna. Lieutenant Colonel Barry wrote to 138 Squadron's Air Operations officer Woolmer at Tempsford:

> In view of the importance and urgency of this party, the personnel are prepared to take any risk to reach their destination. I request, therefore, that the usual considerations for safety of dropping be waived when deciding whether this operation shall take place or not on a particular day. Consideration of aircraft security will NOT, of course, be changed.[4]

Woolmer agreed that the best point to drop the Whiskey agents was within a 5-mile radius of Laaben, about 20 miles from Vienna. As the men knew nothing of the defences around Vienna, they asked if they could be dropped near Alland, about 10 miles east of Laaben. When they were told that it was in a valley and susceptible to cloud, they agreed a point west or south of Alland.

On 27 February, Captain Woolmer at Tempsford was told that two agents and three conducting officers would leave London at 1400 hours on or after 28 February and arrive at STS 61 (Gaynes Hall) for a meal at 1530. 'There is a chance that this party might depart from the South Coast [RAF Tangmere], in which case different arrangements for the feeding would have to be made, but this would be done by Major Dodds-Parker.'[5] However, the mission did not depart.

The failure to send this mission on 27 February caused the NKVD great concern. In Sweet-Escott's opinion, the NKVD in both London and Moscow were furious at SOE's failure to carry out the operation, and were insinuating that they were deliberately holding it up. This was despite the fact that there were two or three nights at the beginning of the February moon period when the weather conditions were so bad all flights had to be cancelled. 'By this time the rage of the Russians was practically uncontrollable, and the question of their sortie had reached ambassadorial level in London.'[6]

Staritsky, meanwhile, had expressed concern about the quality of his forged *Wehrpass* and *Maschinenfabrik* letter under his new name of 'Rudolf Hofstadter'. The SOE considered they would pass all but the closest scrutiny, but were prepared to make some alterations as time permitted.

On 8 March 1942, Staritsky and Troussevitch were taken to Gumley Hall (STS 44), a large eighteenth-century mansion near Market Harborough in Leicestershire, set in 2,000 acres. Agents accommodated there received intensive weapons training and unarmed combat lessons under the command of Major J. H. Drumbell. Three days later, a note was sent to Chichaev commenting that, as Staritsky's original *Wehrpass* was an NKVD forgery, he was requested to ask Moscow to provide original documents from Germany and Austria in future.

The Air Transport form for Whiskey's rescheduled flight showed that it was to leave from Tempsford during the next moon period, between 25 March and 5 April, despite the earlier assertion that a longer period of daylight meant that the planes would be easily spotted by enemy flak on the return journey across Germany and the Low Countries. The agents were to have two containers of supplies weighing 105 pounds and 115 pounds.

The records show that on 16 March the two agents and 'Torop' (Toropchenko) were taken by train from Liverpool Street in the company of Second Lieutenant R. L. Hingley to stay at The Lamb Hotel in Ely, Cambridgeshire, to relax before their mission. But, again, there were delays. On 22 March, they were taken back to London where they stayed at 40 Porchester Court. Then, on the evening of 25 March, they were told the mission was on. Clark comments that it was the first time three Halifax bombers were sent in one night. SOE records suggest the plane left from 'Borne', probably Bourne Airfield, about 10 miles east of Tempsford. The first Halifax, L9976, piloted by 26-year-old Polish Flight Officer Ryszard Zygmuntowicz and his Polish crew, took off at 2000 hours on Operation Whiskey, his first mission to Austria. On board were the two Pickaxe agents.

These were Sevolod Troussevitch (Johann Traun) and Peter Staritsky (Peter Schulmburg). Crossing the enemy coast at le Touquet at 21.27 hours the weather was good until they reached south of Mannheim, from here to the target the ground was covered in mist. Over the target area they searched for one hour and being unable to identify their pinpoint, abandoned their operation and returned home, landing at Tangmere at 06.00 hours.[7]

It must have been a particularly difficult job for the officer reporting to Chichaev that the plane had returned 'DNCO' (Duties Not Carried Out). On 3 April, Chichaev received an urgent telegram from Moscow which prompted him to visit Baker Street personally. A note in the file read:

Will we please consider the WHISKEY operation to be one of first-rate military importance. It is essential that the two agents should be at their posts and ready to act before the German spring offensive begins. In view of the heavy Russian sacrifices, they ask us to make a very special effort in this case.

...I am personally convinced that our inability to carry out this one operation, in spite of difficulties, will have the most serious repercussions and may actually jeopardise Anglo-Soviet relations at a crucial moment. The failure on our part in such a small matter will assuredly be placed in the scale against us, should the Russians ever find themselves in a critical military situation. As so little time remains, may this matter please be treated as urgent?[8]

The following day, Chichaev asked Major Milnes-Gaskell for an urgent meeting with the War Office. It worked. Lieutenant Colonel Barry was contacted, who given the pressure, decided that as Operation Binocular had been postponed indefinitely, it was possible to combine Operation Whiskey with the plane carrying Operation Bivouac to Czechoslovakia.

The men were duly driven to Tempsford where, according to Clark, on the evening of 8/9 April, Pilot Officer Anderle made a second attempt to complete Operation Whiskey and drop Troussevitch and Staritsky. The proposed pinpoint was between Laaben and Wallensdorf in Austria, about 22 miles west of Vienna. An alternative site, if Anderle could not locate the pinpoint, was in the valley between Linz and Vienna.

Flying at 10,000 feet he [Pilot Officer Anderle] encountered heavy cloud and icing. He recognised Mannheim in the north and near Karlsruhe met with two searchlights and flak. However icing and cloud prevented him from finding the pinpoint and he returned north of Mannheim, and unknowingly flew over Paris. Channel conditions were very bad before he landed at Tangmere at 04.40 hours. The Russian agents had now spent over 18 hours in the air![9]

The flight was rescheduled for the evening of the 17/18 April but it had to be cancelled because of appalling weather conditions. It was rescheduled again for 20/21 April.

The Soviets were intensely frustrated as tens of thousands of their troops were dying on the Eastern Front and the British were not prepared to risk one aircraft. The Soviet ambassador insisted a plane was allocated, despite the conditions. The SOE planners were concerned about the success of a long flight over part of Europe that had had little reconnaissance of anti-aircraft positions and where the weather was poor at that time of the year.[10]

SOE officer Sweet-Escott later wrote,

Finally, when there were only two more nights of the moon period to go, I got a message from the minister's office in Berkeley Square that the Foreign Office insisted in the interest of Anglo-Russian relations that the operation should go ahead if it were humanly possible. I telephoned the message through to the station commander at Tempsford, Wing-Commander Benham, a distinguished pilot with great experience of our work. That night the weather was as bad as ever. Benham refused to allow any of his pilots to take the risk of the flight and said that as it had to take place he would pilot the aircraft himself. He took off in the rain. They plotted a course for Czechoslovakia, but he and his crew never returned. All the thanks we got from the Russians was the suggestion that we had deliberately made away with their men.[11]

Both Sweet-Escott and McCall state Benham piloted the plane, but according to Clark, who had access to the squadrons' log books, on 20 April, the end of the April moon period, Ryszard Zygmuntowicz and his crew were briefed for a mission for Czechoslovakia. Squadron Leader Ron Hockey was going to be the second pilot but transport delays caused by the bad weather meant that he was not at Tempsford for the briefing session. In fact, the conditions were so dire that night that all RAF Bomber Command flights had been cancelled. Any flying out of Tempsford was considered out of the question. However, according to Verity, one of the 161 Squadron pilots, 38-year-old Wing Commander Walter R. 'Wally' Farley, the then Commander of 138 Squadron, stepped in and 'to his eternal credit ... decided he could not ask them to fly on such a night unless he accompanied them ... as 2nd pilot'.[12]

In Ken Merrick's *Flights of the Forgotten*, he mentions that Hockey arrived just before the flight of Halifax V9976 and was all prepared to fly. His crew pleaded he be allowed to pilot the plane but Farley, as senior officer, overruled them. He took off with Staritsky and Troussevitch on board. A note on the Air Transport form dated 21 April stated that at 0820 the following morning, the aircraft was 2¼ hours overdue. D/Q.14, an unidentified officer in the SOE's Baker Street headquarters, wrote to Milnes-Gaskell:

I have just received a message giving the following extract from yesterday's Berlin Communiqué issued by D.N.B. [Deutsches Nachrichten Bureau] yesterday afternoon:-

'A single British aircraft which undertook a harassing flight last night into the Ruhr territory was shot down in Southern Germany.'

It looks as if this may be your missing 'plane. I have asked the B.B.C. Monitoring Service to keep a sharp lookout for further details.[13]

According to Clark, Farley crashed in dense fog 66 feet below the crest of a ridge, south of Lake Tegernsee in the Blue Mountains separating Germany from

Bavaria. Dr Michael Heim, a German TV researcher who lived near the crash site, researched the incident and sent me an article detailing his findings:

> The German air defence services detected the noise of the Halifax upon entering the air space of the German Reich south of Strasbourg 2 minutes before midnight ... Altitude between 1,500 and 3,000 metres [4,875-9,750 ft], cloud cover 1,000-1,500 metres [3,250-4,875 ft], visibility 10 km [6 miles]. The machine held a constant easterly course (Ravensburg-Kempten-Augsburg). Noise detected until approx. 25 km [15.6 miles] south east of Starnberg Lake, last report at 1.08 am ... no return flight recognised.[14]

He thought it was a mysterious flight and told me that, in the 1980s, he had interviewed Hockey:

> My crew was furious. Farley was not all familiar with a Halifax. He only knew it from the outside. The Poles pressed me to dissuade Farley from commanding the flight and I tried to do so several times. I don't know whether it was just his stubbornness which made him hold on to the flight and lead the men to their deaths ... or was it because I wasn't to know who the passengers were?[15]

Heim pointed out that the plane kept an easterly course until it suddenly veered off to the south, just south of Munich. He thought it strange that Farley took this decision, but he did not suggest that the plane was under attack and had been damaged. The stated dropzone was about 150 miles east of the crash site. If the Halifax had not hit the mountain, it was only a few minutes from Jenbach in the Tirolean Inn valley, 17½ miles to the south. Here, according to Heim, the Nazis were manufacturing V2 rocket components at the Heinkel factory in an underground aircraft plant and hangars at Ernst Heinkel's high-technology armaments factory near the iron and steel works.

Heim thought that the two agents were one of the 'suicide squads ordered from the very top'. Instead of being dropped in the Vienna area to establish communist cells, he suggested that this was a decoy and that they might have been on another secret mission to investigate the Germans' plans for building an atomic bomb. No corroborating evidence has emerged in the SOE files but details of their missions, as we have seen, were rarely disseminated by the NKVD. In McCall's *Flight Most Secret,* he hinted that the NKVD believed that their agents had been spirited away and disposed of by an SOE 'hit' team.

Karl Vogels, a hunter from Wildbad Kreuth, got to the crash site, and according to Heim, found everyone on the plane dead. He is reported to have stated that they were all wearing civilian clothing, had parachutes, food ration cards and various currencies on them. He also found papers, which he handed over to the German police. In appreciation, Hermann Göring, Commander-in-Chief of the Luftwaffe, awarded him a war merit cross and 500 Reichmarks. There was no mention of containers. Were there any? Had they already been dropped? Could Whiskey have been a team meant to gather information or to sabotage the atomic bomb plant? What was most interesting for the Germans, said Heim, was that they discovered for the first time that British flights over the Third Reich were not only to bomb and disrupt production, but also to carry out secret operations.

The crash was the Special Duties Squadrons' first loss of a Halifax crew and Clark duly listed their names in *Agents by Moonlight,* but for years their identity remained a mystery for people in Bavaria. All the bodies of the eight-man crew were recovered and buried at Kreuth. The two Soviet agents were unnamed but the Roll of Honour website gives their names as Peter Staritsky and Vselovod Troussevitch, agents of the Peoples Commissariat for Internal Affairs. Their bodies were subsequently disinterred and buried at Dürnbach Commonwealth Cemetery at Ternsee. However, research by Henk Welting, reported in *Bomber Command Losses*, suggests the two agents had been members of the OeFF (Oesterreichischen Freiheitsfront) in Moscow; Austrian Marxists, who were veterans of the Spanish Civil War and agents of Stalin.[16]

Staritsky's real name was Lorenz Mraz, a 43-year-old typesetter, whose underground cover names included Moritz Lorenz and Hofstädter Lorenz. He was part of the 'Schutzbund' exiles in Moscow and was wounded while serving as a Political Commissar for an Austrian battalion in Spain. In 1939, he returned to Moscow where he adopted Soviet citizenship. As part of his mission, he was instructed to inspect weapons factories in Austria as engineer Ing Rudolf Hofstädtler.

Troussevitch's real name was Franz Löschl, a 29-year-old typesetter, alias Maschinentechniker Franz Mayer, underground cover name Donner Franz. His instructions were to conduct espionage in factories in Vienna.[17]

'DIE ROTE KAPELLE'

The Soviets had an extensive intelligence network across Europe before the Second World War. It was headed by Leopold Trepper, a Polish Jew who became active in the Palestine Communist party in the 1920s and '30s. When his underground political organisation was broken up by the French intelligence service in 1932, he escaped to Moscow where he worked as an NKVD agent, liaising between French communists and the Soviets.

In 1938, Trepper was sent to Brussels where he became known as 'Grand Chef', with Anatolii 'Victor' Gurevich as 'Petit Chef'. Between them they set up numerous communist cells in Belgium under the cover of the 'Foreign Excellent Trenchcoat Company'. They also developed links with Harro Schulze-Boysen, an anti-Hitler German who worked on the General Staff of Göring's Luftwaffe in Berlin.

Trepper travelled extensively, organising underground operations in Holland, France, Germany, and Switzerland. His network even managed to infiltrate the Abwehr, the German military intelligence service. They tapped the phones of the Abwehr in Paris.

Through the Soviet military attaché in Paris, Trepper supplied Moscow with thirty reports containing detailed information on German troop transfers for Operation Barbarossa, plans for the German T6 Tiger tanks, air attacks on Germany, German aircraft production, German fuel shipments, and the production capacity of German industry. However, Marshal Goikov, the head of Soviet Intelligence Services, ignored the information. He suspected Trepper to be a double agent and his information to have come from a British source.[1]

In early 1939, the Soviets sent three officers, Makarov, Danilov and Yefremov, to help Trepper's network, each supplied with new identities. Despite not being able to speak Finnish, Yefremov posed as a Finnish student named Eric Jernstroem. The other two, codenamed 'Bordo' and 'Pascal', had to report on German military installations in Belgium, Holland and France, to locate and report where General von Rundstedt and his troops were, and to identify armaments factories manufacturing weapons for the German military.

Between May 1940 and November 1942, about 1,500 messages were transmitted to Moscow, some of which included information on many of the most critical plans of the German High Command. The deployment, strength, capability, and morale of the Wehrmacht stationed in Western Europe were of great interest to Moscow. They needed to assess the possibility of additional German divisions being sent to the Eastern front. The situation in Holland, Belgium, and France was also of interest as many German troops were sent there for rest and recuperation. Information was collected on weapons, military aircraft construction, shipbuilding, radio and electronic equipment, and chemical and nuclear technology.

A coded message sent from the 'Direktor' in Moscow, Pavel Fitin, to Gurevich, an NKVD agent codenamed 'Kent', in Brussels, dated 26 August 1941, instructed him to make contact with Berlin to determine the causes of a break in their radio link. Three addresses were provided. He met with Schulze-Boysen who provided him with much top secret information, which, on Moscow's specific instructions, he had to transmit for five hours every night when he got back to Brussels.[2]

This was a grave mistake as such long transmissions were very easily picked up by German goniometrists, wireless detection experts who used signal tracers. A suitcase-sized detection unit was carried onto a plane which then circled Brussels allowing the location of the transmissions to be triangulated. Once a transmission was picked up, the signal tracer provided a compass bearing that was plotted on a street map. The plane flew on and the signal tracer picked up the same transmission, allowing its compass bearing to be plotted. Where the two lines intersected gave the estimated location of the building the transmission was coming from. To confirm it, a third bearing was taken from a different location. It was more successful in rural areas with isolated buildings. In urban areas, a detection team was sent in to search the buildings, often driving around in disguised delivery vans. They also operated from rooftops and walked the streets with the equipment under their coat and wires threaded through their sleeves.

If the transmissions were coming from an apartment block, unscrewing the fuses one at a time from the box on the outside of the building helped the German investigators to identify exactly which apartment the wireless was being operated from. Once the building was located, they sent in a hit squad with sledgehammers and revolvers.

Gurevich's wireless operator, Johannes Wenzel, was captured in this way on 14 July 1942. Under torture, he revealed the location of Konstantin Yefremov, the agent posing as a Finnish student, and 'co-operated' with the Gestapo to provide them with the codes and deciphers needed to decrypt the five figure codes. Yefremov was caught with his wireless set, and under threat of torture and execution at Fort Breendonck, he too agreed to give his ciphers to the Gestapo.

As wireless operators were known as 'pianists' because of their dexterity with the Morse key, the Gestapo termed the Soviet intelligence network as *die Rote Kapelle*, the Red Orchestra. They considered it so important that they created the *Sonderkommando Rote Kapelle* (Red Orchestra Special Detachment) with a staff of seventy, headed by Horst Kopkow. At the Gestapo headquarters in Vienna, under Kopkow's supervision, Kriminalrat Thomas Ampletzer used five captured Soviet wireless sets to play back messages to Moscow in what was called 'Buche-Pascal' of the *Sonderkommando*

Pannwitz. Along with sets captured in Germany, Belgium, and Holland, they began their mission to completely destroy the Soviet intelligence network.[3]

This breakthrough and the defections of Soviet agents Samuel Ginsberg, alias Walter Krivitsky, and Ignace Poretsky, alias Reiss, allowed the Gestapo to liquidate the *Rote Kapelle* in Belgium, Holland, and Germany.[4]

Although the 'Grand Chef' and 'Petit Chef' escaped to France and attempted to rebuild the network, Gurevich was found and arrested in Marseilles. Trepper was arrested in a dentist's chair on 16 November 1942. Instead of being tortured to betray other agents, the Gestapo tried to turn him into a double agent. He later wrote a book, *The Great Game*, about his experiences. The Gestapo wanted him to deceive Moscow's 'Direktor' by providing him with false information, but Trepper managed to alert them that he was compromised. He escaped from the Gestapo in September 1943 and worked closely with the communists in the French Resistance. He participated in the liberation of Paris.

According to Trepper's own investigations after the war, 217 'musicians' in his orchestra were arrested, of whom 143 were executed, many following terrible torture. Whether the figure included those captured in the Schulze-Boysen group is unknown.

While it was not documented in the SOE files, it has been suggested that many of the Pickaxes were sent on missions to rebuild the *Rote Kapelle*. However, as Berlin had already obtained several Soviet code and cipher systems, they were able to capture many of the Soviet agents, and in some cases 'persuade' them to divulge their codes and ciphers and transmit messages back to Moscow.

Kriminal Inspektor Willi Lehmann, the only Soviet agent inside the Gestapo, was one of the most important agents to be captured. Recruited in the mid-1930s and retained on 580 Reichmarks a month, he supplied his 'handler', Alexander Korotkov (NKVD's man in Berlin), with the exact time and date of Germany's attack on the USSR. As it happened, Stalin chose to ignore it, suspicious that it was disinformation. After Lehmann's 'confession', rather than have a show trial that would reveal the Soviet success and publicly embarrass the Gestapo, he was executed in a cellar and the media informed that he had died for his 'Fuhrer and Fatherland' on the Eastern Front.[5]

Many Soviet agents were captured because they were amateurs in clandestine activities. They communicated by phone and regular mail and many were long-term friends who often met up. Few were able to hide from the subtle and more experienced Gestapo investigators. Once one had fallen under interrogation, there was a domino effect. Within a week of Schulze-Boysen being captured, 118 suspects were arrested and placed in Gestapo cells for questioning. Stool pigeons (decoys), psychological pressure, and physical torture were used. Estimates of their playback schemes, called the *Funkspiel,* whereby captured Soviet agents would be forced to relay false messages to Moscow, range between 100 and 160.

Towards the end of the war, perhaps aware that the network was compromised, the NKVD insisted on Pickaxes being dropped blind, without any reception committee, to avoid them falling directly into the hands of the Gestapo.[6]

OPERATIONS BARSAC
AND BURGUNDY

At the beginning of April 1942, SOE's Russian Section received a telegram from SAM informing them that two more Pickaxes were being prepared, destined for Holland and Belgium. On 18 April, the Russian Section made a request to the Royal Navy to inform the Senior Naval Officer at Murmansk to arrange the passage of 'Willi von Krumin' and 'Nikolai Kravets'. The Admiralty was asked to signal the message that it was 'essential that [the arrangement] should not be done through the Russian Government.' On 11 May, the two men disembarked at Greenock in Scotland after a traumatic voyage on HMS *Bulldog*, a British destroyer, which had taken a prominent part in the defence of convoy QP.11 from Murmansk. Although there had been a number of casualties, the two men were unharmed.

Willi von Krumin's papers identified him as 'Frederik Schmidt', born in 1910 in Lucerne, and Nikolai Kravets was identified as 'Jean Philippe Castaigne', born in 1911 in Lausanne. Von Krumin's mission was allocated the codename Barsac and Kravets's was Burgundy. Both codenames and aliases were later mixed up with dire consequences. Initially unknown to the SOE, Willi's real name was Willi Kruyt and Nikolai was his son, Niko Kruyt.

There were problems finding them suitable accommodation. A memo from a Russian Section official stated, 'I do not think we can hold these students anywhere other than S.T.S. 46 [Chicheley Hall]. Will there be any objection to them mixing with the present party now being held there?' The response was negative as they would have to move the Coffee party who were then staying in the Rectory at Chicheley Hall. SOE's policy was that Pickaxe agents should not be allowed to mix, not only with other Pickaxes, but especially not with SOE agents. The arrangement between Churchill and Stalin had to be kept secret.

It was urgent that alternative accommodation was found. Major A. D. Seddon (A/D.3), the new head of the Russian Section, decided that SOE should rent cottages near to the country houses that had outside training facilities. In a meeting on 23 May, it was decided that Gorse Hill, an Edwardian country house in Godalming, Surrey, should be obtained for their use.[1]

In the meantime, the Pickaxe agents were accommodated in rented rooms at 79 Bryanston Court in Paddington, W.1. Meetings were conducted at this address.[2]

Lieutenant Walshe, Barsac and Burgundy's conducting officer, put in a request for four pairs of socks, two suits, four shirts, two vests, two pairs of shoes, two pairs of pyjamas and two Mackintoshes. He also made a request for them to be taken by boat, not by plane.

Willi von Krumin, the older of the two, had not been born in 1910 as the original document stated. He was in his 60s and had never done a parachute jump before, but the possibility of a sea crossing was considered out of the question as, by that time, the Germans had established the 'Atlantik Wall,' a coastal defence network that stretched from south-west France to northern Norway. They had to go by plane.

While in London, von Krumin had a visit from a member of 'N' (Dutch) Section who gave him some general information about conditions in Holland. He reported that von Krumin's Dutch was 'rusty, although his speech gave a rather more German impression than any other. Otherwise he seems a good type, looks the part.'[3]

Once again there were concerns regarding documentation. Under the heading Operation Barsac, D/HV, an unidentified officer at SOE's Baker Street headquarters, wrote to George Taylor, director of SOE's overseas groups and missions, mentioning:

> This man, who has just arrived, has no papers with him at all. In Sam's telegram 0220 he stated that two agents for Holland and Belgium were fully trained, documented and equipped. When BARSAC arrived, however, it was found that he only had a birth certificate and had never been given an identity card, which is absolutely essential.
>
> Dutch identity cards are unfortunately only issued by 'C' [the SIS] who are likely to raise strong objections to issuing one for a Pickaxe. We shall certainly not obtain one unless we approach them on the highest level.
>
> The only alternative before us seems to be:-
> To send the man back to Russia.
> To hold him until the documents arrive from Russia. (judging by the history of COFFEE this may well take six months).
> To send him without any specific documents (which he will probably not consent to do).
> We would be grateful, therefore, if you could take this matter up personally as soon as possible.[4]

Wiskeman, the head of the Scandinavian Section, passed their concerns up the line to Sir Stewart Menzies, C, ('C' was codename for both Menzies and the SIS, the organisation he headed), adding that sending Barsac back to the Soviet Union was absurd and sending him in without documents was suicidal.

Hearing the bad news about the transport arrangements, on 24 May, von Krumin (Willi Kruyt) and Kravets (Niko Kruyt) were taken to Ringway for parachute training. The Commandant was sent a note from Major Milnes-Gaskell.

I am afraid that we are sending you once again two unusual specimens. I feel I should give you some notes about these two, for your guidance.

The boy has already received some superficial training and has made a jump. All he requires is to see our equipment and to have one trial jump. If the weather is absolutely impossible, he will have to be satisfied with a jump from a balloon.

The older person has had no experience at all. On account of his age, I think that it would be best if he were not put to any great strain. I feel myself that if he could be taken up in an aeroplane and shown exactly how someone jumps, i.e. the boy mentioned in para. 2, this would give him all he requires as he is a man of great ability. He should however make one jump from the balloon and, if it is possible, might the largest type of parachute be used?

We should be most grateful if these two could both have the opportunity of burying parachutes and also an opportunity of having a little elementary compass work in the evening. If you have a range, might they have a few shots?

I am afraid, as I said before, that we are sending you unusual specimens but you will, at any rate find them extremely charming and really interested in their work.

I am asking our Conducting Officer, Lieut. Walshe, to deliver this letter to you.[5]

Although they would have learned the theory and been 'shown the ropes', bad weather prevented them from jumping and they were returned to London on 28 May. The Russian Section provided them with maps and photographs of potential dropzones and, after liaising with Air Transport at Tempsford, it was decided that 'Niko' should land in a clearing in a wood at Hulshort, near Harderwijk, and 'Willy' 6¼ miles north-north-west of Marche, just less than a mile north-east of Melreux.

Seddon, who had taken over Milnes-Gaskell's role as head of the Russian Section, wrote a memo two days later to MO/C.1, Captain J. R. Hare:

I must apologise for all the trouble which we have given you. We were hoping that BARSAC would leave for a better world immediately, but life is not as easy as that. On its return to London yesterday, BURGUNDY declared that one party could not go without the other and the personnel of this party is not ready to leave. So BURGUNDY and BARSAC are co-equal and probably co-eternal; both I hope will leave during the month of June. Once again, I apologise for our last minute rush.[6]

The delay gave them time to complete their parachute training so, on 1 June, they returned to Ringway with Major Seddon and Toropchenko. In the Commandant's report their names had been reversed. He stated that 'Schmidt' (Nikolai Kravets, whose alias was actually Castaigne) dropped from 800 feet through the hole and made quite a successful drop, though not a good landing.

Castaigne [Willi von Krumin, whose alias was actually Schmidt] was driven to Tatton Park and the Balloon was especially flown for him. Captain Tice went up with him and jumped first to give him confidence. Castaigne made a fair egress but after that he failed to obey any instructions and he landed quite heavily full length on his back where he lay slightly stunned. However, he soon got up but was very dizzy, recovering rapidly afterwards at Fulshaw Hall where I took him back to tea. I think he had a slight concussion as he seemed to remember very little about the jump at all.

After a night's rest he seemed to have recovered and Major Seddon departed with them by the 10.50 hrs. train in the morning.

I consider Castaigne had a very lucky escape from injury.[7]

After three days in London, Willi (Burgundy) and Niko (Barsac) were transferred to Little Berkhamstead Manor, a late-sixteenth-century farmhouse, north-west of Hertford in Hertfordshire, where they were kept on stand-by until 17 June. By this time Lieutenant Walshe had realised that they were father and son. His character assessments also shed light onto the contemporary attitudes towards the Soviets.

Nikolai KRAVETS

Aged 22. Eldest son of BURGUNDY and probably born a Dutch subject. His mother, who died recently in Moscow, was German. Has left two younger brothers in Moscow.

Left Holland as a small child and was partly educated in Germany. Has lived most of his life in Russia and at the outbreak of war was working in a furniture factory.

Speaks perfect German and Dutch, very fluent Russian and adequate English.

A typical Dutchman to look at, having fair hair, blue eyes and broad face; but he also has picked up the pronounced stoop and rather furtive ambling gait, which is a general characteristic of the Soviet worker, and which seems to be an unconscious expression of being downtrodden for generations. Very young, both in appearance and habits, he is quite uninterested in any of the things which normally interest those of his age, except politics, in which he never shows any very marked enthusiasm for Communism. He neither smokes nor drinks, is a most conscientious worker, quick witted, hard and keen on carrying out the job allocated to him.

A first-class lad, who should make an excellent agent.

Von KRUMIN

Aged 64. Probably born a Dutch subject. His wife who was German, died recently in Moscow; he has two sons still in Moscow. For his eldest child, see under 'BARSAC'.

A man of very considerable intellectual powers, who must have spent most of his life wandering about Europe, lecturing at various universities. By nature a savant, he is probably a well-known man (he was a personal friend of Lenin, and also knows Nehru well), and this is rather borne out by his genuine anxiety about being recognised either in England or Holland. He spent a year at an English school as a child, and has kept up his knowledge of the language by mixing with English people ever since; his knowledge of English literature is quite phenomenal. He was last in Holland in approximately 1923, when it seems that he went to Russia, where he basked in a certain amount of reflected glory, owing to his association with Lenin. Some time after Lenin's death, he went to Germany, where he spent some years, and his children all learnt to speak perfect German; then about thirteen years ago, he accepted the post of Professor of Scandinavian Languages at Moscow University, where he has remained up to this present time. His Russian is very poor, but he speaks fluent English, French, German, Dutch, Flemish, Swedish, Norwegian and Danish; however, like most people who speak many languages, he speaks with a strong accent in all of them, except Dutch.

A very charming person, but not accustomed to his new profession and in no way fitted for it, either in age or mentality. A remarkably well-preserved man for his age, he has the courage of a lion and did his jump at S.T.S. 51 with complete calmness – a considerable feat for a man of 64. He never expressed any doubts or fears about the future, and was obviously quite indifferent as to his own fate; in fact, his only anxiety was for his son (BARSAC), to whom he was devoted, and it is most probable that he undertook his dangerous mission, more to look after his son, rather than from any ideological motives.

On the other hand, his idea of security and of how an agent should behave, were worse than elementary. While in England, he was given a Swiss name and nationality, but he generally forgot this and gave his Russian name when asked. As a liar he was hopeless, and was several times caught telling a different story about the same thing; in the end, without being pressed, he usually admitted that he was becoming rather involved and produced the truth. Finally, he was inclined to leave his private papers, maps, etc., lying about, for anyone to see. We tried to point out on several occasions that such behaviour could only have one end in Belgium, and it is to be hoped that our warnings had some effect.

The man is unfortunately too honest and cannot believe that other people have different ideas from his own. A firm believer in Communism, particularly from the international standpoint, he was once naïve enough to say that he had been given to understand that we were very near a revolution in England; having stayed here a few weeks, however, he was disappointed to see that we were not quite as near the expected revolution as he had hoped.

He should not have been allowed to undertake this job, of course, and one can only assume that he insisted on being permitted to accompany his son. One can only hope he will get through.[8]

When Nikolai was told his flight was scheduled for the June moon period, he was taken to London. SIS supplied him with a Dutch identity card in the name of 'Jan W. Schouten'. SOE provided him with appropriate clothing for Holland and he was given 500 Dutch florins. No doubt he was given a cover story to learn and a final briefing before being taken for his flight.[9]

On 21 June, he was driven up to Tempsford with his wireless transmitter, 50,000 Belgian francs Chichaev had given him, and identity papers in the name of 'Henri Despotter'. Before take-off, agents were plied with alcohol in a farewell party in the hope that they might divulge something of their mission. From the information gathered, they determined that few of the agents would survive as they had been inadequately prepared for outsmarting the Gestapo.[10]

On the night of 21 June 1942, exactly a year after the start of Operation Barbarossa, two operations were planned for 138 Squadron. Flight Lieutenant Smith's operation Periwig 4 to Belgium failed because of bad weather, but Squadron Leader Davies flew a Pickaxe operation to Holland to drop a Soviet NKVD agent which had been scheduled for May. Taking off at 2332 hours, the plane crossed the Dutch coast at Callanstoog, flew down to Hoorn and on to Harderwijk. After searching for 16 minutes, Niko was dropped blind from 500 feet.[11]

According to the Air Transport operation report, the plane reached the dropzone at 0142 hours and the despatcher commented that the 'agent jumped without hesitation on signal, and appeared quite happy during trip out.' The rear gunner noted that the 'chute seen to open, and agent believed to land between small wood and boundary of clearing.'[12]

However, there was an additional note at the bottom of the report:

> By a most unfortunate oversight, at the packing station, BARSAC's luggage and W/T set were confused with those of BURGUNDY and the mistake was not discovered until after he had dropped. After careful consideration, it was considered that, if we admitted such an inexcusable error to the N.K.V.D., the results upon our relations with them would be disastrous, not to mention the affect which it would certainly have upon BURGUNDY's morale, just before he was due to leave us. It was decided therefore to say nothing about it, and to send BURGUNDY (who was dropped three days later) with the luggage which should have been sent with BARSAC, in the hope that they would be able to straighten matters out later.
>
> BARSAC and BURGUNDY were in any case working in close conjunction with each other, and had arranged regular meeting places. It may therefore be possible for them to exchange their luggage, and it only remains for us to hope that they do not have the opportunity of telling the N.K.V.D. about the ghastly mistake which we made.[13]

Clark commented that SOE's failure to send Niko with the right luggage was the cause of extensive complaint by the Soviet Union. The Special Duties Squadron's records reveal that there were no instructions in the cargo manifest for this flight for a container or a package to be dropped with Barsac.[14]

The issue about the mix-up was not able to be brushed under the carpet. Seddon wanted the SOE's regrets to be conveyed to the Soviets at the very highest level but concluded:

> I feel that, as this section cannot be held responsible for the mistake ... it is likely to produce a grave situation in our relations with the N.K.V.D.... Furthermore, DPR.1 [Chichaev] should be informed that we are prepared to do anything in our power to rectify the mistake, even to the extent of dropping another W/T set at any point specified.[15]

Chichaev was not informed of the mistake about the luggage mix up. But the matter did not stop there. Sir Charles Hambro, the head of SOE, wrote to M. P. Murray, one of his deputies at Baker Street, codenamed D/CD:

> I understand that you are instituting a proper court of enquiry over this evidence of a lack of supervision on somebody's part and I hope it will be a very careful and detailed one in view of the importance of maintaining our good relationship with the persons for whom we are acting.[16]
>
> ...One must also remember that we are a secret organisation about which nobody knows or should know anything and therefore we are liable to be shot at for any mistakes we make ... Mistakes made by us are usually connected with loss of life so that we have got to be all the more careful to avoid any criticism.[17]

One imagines that, as a consequence, there were much stricter controls introduced relating to agents' luggage.

Niko's arrival in Holland was during a time of heightened tension. On the day that he landed, 22 June 1942, an order was issued to deport all Jews to work in the Third Reich. The *Englandspiel*, the Dutch version of the *Funkspiel*, was already in full swing, which meant that many resistance groups had been infiltrated and members arrested.

After burying his parachute, Niko caught the train to Amsterdam where all three safe houses were located. He called at Jap Smeding's barber shop at Aalsmeerweg 17, and after waiting for the other customers to leave, he gave the password in German: '*Ich komme von einer Bleistiftfabrik in Koln. Brauchen Sie noch Bleisifte?*' ('I come from a pencil factory in Cologne. Do you need pencils?') As the Germans had warned the Dutch that harbouring a foreign parachutist would be punishable by death, Jap was worried. Consequently, Niko went to see Bart Rissouw who worked for *De Waarheid*, an illegally produced Communist newspaper. The group provided him with new clothes and a 'safe house' in Riverlaan 6 with Ben Polak, a physician, and his wife, Petra Eldering. He did not stay long as other communists used to meet there with little regard for security.[18]

He then stayed with a number of other contacts, some of whom commented on his views about the USSR. Joop van Santed, who Niko gave Russian lessons to, noted that he found it 'very interesting that he made some critical remarks about the Soviet Union, the missing freedom there.' Years later, Niko's brother reported that he wanted 'to do everything to prevent Stalinism coming to power in the Netherlands' and that 'he was full of hate against the system of Stalin.'[19]

Having managed to make contact with Daniel Guolooze, the main Soviet agent in Holland, Niko was sent a Moscow-trained radio operator. When this man was arrested, the NKVD arranged for Bruno Kühn to be sent as a replacement. (Bruno Kühn was an alias of Pyetr Kousnetsov, aka Ivan Roberts, the Pickaxe agent who was admitted into Ely hospital after his plane crashed on 27 December 1941, killing his fellow Pickaxe II agent, Pavel Koubitsky). Niko was lucky to escape arrest.

Research by Igor Cornelissen, a Dutch journalist, revealed how Niko arrived at the house where Kühn, codenamed Sauterne, transmitted from. When he rang the doorbell, Gestapo officers opened the door. He told them that he had just stopped by to see if his friend, Tonnie van Rijk, wanted to go swimming with him. Having been taught to have a good cover story for any eventuality, he carried his swimming trunks and a towel with him. It worked and they let him go, but the experience made him a lot more cautious.

Abandoning his mission to locate safe houses, Niko moved into his brother's house in Hilversum. He was one of very few 'Pickaxes' to survive the war.[20]

In *The Greatest Treason*, Richard Deacon alleges that Niko was involved in arranging for George Behar to be taken down one of the SIS-supported escape lines through France and Spain and back to Britain. Behar was one of fourteen Soviet agents brought out of Holland in this way, and he worked as a double agent for the SOE until his arrest in 1961.[21]

It was not until 23 July 1943, just over a year after Niko had been dropped, that Chichaev reported to Wiskeman, head of the Scandinavian Section, that he had 'come up' on the wireless and had reported being dropped with the wrong kit. There was no mention that he had met up with his father. Presumably, he had been able to make contact with other Soviet agents in Holland and get a message back to Moscow or London.

More information on Niko's mission came from a report in SOE's Russian file headed 'Pickaxes: Soviet Agents in Holland'. The British successfully intercepted the Comintern's wireless transmissions. This traffic was known as ISCOT and the SOE was sent decoded Pickaxe transmissions. Barsac and Burgundy's file included transcriptions of a series of wireless messages from '05' to Moscow, presumed to have come from Niko once Kühn (Kousnetsov) had given him the replacement wireless set. Colonel Chichaev had asked SOE for spare wireless crystals to be dropped for Kühn and 100 sheets of various German ration tickets to enable him to proceed to Germany.

In May 1944, an SIS agent in Holland was given a coded message by a Soviet agent who called himself 'Hermann von Holland'. He was asked to transmit the message to the Soviet Embassy in London. SIS in Holland mentioned it to the Dutch Intelligence and SOE's Dutch Section. They knew nothing about any Soviet agents operating in Holland. Because of the secret nature of SOE's agreement with the NKVD, the Russian Section had not informed them. In fact, their response was to officially deny it. They telegrammed SAM to tell him to deny it as well.[22]

In the meantime, the Russian Section asked Chichaev whether he thought the message came from Barsac, Sauterne (Bruno Kühn) or an 'agent provocateur'. He said he could not be sure, and in response to enquiries from Dutch Intelligence, he told them that he presumed the agent was either forced into Holland on his way to Germany, or that he might have escaped from Germany. By August 1944, the Dutch sent the NKVD a description of the agent. An anonymous note in the 'Pickaxes' file mentions:

> It appears that the description does not in any way tally up with the agent who was dropped by us and DPR.1 [Chichaev] is somewhat worried about the position. I emphasised the necessity of DPR.1's keeping us fully informed of any developments, so that his and our version to the Dutch government accounting for the presence of a Russian agent in Holland should be the same. He promised to do so without fail. [23]

No hint of the *Englandspiel*, the Gestapo's playback scheme using agents captured in Holland, was mentioned in the file, but by that time, the upper echelons of SOE knew all about it.

Further light was shed on the fate of Willi and Niko after the war when MI5 were investigating what became of the Soviet agents SOE had sent into Europe. There was a worry that, if they had survived the war, they might be a potential threat to Britain. In a copy of an unsigned letter sent to Miss Small, presumably the person putting together the files on the Pickaxes, she was informed:

> ... when Franz aka Pyetr KOUSNETZOV was arrested by the Germans on 28.7.43. young KRUYT only escaped by a timely warning by one of his neighbours. He then went to stay with his brother in Hilversum.
> We had asked for further information of the brother.
> As regards his father, young KRUYT says he was a well known clergyman (the first we've heard of this!), that he was a Socialist and a member of the Dutch Second Chamber. In 1935 he and a young KRUYT went to Russia. During the war they were both evacuated from Moscow to Tashkent. They asked to be allowed to be returned to Holland which was agreed on condition they worked for the Soviet Intelligence Service there.
> Young KRUYT has told the Dutch that when he landed in Holland on 22.6.42, he was met by Bart RISSOUW or RIZAUW, editor of 'Waarheld'. We have no

information about RISSOUW, who must presumably have been a trusted Soviet agent at that time and with foreknowledge of the arrival of KRUYT. We have asked the Dutch for more information and a photograph. We do know that RISSOUW survived the war.[24]

Research by Dutch investigators after the war, detailed in O'Sullivan's '*Dealing with the Devil',* reveals that the Soviets tried to locate Niko and encourage him to return to the Soviet Union. They suspected him of working with Dutch intelligence and, when he was reported having committed suicide on 18 July 1954, some suspected foul play. Found in his wardrobe was the pair of boots that he had been given for his parachute jump.[25]

On 24 June 1942, two days after his son's flight, it was Willi's turn. Although the kit he was given included a Russian wireless set, he was not a fully trained operator. SOE tested the set and considered that it would be used for communicating between the Belgian and Dutch organisations.

Foot thought that the plan to drop Willi Kruyt into Belgium did not take place, partly due to the mix-up with the containers but also because of 'the unsuitability of the agent himself'.[26] The mission did take place in fact. Clark reported that the instructions on the cargo manifest, dated May 1942, said one person was to be dropped 10 km north-north-east of Marche-en-Famenne in Belgium, 1 km north-east of Melreux. The alternative dropzone was a suitable spot in the same neighbourhood, as near as possible to a station on the Marche-Durbuy railway line.[27]

Flight Lieutenant Smith took off from RAF Tempsford in his converted Whitley bomber Z9287 at 2307 hours with Sergeant Keen as the despatcher. They reached the French coast at Crotoy 70 minutes later. Setting course for Givet, south of Dinant, he then made for the target area, where 'low cloud made accurate map reading impossible but dropped passenger from 600 feet about 10 km north or west of pinpoint' along with a package.[28] The despatcher commented that his passenger was 'a little nervous at one stage but jumped immediately on the green light'. Both his and his container's parachute were seen to open.[29]

Willi's dropzone was 4 km west of Ferrieres and 9 km north-east of Durbuy in the Belgian Ardennes. The Biographical Dictionary of Socialism and the Labour Movement in the Netherlands (BWSA) stated that he fractured his leg on landing in Ciney, near Namur, and was arrested by the Gestapo three days later and taken to Fort Breendonck Prison outside Brussels. However, eyewitnesses stated that he reached Brussels on 26 June and walked round the city all day long. After making contact with the Otten-Wynants family, he was warned that it was not safe and he was urged to leave. They refused to take his money so he went to see Marie Jeanne Compere. On Monday 29 June he went out, presumably to meet other contacts and distribute money. When he returned at midnight there was a long argument which lasted until the Gestapo arrived at 4 a.m. and arrested him.[30] The testimony of Georg Eppstein, a Gestapo officer who served time for war crimes in St Gilles prison in Brussels, shed more light on the arrest.

Eppstein received orders from Kommissar Pütz in June 1942 to go to 56 Avenue Charles Quint in Brussels and arrest a parachutist who was hiding there. After contacting Charles Bocar, the man who had denounced the agent, Eppstein's three-man team arrived at 4.30 a.m. on 30 June 1942. When Bocar opened the door, specially greased to ensure a silent entry, his men ran up to the third floor. The Gestapo surprised Willi Kruyt in his bed. Claiming he needed to go to the toilet, he swallowed his cyanide pill. When he returned and collapsed back in the room, Eppstein knew what he had done. They immediately took him to the Bruggmann hospital where they succeeded in resuscitating him. No mention was made of attempting to interrogate Kruyt before he was transferred to Breendonck fortress. Afterwards, Bocar married Marie Jeanne Pierre and moved to Antwerp, probably using the reward he had received from the Gestapo to start a new life.[31]

Research by Frans Kluiters into the agents parachuted into Holland suggests that Willi committed suicide. With no regard for age or gender, the Gestapo used psychological and physical pressure to persuade prisoners to divulge their information and work for them. Despite 'heavy torture under interrogations', Willi did not betray his son and resisted their attempts to make him work for them in their *Funkspiel*. In July 1943, Willi was taken to Moabit prison in Berlin and executed.[32] His daughter Elske did not think he was a secret agent and another daughter, Truske, later said, 'My father was an idealist who saw everything through rose-tinted glasses. For me, he was a tragic figure.'[33]

Additional information, not known by the SOE, was found by Günter Nollau, a former head of the West German secret service, and Ludwig Zindel, a military historian. Their work, *Gestapo ruft Moskau,* revealed that 'Krumin' was also known as Johan 'Willy' Kruyt in Holland and Willi Kruijt in Germany. Born in Amsterdam in 1877, he became a preacher in Nijmegen before taking an interest in left-wing politics. He became actively involved with the *Internationale Arbeithilfe*, a Soviet organisation set up in the 1920s, and moved to Berlin to represent the Dutch section on their Central Committee. When the Nazi party closed down the main trade union organisations in 1933, he was taken on by the Soviet Trade Mission and moved with his wife Gustel and eldest son Niko to Moscow where he worked as a translator for the Dutch section of Radio Moscow. Following the German invasion, Volga Germans were transported to Kazakhstan, but after the apparent suicide of his second wife, they were taken to Tashkent.

Being fluent in several European languages, Willi and his son Niko were approached by the NKVD about being Soviet agents; they agreed and received parachute training in Kuibyshev. The codenames 'Willi von Krumin' and 'Nikolai Kravets' were allocated and they were told that should they fail in their mission or betray their secrets, they would be severely punished. O'Sullivan mentions that SIS had known about Willi Kruyt since 1920, but their file on him was not shown to SOE.[34]

There is evidence in the SOE documents suggesting that in early 1942, some in the Russian Section were beginning to wonder whether the Soviet agents were operating according to a different agenda. In a note in one of the Pickaxe folders it was admitted that von Krumin's room had been searched to 'assist us in penetrating part of the Communist organisation' but that nothing significant was found. What was found in Niko's room was not stated, but it was determined that his mission was to report on the political situation in Holland and the scope of the Dutch resistance, and to organise resistance against the Germans.[35]

However, Willi's file does contain a translation of his diary, which covered the time they spent in the Soviet Union, their journey from Murmansk to England, and their stay under SOE's hospitality. The latter part is included as an appendix; it provides a fascinating insight into the day-to-day events of one of the Pickaxes and the extent to which their conducting officers ensured that their stay in this country was filled with as many rich and varied experiences as possible. This was despite the strict rationing that was in place for the general population. Visits were arranged to Italian, French, Turkish, Czech, and Hungarian restaurants. Shooting practice was arranged at various underground London gun clubs. They were taken to the cinema and round places of interest in London, including St Paul's Cathedral and Madame Tussauds, and generally kept occupied in some rather pleasant company.

OPERATION SAUTERNE

On 5 February 1942, the NKVD asked the Comintern for more foreign agents. According to O'Sullivan, they sacrificed preparation and training in favour of politics, considering some as 'expendable assets'. It appeared that the NKVD had not realised that captured and 'turned' agents could prove disastrous to the whole Pickaxe programme.[1]

The following day, doctors from Ely Hospital informed SOE that Petyr Kousnetsov, alias Corporal Ivan Roberts, the Pickaxe agent who had been seriously injured in the plane crash on 27 December 1941, was now fit enough to leave hospital. Arrangements were made for him to be taken to Little Berkhamstead Manor. When the SOE officer arrived to pick him up on 11 February, the adjutant, Flight Lieutenant Harris, told the officer that Kousnetsov had been 'surrounded with an aura of mystery which had merely aroused curiosity and caused inconvenience to the hospital staff.' He was known only as 'Mr X' but had admitted to some in the hospital that he was from the Soviet Union, contributing to rumours that he was a spy. When all his documents were handed over, the hospital was requested to 'regard the case as never having existed'.[2]

A new landing certificate was provided, dated 14 October 1941, giving his name as Ivan Roberts but with a cover name of Robert Josef, a Swiss engineer. He was also supplied with a new identity card and ration book. His file states that he returned to Ely for check-ups in late February and early April. A flight was arranged for the May moon, and on 3 May, he was taken to stay at 79 Bryanston Court. But when he learned that he would be the only passenger he refused to fly. He had expected that another agent would be dropped with him.[3]

On 11 May 1942, he was taken back to Berkhamstead Manor, but with no clear order from Moscow, he was getting impatient and SOE was worried about his morale. A month later he was taken to stay at Roughwood Park, Chalfont St Giles, Buckinghamshire, (STS 42), where he underwent further wireless training. On 17 June, he was taken back to Bryanston Court. Part of his cover included various forged papers including a Dutch identity card, six business letters, and an amended *Wehrpass*. He was also given 2,000 guilders for Niko Kruyt and a 75-watt Polish field wireless set capable of reaching Moscow. There were also spares, a receiver, a vibrator pack, and 6-volt batteries. The transmitter worked off AC mains and the receiver off AC mains or battery. Arrangements were made for Kousnetsov to practise making transmissions.[4]

The planned dropzone was in the Wahlrod/Hochstenbach area close to the Baltic Sea in open ground near the edge of a wood about 6 miles south-east of Altenkirchen. On 22 April, Kousnetsov's new mission was codenamed Sauterne.[5]

While waiting for his injuries to recover, his SOE 'minders' were able to build up a character assessment.

Age, about 38. Probably born a German subject, spoke fluent Russian though his accent was not impeccable, good English and some Spanish.

A very extraordinary personality, who seemed to have had a very varied career. An ardent Communist and very security-minded. There is little which is known for certain about his past life. He fought in Spain on the Republican side and seems to have gone from there to Russia, though he may have been in that country already, because his German accent, apparently Saxon, had got somewhat blunted. He was never at a loss for words – indeed on subjects which interested him, such as politics (with special reference to Dialectical Materialism) he became rather enervating to those unaccustomed to totalitarian ideas of politics. But his character was, nevertheless, a very pleasant one. He liked England and the English – indeed he once affirmed that England was the only capitalistic power whose future he viewed with some hope. On discussions of the war, his ideas on occasion were sound and, by no means, entirely Red. He could never be got to explain the difference between Fascism and Communism, the former of which he viewed with very great disfavour.

All those people with whom he came into contact found him easy to get on with and he was fond of children. The Army officer's family with whom he stayed in Guildford were devoted to him and he took it for granted that here he had found a typical English family and he reciprocated this feeling.

He was always most grateful for what was done for him in an official way by the British and his few grumbles were always well founded. He was liberally supplied with documents by us, which was made necessary by the fact that he had three separate covers, i.e. a German in Holland, a Dutchman in Holland and a German in Germany....

His calmness was always surprising – even when three weeks before he left he was ordered to go to Holland, he immediately set to to learn Dutch from scratch. As an agent, he would be a credit to any country for which he worked.[6]

In October, following Kousnetsov's refusal to fly unaccompanied, Chichaev informed the Russian Section of a change of plan. They may have heard that Johannes Wenzel, Gurevich's wireless operator, had been arrested in Brussels in July. What they possibly did not know was that, under torture, Wenzel had revealed the information needed to decrypt Moscow's messages and to arrest other members of the network. They decided to send 'Ivan' to Holland to take Wenzel's place.

Major General Colin Gubbins, the deputy head of the SOE, expressed concern about dropping Pickaxes into Holland, arguing that 'it was a small country in which our operations were going well. Our relations with the Dutch were now excellent, but this satisfactory state of affairs could not last if they found out that we were introducing communists into their country.'[7] While Wiskeman, head of the Scandinavian Section, was not pleased about the proposal, he decided that they had to go ahead with it as he felt 'morally bound to accept their proposition, if only in reparation [for the error made in mixing up Barsac and Burgundy's luggage].' He sent a telegram to Lieutenant Colonel Ralph Brooks, codenamed D.R., the deputy head of operations in Northwest Europe, saying, 'We have already committed ourselves to the dropping of the W/T set and stores an do not see how we can avoid accepting the new agent.'[8]

After much discussion, the Russian Section decided on using the same dropzone used by Niko Kruyt who, by this time, had made contact with someone in Holland with a transmitter. Kousnetsov was informed that there was going to be a reception committee waiting for him. The signal from the ground was to be three short blue flashes from a hand-held torch.

In Holland he was to be known as Bruno Kühn, while in Germany he was to be Frederick Müller. The SOE were unaware at the time that Bruno Kühn was Kousnetsov's real name (he is referred to as Bruno Kühn hereafter), that he was a well-known member of the German communist elite, and that the Gestapo already had a file on him. Forged documents had to be created and cover stories for both his German and Dutch identities were carefully worked out by trained SOE staff.

The luggage for the trip was packed into two small brown suitcases and sent to the packing station, then at Gaynes Hall, where they were put into a container, along with a spade to bury the container. Also inside was Niko Kruyt's replacement luggage and a wireless set.

On 29 November 1942, Bruno Kühn (Petyr Kousnetsov) was driven up to Tempsford. According to Major Wooler's Air Transport Operation report, Chichaev informed the base at 0130 hours that there was not, in fact, going to be a reception committee. Pilot Officer Bunting took off at 0240 hours on Operation Sauterne; to disguise the nature of the mission, the despatcher dropped propaganda leaflets at Apeldoorn. On the return flight, they reached the dropzone at 0505. The agent was informed of his whereabouts and dropped with his package from 500 feet while the aircraft was heading north.[9]

On landing and burying his container and parachute, Bruno was met by Joop Janama, the brother-in-law of the Dankaart brothers, well-known Dutch Communists. They took him by train to Amersfoot where he was introduced to Piet Dankaart and Bart Riezouw, the editor of *De Waarheid*. Dankaart cycled back to Hulshortsche, dug up the wireless set and successfully got through several checkpoints without it being spotted. He later recalled how Bruno, 'showed me the poison pill triumphantly and said: "If something happens, I will swallow this."' Two days later, Bruno was introduced to Daniel Guolooze, Moscow's 'Grand Chef' in Holland.[10]

As a Dutch member of Comintern before the war, Guolooze had been sent to Moscow where he was given training in codes and radio operations by military intelligence experts. Having returned to Holland with Johannes van Proosdij in 1937, he worked for the Soviets from a philately shop, providing a communications link between the Dutch Communist Party and Comintern headquarters in Moscow.[11]

It was not until 8 March 1943 that the NKVD informed SOE that Sauterne had come on air and stated that, when he was dropped, the spare crystals for his W/T set were not packed with it. They suggested that they could provide a dropzone and a reception committee if SOE could provide the plane. Not understanding this message and unsure of its veracity, the SOE officer replied that they would look into it. The Air Ministry's response was that they would need to check out the dropzone first, commenting that 'Holland especially is difficult from the point of view of Reception Committees owing to the strong enemy defences. Consequently, only certain areas are permitted.'[12]

Here was a slight indication that all was not well in Holland. On 6 March 1942, Pilot Officer Russell had taken off from Tempsford and flew to the Hindeloopen area of Holland where he dropped six containers and six packages straight into German hands. (Unlike a container, a package was a wire-framed, padded basket that contained larger, more delicate supplies like wireless sets, printing presses, machine parts etc.). He was unaware that Hubert Lauwers, a Dutch radio operator who had been parachuted into Holland in November 1941, had been captured and was transmitting back to London under duress. Thijs Taconis, the agent who had been dropped with him, had gone to Arnhem to set up an SOE circuit where he had unwittingly recruited a *V-Manner*, the term used for a police informer. His betrayal, presumably for many Dutch guilders, led to Lauwers' arrest at his wireless set. Three ciphered texts contained the code he was using to transmit to London. Under torture and threat of execution, Lauwers agreed to work for the Germans under the control of Obersleutenant Hermann J. Giskes, the Chief of the Abwehr III/F counter-espionage operations in Holland and Belgium.

Having been thoroughly trained in England before he was dropped, Lauwers deliberately sent his messages back to London without the correct security checks, hoping that it might provide a clue that the operation was compromised. He inserted the letters CAU and GHT as often as he could among the jumbled letters. These normally preceded and terminated each message. However, the discrepancy went unnoticed. The signals that came back from Major Charles Blizard, head of SOE's Dutch Section, read 'Instruct new operator in use of security check'. His attempts at warning SOE had been exposed.

So began what Giskes described as *Der Englandspiel* and later 'Operation Nordpol'. Between 1942 and 1944, the Germans made arrangements for the SOE to send in more than fifty agents, supplies and money straight into their hands. Those manning anti-aircraft batteries were said to have been informed when incoming flights from Tempsford were scheduled and ordered not to shoot them down until they had dropped their passengers and containers and were returning to Britain. Eight of Tempsford's planes were lost in this way.

Having been dropped blind, Bruno Kühn was not captured on landing and went on to make contact with Niko Kruyt. Another request came on 11 March for 100 sheets of butter, meat, margarine and bread Reisenmarken, needed to help him proceed into Germany. The British had intercepted a message from 'Paul', thought by O'Sullivan to have been Pavel Fitin, the Direktor in Moscow, to a radio operator in Holland, announcing the arrival of batteries, money and ration cards for 'Franz'.

Dates and times for a reception committee were supplied but SOE's request to the Air Ministry for a plane was turned down. Negotiations ensued whereby they eventually agreed to parachute the container at the same dropzone as part of another planned operation over Holland.

> The Reception times must be from midnight to 0200 hours G.M.T. on the 15/21st April. The man must stand in the clearing well away from the trees and on hearing the aircraft must flash alternative red and white flashes on torches held in each hand, one red and one white. The package will be despatched from the aircraft during these times and dates irrespective of whether the lights are observed or not, provided that the dropping point is correctly identified.[13]

Another wireless set, six dry batteries and another 2,000 Dutch guilders (equivalent in April 1943 to £106 13s. 4d or $429.33) were prepared to be sent in two packages. To help Bruno cross the border into Belgium, an annotated sketch map obtained from another SOE agent was added.

New forged documents were prepared and fifty sheets of travellers' ration cards for bread, butter, meat, cheese, margarine, and *Nährmittel* (cereals). To explain his injuries from his plane crash of December 1941, Bruno was provided with additional paragraphs for his cover story:

> In June 39, you were involved in a motor accident just outside Kiel, while engaged on a job at the Germania worft. You were in hospital in the Krankenstalt, Wetzstr. 55, where you remained for three and a half months.[14]

Despite having collected all the paperwork, Captain Tice at Tempsford was not able to find a plane destined for Holland by 19 April. The delay was cause for concern for Colonel Graur, Chichaev's replacement as head of the DPR Mission while he returned to Moscow on holiday. Captain McLaughlin wrote to Lieutenant Colonel J. S. Pearson (D/HV) at Baker Street stating:

> DPR.2 [Graur] treats this operation as one of the utmost urgency and it is felt by this section that a small sop to DPR Section, under the present circumstances, would be of the greatest value. The reception committee has been standing by since last Friday. We would be grateful if you could impress this on M/CD [Gubbins] and ask for first priority.[15]

The April moon period passed without any planes being made available, and bad weather prevented any flights being taken on the following May moon. On 19 June, a plane took off from Tempsford at 2335 hours. On its return just over three hours later, the captain reported that 'after crossing Vlieland and before reaching the dam, the night was too bright for Holland, so operation abandoned. Load brought back to base.' One of the crew added that they 'might as well have gone over in the afternoon'.[16]

The drop was never made. Leo Marks, SOE's code master, realised that the radio messages being received from Holland contained no mistakes, which was rare among SOE 'pianists'. He was so sure that they must have been sent by expert German radio operators who had copied the pianist's 'hand', that he deliberately sent an indecipherable message. When he received a reply, his fears were confirmed. However, Marks was unable to persuade the upper echelons of the SOE to stop sending agents into Holland. Eventually, it was the Special Duties Squadrons who imposed a ban on flights to Holland as twelve of their planes had been shot down after dropping containers and agents during the winter of 1942-3.[17]

The NKVD was told that the halt in sending agents to Holland was due to a regrouping of anti-aircraft defences.[18] The guilders were returned to D/FIN, Group Captain John Venner, head of the Finance Section, and the forged documents were returned to Bruno Kühn's file.

Most Dutch Communists had no training in clandestine operations and, as they were known by the Gestapo, they could easily be followed. Co Dankaart was arrested in July 1943 following the arrest of Johannes van Proosdij. Dankaart confessed during his interrogation that he knew the safe house of a German agent working for the NKVD. On 28 July 1943, Gestapo officers surprised Bruno Kühn at Number 4, Voglenzangstraat. Their report stated:

> His pistol was loaded with seven bullets, and it was ready to shoot. During the search of his room the wireless set was discovered built into the chimney.... Because Kühn was obviously an intelligence agent, further investigations were undertaken by a special department.[19]

Bruno Kühn had managed to stay in hiding for eight months, a record for a Pickaxe agent. Although a number of sources say that he took his poison pill, O'Sullivan claims otherwise. Gestapo papers identified him as Frederick Müller and he was taken to Breendonck prison in Brussels where the radio games were being played. On 6 July 1944, a year after his arrest, he and Anton Winterink, another Soviet radio operator, were taken to a firing range at the Tir National, Boulevard August Reyers, and shot.[20]

Kühn was probably the most important of all the Pickaxe agents. From the age of 17, he had been prominent in the German Communist party and at the time of the Weimar Republic, he was an official in the Young Communist League of Germany. His Communist ideals inspired his younger sister, Charlotte Kühn, to join the Socialist movement in 1921. After working at the Soviet Trade Mission for four years, she moved to Moscow in 1931, where she fell in love with and eventually married Walter Ulbricht, another German communist who had also emigrated to the USSR.

After the war, Ulbricht became the first Chairman of the German Socialist Union Party. Bruno Kühn was honoured by the German Democratic Republic by having an army unit and a school in Gera named after him. Stephan Hermlin, one of the East German propaganda writers, portrayed him to the nation's youth as one of the republic's revolutionary martyrs, falsely claiming that he committed suicide rather than confess to the Nazis.[21] Whether he did reveal anything to the Gestapo was not documented in his personnel file or SOE documents.

Following the release of British documents, Lotte Ulbricht discovered the details of her brother's death. On 21 June 1989, she wrote to Erich Honecker, the Chairman of the East German Communist Party, giving him all the details and asking that instead of her brother's grave being known as 'Inconnu Nr.311', his real name should be engraved. It did not happen. After the breaking of the Berlin Wall and reunification of Germany, all traces of Bruno Kühn were removed. His army unit was disbanded, the school was renamed, and a relief depicting him was removed from its wall in 1990. Although the Belgian Radio station stands on the site of the nineteenth-century firing range where he was killed, a small plaque with his name on has been added in the cemetery next to it.[22]

INFILTRATIONS AND PREVARICATIONS

By the end of March 1942, the SOE had dropped thirteen Soviet agents into Belgium, Holland, France, Austria and Germany. Meanwhile, the NKVD had managed to drop several agents into Poland to work with the Polish Communist Party, seven agents over Czechoslovakian territory and six Sudeten Germans, five Austrians, ten Poles and five Romanians.[1] Soviet agents were sent by plane from the Soviet Union. The stories of three agents, Willi Börner, Albert Hössler, and Robert Barth, are especially interesting.

Willi Börner, alias Anton Belski, and two comrades were dropped with a wireless set near Insterburg in East Prussia on 16/17 May 1942. When his comrades were captured, Börner managed to make his way to Vienna before he too was caught on 18 July. Threatened with execution, he agreed to send false messages to Moscow, helping the Gestapo to trap yet more parachutists. After months of waiting, Börner received a message from Direktor Fitin to expect two agents, called by the SOE the 'Everest' mission, which will be referred to later.[2]

Two other agents, Albert Hössler and Robert Barth, were dropped behind German lines near Bryansk in August 1942. Pretending to be German soldiers on home leave, they made their way by train to Berlin. Their mission was to re-establish contact with Schulze-Boysen and Arvid Harnack, an official in the Reich's Economics Ministry who was also anti-Hitler. Hössler was a German Communist exile who, like most of the Pickaxes, had fought in Spain. Back in the Soviet Union he volunteered for NKVD training in wireless operations, ciphers, and deciphering. Barth was a German soldier who had been captured by the Soviets in March 1942 and successfully 'turned'.[3]

The first message sent back at the end of August stated that they had reached Berlin and made contact with Soviet agents. However, the Gestapo captured Schulze-Boysen on 31 August 1942, and most of his comrades within a few weeks. Hössler was arrested in September and Barth the following month. When his wife and her parents were threatened, Barth agreed to give the Gestapo his ciphers and co-operate. Thus began another *Funkspiel*, sending Nazi-inspired messages to Moscow on Hössler's frequencies and receiving their responses. It was thus possible for the Gestapo to arrange reception committees for new Pickaxes and meet them if they parachuted accurately into the dropzone.

Gestapo Officer Horst Kopkow's post-war testimony has shed some interesting light on the transmissions sent under duress by Hössler and Barth. Hössler only agreed to co-operate so that he could alert Moscow to what had happened. He and Barth had both been given a 'security check', but despite this Moscow didn't recognise Hössler's warnings. When he realised this, Hössler refused to co-operate further and was shot on Himmler's orders in December 1942. The Gestapo were forced to use a substitute operator – an unsatisfactory measure – but to the surprise of Horst Kopkow, head of *Sonderkommando Rote Kapelle* (Red Orchestra Special Detachment), Moscow did still not detect that it was not Hössler who was transmitting. Barth, meanwhile, continued to send messages and was rewarded by the Gestapo with extra food and visits from his wife.[4]

The Gestapo released Barth and sent him to the Western Front where he was taken prisoner by US troops. When he told them that he had been an NKVD agent, they handed him over to the Soviets. They did not believe his claims that he had included security checks in his transmissions; he was charged with treason and executed in Moscow in November 1945.[5]

Theodore Winter and Katja Niederkirchner were the first male/female pair of NKVD agents to be dropped into Germany from the Soviet Union. Winter was the son-in-law of Wilhelm Pieck, the chairman of the German Communist Party exiled in Moscow. He complained to the NKVD that they were ill-prepared for their mission as they had only been given shoddy clothes. Winter was duly provided with a tailor-made suit, but there was no mention of Niederkirchner receiving a new outfit.[6]

On 7 October 1943, they were parachuted into Poland with a short-wave transmitter to collect information about the situation in Germany and to transmit reports back to Moscow. With the help of Polish partisans, they made their way to Konigsberg. However, before they could reach Berlin, they were arrested by the German police. The police quickly discovered discrepancies in Niederkirchner's forged identity card and expired ration cards. They were both tortured and interrogated at the Sachsenhousen concentration camp. Winter was transferred to Berlin and it is unknown what happened to him, while Niederkirchner was transferred to Ravensbrück concentration camp and was shot by the SS in the early hours of 28 September 1944.[7]

Commenting on their case, O'Sullivan made the point that 'none of the NKVD desk officers had to answer for these mistakes, a stark contrast to the pre-war purges for non-existent crimes. But professional mistakes went unpunished. The parachute agents relied on the NKVD and paid the price.'[8]

In March 1943, probably because of the misfortune of their NKVD agents, the Russians allowed Special Duties Squadron planes to fly operations to Eastern Europe from Soviet air bases. To reach Russia, the pilots of the Halifaxes and Stirlings had to fly over Northern Norway and Finland to avoid German-controlled air space. However, the operations were short-lived.

Even though SOE had been given clearance, in extreme circumstances, to fly long-range missions to northern Norway from Murmansk, the Soviet success in attacking the isolated German troops in Russia meant that they could undertake their own operations using Russian planes.[9]

On 8 July, Moscow received an SIS document from a British agent which pointed out that the differences between the USSR and Great Britain were just as large as those between Germany and Britain. The Soviet Union would only be an ally as long as it was in Moscow's interests. They did not trust London and organised active intelligence against Britain. The SIS's opinion was that, 'We cannot trust the Russians like we trust the Czechs or the Americans or give them information which may reveal an important or delicate source.' Some Russians, it appears, did not differentiate between the SIS and SOE at this time.[10]

A Soviet document referred to by O'Sullivan sheds light on Chichaev's attitude to Hill, who returned to London for 'discussions' in August 1942. He was not impressed at how quickly Hill admitted mistakes. In a telegram to London he commented: 'The British want to continue the cooperation and try to improve their performance.'[11] However, he also intimated that SOE was planning to sabotage the Pickaxe missions by delaying their departure deliberately to give them a chance to find out the agents' objectives and persuade them to defect.

With the RAF banning flights to Holland and the Foreign Office insisting on permission being given before Soviet agents could be infiltrated into France, Belgium, and Switzerland, the NKVD intimated that SOE was not acting according to the terms of the treaty. In early August 1942, Sir Stewart Menzies, the head of SIS, stated:

> The fact that communists are introduced into France cannot, I submit, be very dangerous in view of the fact that such elements are recognised to be united in their effort against the Axis. Our chief aim is primarily to fight against the Axis by all means in our power, leaving the long-term political problems to the F.O. [Foreign Office] It would, I think, be regrettable if the F.O. were invited to reconsider their decision on principle [that permission is required for Pickaxe operations into France, Belgium, and Switzerland]. Presumably they are satisfied that the danger to the future set-up of French government is outbalanced by the possible subversive value of these agents in enemy-occupied territory. Furthermore any potential danger is lessened by the fact that we have a 'tally' on these agents by reason of our position as intermediaries.[12]

The SAM mission was augmented when Milnes-Gaskell was flown out to Moscow in August 1942 with the rank of Lieutenant-Colonel to give him more standing among the Russians. Probably accompanying him on the flight was Hill, who had paid a brief visit to London and had been assured by Sir Charles Hambro and Lord Selbourne, who had taken over from Dr Dalton as Minister of Economic Warfare, that a better service from now on would be accorded to the NKVD.[13] When Hill arrived, Captain Graham told him that his mistress Luba had been missing for ten days. Hill suspected an NKVD plot but admitted that his liaison with NKVD came foremost, even if it meant torture and death for Luba. She had been sent to the Intourist Hotel in Omsk, Siberia. After four days she was sent to do unpaid work in the forest.[14]

In a telegram from SAM on 10 November 1942, London was informed that 'NKVD anxious to send group of 3 or 4 repeat 3 or 4 trained parachutists to Austria.'[15] In response, Lieutenant Colonel Ralph Brooks, codenamed D.R., the deputy head of operations in Northwest Europe, wrote a note to Gubbins, deputy head of SOE, hoping it might be used to 'stall' their arrival:

I have no objection to furnishing whatever aid is possible to the Russian section when they wish to drop agents in my territory. This telegram raises the issue of whether the game is worth the candle on a bigger scale, since four agents is a large order by any standard.

I would therefore be grateful if you would ask C.D. [Hambro] for a ruling on our position vis-à-vis the Russians. To enable him to assess the position, I should like to table the following considerations, leaving the D/P [Russian] Section to make good their own use from the other side.

a) We are at present extremely pressed for aircraft owing to the recent developments, and also to the bad weather of the season.

b) Eventually of course there will be undesirable comebacks from these operations e.g.

i) If F.F. [De Gaulle's Fighting French] Headquarters ever spot these droppings, they will accuse us of fomenting further division among French resistance groups.

ii) After the war, the French regime is likely to bring it up against the British government that Communists were imported by us.

iii) A similar argument applies a fortiori with regard to the Dutch, from whom we have to conceal these operations even more stringently.

c) It is also clear that the Russians are using our original favours as the thin end of a very palpable wedge. Thus a current operation originally proposed to take a wireless set to the agent previously dropped by us in Holland (operation BARSAC), with the proviso that the agent should pass on immediately into Germany, has now been extended to cover the dropping of two sets as well as the operator, who will remain for not less than six months (at the end of which time of course his papers will be out of date, and he will be unable to proceed to Germany). In other words, we are being 'worked' for the introduction of a second operator and set.

d) I wish to make it clear that I am still perfectly willing to execute any orders on this head, but I wish to be assured that it is officially considered that we are getting sufficient dividend for our trouble and risk.[16]

In response to Lieutenant Colonel Brooks' concerns, Gubbins passed a note to Hambro saying that he was not worried as much about France. Holland, however, was a different matter:

> …[Holland] is a small country in which our own operations are going well despite the limited number of suitable dropping points. Our relations with the Dutch are now excellent and they trust us implicitly, but this satisfactory state of affairs cannot last if they find out we are introducing Communists into their country. I consider that Norway, and to a lesser degree Belgium, come into the same category and feel that we should make every effort to avoid being instrumental in introducing Communists into any of these three countries.
>
> If you agree with the above would you let me know what excuse you think we should give for 'stalling.'
>
> Personally, I can see no objection to the introduction of Russians into Denmark, France and enemy country.[17]

A meeting was arranged with Sir Alexander Cadogan of the Foreign Office and Sir Stewart Menzies, the head of SIS. The result was a statement of SOE policy towards introducing NKVD agents into Europe:

> a) Into all countries fighting with the Axis including Hungary we shall be willing to introduce agents as required by them.
> b) Into Allied countries occupied by the Axis, whose Governments are refugee, we shall only introduce NKVD agents with the consent of the Governments concerned.
> c) Into Occupied France. We shall judge each case on its merits but in general we shall not agree to introduce NKVD agents without consulting the Fighting French.
> d) Into neutral countries. We shall in each case consult the Foreign Office but it would be normally our intention to refuse to introduce NKVD agents into these countries.
> Denmark I think is the only country which I have not covered and should a request be received for the introduction of an agent into this country I intend to leave the matter to be decided in the light of events.[18]

In a letter to Hambro, Menzies expressed his hope that 'SOE agreed that all operations to put in Soviet agents should be subordinate in priority to both S.I.S. and S.O.E. operations for other agents.'[19] In a note five days later, Gubbins wrote to Hambro:

> 'C' [Sir Stewart Menzies] has at the most four or five operations a month and there are seven Halifaxes in 161 Squadron on which he has a prior claim, in

addition to the twelve in 138 Squadron which are for our work. I cannot see how any situation could arise by which any air operation for 'C' could possibly be postponed because we wanted to deliver a Russian. In regards operations by boat, there 'C' has prior claim and prior facilities in every way, and we could not possibly interfere.

As regards subordination and priority of NKVD agents to SOE operations, naturally, if we have urgent operations and few craft, we might have to put NKVD off for a month or so, but there is little reason why this should occur in the future, although in the past with only one or two long-range aircraft available it was the case. I myself am much happier if we can get them off in reasonable rotation with our own men. Not only does this put us in well with the NKVD which possibly is some advantage, but also it enables us to eliminate early from our training and holding arrangements a feature which can, on occasions, prove extremely embarrassing!

I have written the above merely to put you in the picture, but you can safely answer 'C' that we do not and will not allow NKVD operations to prejudice our own in priority, nor would we be a hand in prejudicing those of 'C'.

Reference last para. of 'C's' letter, de Gaulle naturally hates the Russian connection into which he has been forced owing to pressure of events and has little palate for it.[20]

OPERATIONS TONIC
AND SODAWATER

On 17 July 1942, the Russian Section informed SOE that MI5 had to provide false identities and ration cards for two more agents, 'Elena Nikitina' and 'Pyotr Koltsov'. They were a married couple and their party's codename was to be Tonic.[1] The problem of the Soviet agents arriving without proper papers generated action at high levels.

On 12 August 1942, MAJOR PEARSON sent a minute to MR. HANBURY WILLIAMS through COLONEL TAYLOR concerning the PICKAXE parties. He said that London had had trouble in the past with the Pickaxes owing to the fact that they arrived in this country without the proper documents. It was pointed out that HILL had made representations to the N.K.V.D. in Moscow but they had refused to allow him to interview and check up on their agents before they left. It was agreed that if further Pickaxes arrived without proper documents they would be returned to Russia by the next boat. On his return HILL was told to make it quite clear to the N.K.V.D. that if they did not allow him to check up on their agents before leaving Russia, S.O.E. would not accept any responsibility for their future.[2]

In August, SOE were told that Nikitina and Koltsov had already embarked from Archangel on the SS *Ocean Voice* with three others. Captain Baird (D/CE.5), one of the security section officers, then informed them that the three others were 'Henrik Gorelov' and 'Emilya Novikova', both destined for Bavaria and codenamed Sodawater, and 'Martens' (Alvin Mayr) who was to join the Coffee party. All five had to be registered with the police as Estonians.[3]

Their journey was eventful. After a delayed departure caused by a U-boat attack on their convoy on its way to Archangel – SS *Ocean Voice* needed a 20-foot hole in its hull repaired and the bridge repainted after fire damage – further problems arose when Ossipov complained bitterly that Captain Maund, the Senior Naval Officer, was being most uncooperative. Hill explained to London that the appointment of Krasilnikov, the NKVD's new chief at the port, had led to a clash with the British Naval authorities. When Krasilnikov refused to allow British naval hospital staff to land without visas, Captain Maund retaliated by refusing to carry any NKVD agents.

> Reading between the lines, I think it is quite probable that the Pickaxe parties have been used by both sides as whipping tools ... Generally speaking, we are entering upon a very difficult and trying period, when the nerves of both sides will be considerably frayed. I do not think that under the circumstances this state can be avoided. I am convinced that by keeping to a steady policy, one will weather this particularly unpleasant period.[4]

The convoy finally left Archangel on 14 September 1942 with the British hospital staff and NKVD agents aboard, but the drama was by no means over.

> Tuesday September the 22nd came along and with it a fine morning with a calm sea and a slight swell, which caused the ships to roll a little, but nothing to give any discomfort even to the trawlers. All was quiet until just before the watch below was called out for their breakfasts at seven-thirty. Then in the short space of half an hour or so three ships were hit by torpedoes. The first one was the Ocean Voice, the second the Bellingham and the third the fleet oiler Gray Ranger. The latter two were hit within seconds of each other. The rumble of depth charges sounded and reverberated through the half-empty ships that were left sailing along, they were being dropped by the escorts over on the port side of the convoy, but it was a job to pick up an echo from a submarine in those cold waters with so many fresh water layers hidden away among the salt sea. I saw the stricken ships keel over as they were hit by the exploding torpedoes, for we were fairly close to them.[5]

The crews and twenty-five Soviet passengers were rescued by the escort ships. The five Pickaxes continued their journey on HMS *Bulldog*, arriving in Glasgow on 28 September. However, although they were lucky to have escaped death, their wireless sets, cover documents and those needed by the Coffee party, were at the bottom of the Arctic Ocean. Having been given British clothing and issued with food coupons, they were taken by train to London to meet their NKVD masters and accommodated in a flat at Cropthorne Court, Maida Vale. Moscow sent them a telegram expressing their sympathy.

Whether NKVD was putting pressure on the Russian Section is unknown, but the day following the arrival of the five new Pickaxes, they were informed that there were nine more Pickaxes awaiting transfer from the USSR – four destined for occupied France, three for Austria, and two for Italy. There had been plans for twelve, but pressure must have been brought to bear from higher quarters as the two destined for Lisbon in Portugal and one for Switzerland were refused.

The papers of the 'Estonian' arrivals identified Nikitina as 34-year-old Kersti Poska, an unmarried stenographer from Haapsalu; Koltsov as 36-year-old Juri

Kruus, an unmarried wireless engineer from Tallinn; Novikova as 34-year-old Anna Under, an unmarried governess from Virz-Yarvi; and Gorelov as 37-year-old Otto Ulnoti, an unmarried electrical engineer from Rafla. George Martens, already mentioned, was identified as 34-year-old Jaan Runo, an unmarried timber merchant from Parnu, who by 1 October had been allocated to the Coffee party. His real name was Alvin Mayr. All records of their arrival in Britain in their real names and nationalities were ordered to be expunged from Immigration, Home Office, and National Registration records.[6]

Chichaev informed SOE that Moscow had ordered Colonel Graur to live permanently with the new agents.

> This was unadvisable for security reasons and London asked Moscow to try and get the orders rescinded. Moscow replied that they had talked the matter over with the N.K.V.D. They assumed that the objection had been to GRAU [sic] personally who, owing to his insufficient knowledge of English, etc., was likely to blow cover. This assumption, however, as London pointed out, was not sound. London's objection had not been based on personal grounds but was one of principle. London, however, thought that Moscow need take no further action on the matter.[7]

There was what was termed 'a minor storm' when Chichaev learnt that SOE had taken photographs of all the Pickaxes. They had been taken without his consent during Lieutenant Suvorov's absence from the house. He objected to the fact that they looked like criminals in a police file as the sitter held a serial number with the letter S or F to denote side or front. Major Seddon explained that it was a routine procedure for all SOE agents and disingenuously suggested that they were to be used in their forged documents. When the final copies were shown to Chichaev, he criticised their sloppiness and insisted on better quality ones. As they also had to wait for replacement wireless sets, the agents had time on their hands.[8]

On 5 October, Alvin Mayr left to join the Coffee party at Hansteads. As Gorse Hill had not been acquired, alternative accommodation was needed. Toropchenko and Corporal Morris, their conducting officer, took Tonic and Sodawater to Alderton Hall Farm in Loughton, Essex, where they were looked after by Mr and Mrs Chaffe.

Although Nikitina and Koltsov were grouped togther and given the codename Tonic when they arrived, one can only imagine that Chichaev did not like the fact that they were a married couple. He separated them by swapping Koltsov and Gorelov. The new Tonic party was made up of Nikitina and Gorelov and the new Sodawater party was Novikova and Koltsov.

While at Alderton Hall Farm, the newly paired Tonic and Sodawater parties were provided with maps and they discussed their separate dropzones. Group Captain C. Grierson, one of SOE's conducting officers, fed back to London that they were prepared to go to Freiburg-im-Breisgau, Nieusiedler See in Ostmark, and Rostock in Stralsund, and asked for photographic plates of these districts to be sent.

On 27 October, they were taken to Ringway for their parachute training where, like the others, they stayed at Dunham House. Major Edwards was satisfied with the efforts of all of them except Elena Nikitina (Kersti Poska), who he described as 'a very nervous type of person who was frightened in the ground training and also in the balloon descent. She did well to jump at all.'

While at Alderton, the agents had issues with the Chaffes about food and heating; the SOE sent a Mr Saunder to investigate. He informed Major Seddon that, contrary to orders, the 'guests' had lit coal fires in the dining and sitting room and had electric fires in bedrooms. They went out for meals at a moment's notice after a meal had been ordered and prepared by the Chaffes.

> ...[They] invaded Mrs. Chaffes kitchen at 11 pm. to make tea or coffee for themselves. They go to bed about midnight with the lights and fire going. They have raided the orchard and taken all the pears; they throw the cores of these on the floor when they have finished with them![9]

As for Lance Corporal Morris, the conducting officer, Saunder reported:

> He frequently disappears across the fields near the house and comes back with his boots covered in mud. The other day when walking with one of the lady guests he became very frightened, and ran away from her, to return later looking very much upset – she told Chaffe this, and said she would not go out with him again. He does not appear to show any satisfaction at British or Russian successes. I mention this as I think his antecedents might be interested.[10]

On 8 November, after only a week in Alderton, the agents were taken to The Drokes. Over the next few months they were moved regularly; one imagines to break up the monotony of a long wait. They were sent to Cropthorne on the 17th, back to Alderton on the 19th, and then to Cropthorne the next day where they stayed until 1 December.

During this time, after seven changes of mind, they finally agreed on their dropzones. The Air Transport Form 6 gave Tonic's as 4 kms south-south-east of Endigen, 5¾ kms south-south-west of Reigel and 15 kms north-west of Freiburg. Sodawater's was 4½ kms east of Wimpassing, 2½ km west of Loretta and 8 ½ km north-north-west of Eisenstadt. It was decided that, to increase the chances of a safe delivery, both parties had to be despatched on separate aircraft from Tempsford, and in accordance with their cover story, on a weekend.

At a meeting held on 20 November, having discovered that the documents to be carried by the agents were incomplete or incorrect, Chichaev presented a variety of demands.

London pointed out to him that since the agents were already standing by there was not sufficient time to make all the alterations he asked for, and suggested that a better time for raising these questions would have been when the documents were first received, some twelve days previously. As a result of these alterations the sorties had to be postponed.[11]

Consequently, on 21 November, the Russian Section sent a message to Tempsford requesting that, 'owing to difficulties beyond the control of this section,' the Tonic and Sodawater operations had to be postponed until Friday 27 November. In the meantime, Toropchenko informed the agents that he had cancelled the operation on the grounds that 'SOE were not ready.' Chichaev told them that they were waiting for wireless sets which were being flown by Liberator from Moscow. By the time the plane left Moscow on 27 November with the sets in the Soviet diplomatic bag, the Air Ministry had postponed both flights because of the bad weather.[12]

While they waited to be notified of their flight, on 2 December, instead of going back to The Drokes, the Pickaxes stayed for five days at The Vineyards, (STS 35), another of the large country houses at Beaulieu. Here they were given additional training in wireless and telegraphy before returning to Alderton on 7 December. A week later they went down to Cropthorne Court in London where they spent Christmas and New Year. They went back to Alderton on New Year's Day.

In early January 1943, Major Seddon reported to SAM that he had had 'a most unpleasant interview with Chichaeff'.

... as a result of the TONIC-SODAWATER failure [CHICHAEV] had reviewed the whole situation since the signature of the Charter. CHICHAEFF had drawn attention to the fact that PICKAXE results had been lamentable and that much time and money had been wasted without result. He had pointed out during this period, of parties destined for Austria no successful operations had been carried out and that for the delayed parties the only excuse produced had been the weather. He failed to understand how weather could have been uniformly bad for eighteen months, and had said that this argument was difficult for him to explain to his superiors.

SEDDON had tried to explain that his were not the only operations thus affected. He had accepted this argument but had suggested that if our commitments were so heavy we should not have stressed our ability to deliver the goods. He had added that he had lost confidence in the efficiency of our organisation. SEDDON had been obliged to agree that our results had been poor and CHICHAEFF had asked to be put in touch with a superior officer of S.O.E., failing which he would have to act on the diplomatic level.

Moscow replied that on February 1 the N.K.V.D. in Moscow had made a demarche (clearly most carefully prepared) about the unsatisfactory results of

S.O.E.'s transport arrangements for Pickaxes. He had explained that that the N.K.V.D. did not demand priority in infiltrating agents into western Europe but they did expect "equality of service" and they were convinced they were not getting it. It might be better to end the liaison with S.O.E. Hill said that if this were done it would obviously have to be done on a high level. S.O.E. had come to the U.S.S.R. as a result of a conversation between MOLOTOFF, with the consent of BERIA and the approval of the British Foreign Office, and it was logical that if it were decided to end the liaison the decision should be taken on the same level.[13]

Chichaev managed to get an interview with General Marshall Cornwall to whom he reiterated his concerns at great length. This demanded an equally long attempt to explain SOE's problems.[14] Chichaev, Toropchenko and Graur's correspondence, if it exists, would give a fascinating insight into these incidents. No doubt Chichaev was putting pressure not just on the highest echelons of the SOE, but also on the Soviet Ambassador to consult at the highest levels in the Foreign Office and the War Office.

Although a flight became available on 17 January 1943, there was another hiccup. Form ATF 11, used to help identify each party's luggage for the personnel who packed their containers, was not completed until the day of the flight; a delay which caused some concern. Given what had happened with the luggage of Willi and Niko Kruyt, a lot more care had been taken in identifying Tonic and Sodawater's luggage. Tonic's was described as a clean grey rucksack with lighter pockets, a neutral coloured rucksack with a tear in the front that had been repaired by hand, a small brown imitation leather attaché case, and a dark brown fibre suitcase. Sodawater's included a small tan pigskin suitcase and a dirty grey rucksack with soot marks on the front. The rule that luggage had to be received four days before the actual flight had not been followed, Air Liaison therefore postponed their departure again. It was decided by the Russian Section to curb their apologies for the delay, blaming it on 'our Russian colleagues'.

The agents returned to Cropthorne on 17 January, where they were on stand-by until the 26th. Koltsov was given another alias, Hermann Koehler, sometimes spelt Köhler and Novikova was given Emile Boretzky. While at Cropthorne, Koltsov needed his wristwatch repaired. A Movado was provided as a replacement but the watchmaker was asked by the conducting officer to fix the faulty one and return it as quickly as possible as 'their friend' preferred the old one.

What was unusual about both these missions was a note in their file stating that reception parties would be waiting for them between 19 and 27 January between 2200 and 0200 hours, but that they would not be using light signals. This suggests the NKVD or SOE had received messages from a wireless set transmitting from the field detailing such arrangements. Apart from blind drops, where there was no one to meet them, most agents were met by a group of resistance members on the ground who, on seeing the aircraft approaching, flashed an agreed Morse code recognition letter. When it was returned by the pilot, they would light three torches and align themselves with the wind direction, thus giving the pilot a line to approach for the drop.

On the evening of 24/25 January, everything was in place for the Tonic party (Nikitina and Gorelov). The plane was available, the weather was fine, but Tempsford's Daily Operations Report stated that the mission was postponed because of 'crew difficulty'. One of the crew fell sick and couldn't be replaced, a slip-up attributed to the fact that the aircraft was from 138 Squadron while the crew had been borrowed from 161 Squadron.[15]

They returned to Alderton on 1 February and, on the 10th, were sent to Cropthorne with instructions to stand by. News came through that there was a plane arranged for 13 February. Nikitina and Gorelov were taken up to Tempsford again. Everything seemed to go according to plan and Flight Officer Ruttledge took off at 2005 hours:

> …Taking the route Beachy Head – Pointe du Haur-Banc. A large wood southwest of Valenciennes – Lake Lachaussée (approx. 30 km SW of Metz) – Target. The pinpointed 'junction of canal with River Rhine near Sandhouse'. This must have been the junction of the Leopolds Canal and the River Rhine just 12 km north of both Endingen and Riegel. Here they spent three quarters of an hour over the target area, poor ground visibility preventing them from pinpointing their exact position. This coupled with a calculated ground wind of 30 mph decided them against the drop and they abandoned the operation. They returned home by the same route, landing after some 7.30 hours in the air. There had been no enemy opposition and apart from ground haze weather conditions were good.[16]

To disguise the real purpose of the mission, leaflets were dropped at 0015 hours and the plane returned safely to Tempsford at 0332 hours. The conducting officer reported:

> Passengers quite O.K.… The pilot would have been wise not to have dropped his passengers in this strong wind even if he had located the point exactly.[17]

Whether they were provided with rooms at Gaynes Hall or returned to London was not mentioned.

Three days later, on 16/17 February, Flight Officer Wilkin and his crew tried to complete Operation Tonic. The plane took off from Tempsford at 2000 hours and reached the area by 2253 hours, but according to the pilot's report '10/10 cloud' made it impossible to pinpoint their position and the decision was made to return without making the drop.[18]

Leaflets were dropped at 2300 hours in the Sarrebourg area, north-eastern France, and at 0300 hours in the Arras area. After 6 hours 10 minutes flying time they touched down at Tempsford and were driven back to Gaynes Hall. Again the passengers were described as 'Quite O.K.'[19]

The next rescheduled Tonic mission, due to be flown by Flight Lieutenant Dodkin on the 18/19 February, was cancelled at the last minute. The Daily Operations Report stated that 'one of the party sick before take-off. Their Chief called the trip off.'[20] O'Sullivan commented that Nikitina was sick at the thought of sharing an aeroplane with Belgians.

On 19 February, a flight was scheduled for the Sodawater party. Squadron Leader Boxer took off from Tempsford at 1830 hours. He flew to Beachy Head, over Point du Haut, Banc, Leval and Lake Lachaussée to a pinpoint on the Rhine-Marne Canal. On the next course, the temperature of the port outer engine started to rise just before reaching Tubingen, south of Stuttgart. A second engine began to fail near Lake Constance, so Boxer decided to abort the mission. He feathered the engine and turned for home. 'Owing to difficulty in maintaining height the "A" type package was jettisoned without parachute in a wood. Time 2140, position 10 miles N.E. of Freiburg, height 2,300 feet.' On the return trip, 65 km from Lake Lachaussée, an unidentified twin-engined aircraft was spotted flying parallel to them on the starboard side and flashing a white light. There was no mention that it spotted them. They landed safely at Tempsford after a round trip of 7 hours 45 minutes.[21]

The following day, an unsigned note headed 'URGENT' was sent to Air Liaison at Tempsford telling them that the Russians had been on to them to get Sodawater's remaining luggage back to London so it could be examined to see if any documents were missing.

> In view of the accidents we have had carrying out PICKAXE Operations it is most important that we should not fail to do this. I spoke to C.D. [Hambro] about PICKAXE Operations this morning, and we are most anxious to avoid further troubles with the Russians. I do hope, therefore, you will see that we do not let them down. I cannot exaggerate the URGENCY of the importance of this.[22]

The same day, the NKVD responded to SOE's concern about a supposed Soviet attempt to assassinate Herr von Papen, the German ambassador in Istanbul, with a complaint that they had somehow mixed up the luggage of Barsac and Burgundy and another unfortunate 'Pickaxe' had been dropped without money, papers, and a wireless set. Who this agent was is unknown. It seems they had been misinformed.[23]

While Sodawater waited, they must have been pleased to receive 2 lbs of German tobacco, 400 Dutch cigarettes and a 5U4G valve for their wireless set. Their new luggage was, this time, sent in advance to Holmewood Hall, near Peterborough, for packing.

138 and 161 Squadron Operations Records show that all the SIS's Iridium missions and SOE's Mercury missions to Eastern Europe on the 18/19 and 26/27

January were recorded as NCO (Not Carried Out) due to bad weather or being shot down. To give one an idea of the conditions, the winter of 1942/43 in Norway was described as being one of the severest winters in living memory.

On the night of 24/25 February, the four agents returned to Tempsford. Flight Officer Gebik and his Polish crew took Sodawater. He reported taking off with his Halifax DT-725 'J' at 1850 hours following much the same route as Squadron Leader Boxer.

> At Lake Constance they turned on ETA for Neusiedler See, (Lake) having first made a pinpoint on Chiem See (approximately 50 km west of Salzberg). Neusiedler See is about the same distance SE of Vienna. It was in this area that they parachuted from 700 feet, the two NKVD agents and their parcel. On the way home 21 minutes after leaving the target area flying at 6,000 feet they met with heavy accurate heavy flak from four guns at Steyr (south of Linz). From Lake Constance the weather had been clear with good visibility. They landed at Tempsford at 05.30 having been flying for 10.40 hours. The remarks by the OC No. 138 Squadron on the report was 'Good show!' G/Capt Fielden was more forthcoming with 'Very creditable!'[24]

The despatcher noted that the 'woman delayed too long after the man, who jumped first. Distance estimated as 300 yards at least. Their 'chutes seen to open.'[25]

Flight Sergeant Twardarwa reported taking off in his Halifax DT-727 'K' at 2105 hours on Operation Tonic with Flight Lieutenant Gryglewicz as navigator.[26] It was the Polish crew's first Special Duties mission. They took off at 2105 hours.

> [They] crossed the French coast at a height of 500 feet and afterwards set course for a large wood south of Valenciennes, which they reached on DR [Dead Reckoning]. They pinpointed the lakes west of Sarrebourg (some 50 km east of Nancy), (Meurthe-et-Moselle) and pinpointed the canal joining the River Rhine. From here because of bad visibility they made several runs to the target eventually parachuting load from 1,900 feet indicated, flying due north. Three parachutes were seen to open. The agents must have been relieved to have jumped at last having logged 17.25 hours in the air when they finally left the aeroplane.[27]

The plane returned without incident to Tempsford at 0350. Nikitina and Gorelov had landed safely on their fourth attempt. The pilot's report stated that 'the lady was nervous lest they should be dropped on the wrong place. Also slightly airsick, in spite of pills to counteract same.'[28]

The following day, 25 February, Major Seddon wrote a letter to Chichaev informing him of the success of the Tonic and Sodawater operations. Their certificates of registration, national registration identity cards, clothing books, ration books and I.B. 23s were returned to McLaughlin with an intriguing note:

'We have been fortunate to find the I.B. 23 belonging to Jaan RUNO [Georg Martens/Alvin Mayr], who was one of the party who returned to the U.S.S.R. recently.'[29]

Three days later, Chichaev informed General Marshall Cornwall at a reception at the Soviet Embassy that he was leaving for Moscow the next day. He gave no inkling of the reason for his journey and was unable to say whether it was temporary or permanent.[30]

While the agents had been cooped up with their conducting officers, SOE was able to build up detailed character studies.

Elena NIKITINA (Kersti Poska)

Apparently regarded as the head of the group and certainly possessed the strongest character. Throughout their many trials and tribulations, she maintained a relative calm and only on one occasion – when she was faced with two operational nights running – did events appear to be too much for her. She invariably knew what she wanted and almost as invariably got it. She never allowed her political views be known, indeed she never discussed politics. For most of the men with whom she came into contact, she appeared to exude an ineffable sex appeal, a characteristic which was certainly not based on any misconception of belonging to the weaker sex.

Very little is known of her story; she required a certain amount of alteration to her documents and she was given various additional papers to complete her cover. She, however, did all the filling in herself, as did the other members of both these parties. Towns in which she was interested were Cologne and Berlin, and, amongst other things, she asked to be provided with a wedding ring and a crucifix.

Henrik GORELOV (Otto Ulnoti)

A funny quiet old man, probably aged about 45, who, at first sight, appeared to be permanently depressed. However, longer acquaintance and alcohol produced quite a collection of seemingly funny stories. Apart from these latter, he wasted few words and never spoke, unless spoken to. On all the many occasions of parting, his eyes used to well with tears. His job seems to have been in connection with M.A.N. [sic] Works and he studied various plans of Stuttgart.

Emilya NOVIKOVA (Anna Under)

A very ordinary woman aged about 35; a somewhat nervous type. Indeed she was the only one to hesitate in jumping. Very much the Hausfrau and indeed she used to prepare, on occasion, a very nice tea for D/P 4 [McLaughlin]. She appears to have been the W/T agent for SODAWATER, and on one occasion evinced great technical knowledge of the subject. She often found it exceedingly difficult to make up her mind on any given occasion of doubt, and several times, inflamed the usually placid E/FC [an unidentified SOE officer] – and many are the stories which he will tell on the subject.

Pyotr KOLTSOV (Juri Kruus)

A very typical Viennese, aged about 38, with his native sense of humour remaining intact. On one rather sordid occasion, when a delay in the arrival of baggage occurred, he sat for two hours telling often amusing, and always doubtful stories to Miss Hatfield and D/P 4. Nothing upset him, even the prospect of dropping unexpectedly in an unknown part of Germany. His main interest from our point of view was in the Steyer-Daimler-Puch Works in Vienna. Although he never talked politics, his tendencies appeared to be anything but Communistic, and it seems probable that he was one of the refugees from the 1935 Putsch.

The group stayed together through many trials and tribulations and it must be admitted that they were always in good heart, and, latterly, at any rate, seemed really grateful for any small thing which was done for them – a complete change of atmosphere from the days of their arrival, when Nikitina was heard to disapprove loudly of the quality of goods in the London shops, when opposed to the glittering emporia of Moscow. [31]

Additional information was provided by O'Sullivan, who added that Yelena Nikitina

...was in effect German Communist Elsa Noffke, and Gorelov/Ulnoti her colleague Georg Tietze. Noffke had worked in the Communist paper *Rote Fahne* in Berlin until 1933. She had been trained in a special school for agents near Moscow for nine months in 1942 before travelling to Britain. The Gestapo had advance notice of the arrival of 'Tonic', probably through deciphered messages from the Moscow 'Direktor'.[32]

Nothing more appeared in their files until 9 August 1943, when a note was sent to Colonel Chichaev informing him that SOE had just received a report from a Polish/Austrian refugee who had reached Switzerland. He claimed to be a Professor of Celtic at Berlin University with a Dublin University degree, and had been forced to leave Berlin in 1943 following an order for his arrest as he had Jewish grand-parents. While hiding in Freiburg, he heard that English parachutists dropped near Kaiserstuhl early in 1943 had been captured by local police around Whitsuntide (June 1943). The W/T set and codes were seized intact. SOE confirmed that Nikitina and Gorelov had been dropped near Koenigstuhl.

On 6th June 1943, a man called MÜLLER [Bruno Kühn/Pyetr Kousnetsov] in possession of Swiss papers was arrested at his house in the ALBERT STRASSE,

FREIBURG i. Br., for having sheltered agents who were parachuted by the British and allowing them to set up a wireless transmission set in his house. He is stated to have confessed and the agent believes that the wireless set is now being used by the Germans to deceive the originators of this enterprise.

It seems to us that this party may well be NIKITINA and GORELOV and I should be glad if you would communicate this information to your headquarters as soon as possible, so that they may check with the information given.[33]

NKVD's response was to ask whether there was any information to show how Müller's activities had become known to the Germans and by what means he had been arrested. They also wanted to know who, if anybody, had been arrested with him and whether a certain Ober-Lieutenant Gitter (or Hitter or Hutte) had been arrested at the same time. Presumably Gitter was a Soviet agent.

In SOE parlance, the 'birds had been blown'. There was no mention of the German radio detection teams used to triangulate wireless transmissions. Unable to answer the NKVD's questions, SOE provided additional information that the informant had overheard some German soldiers on a train between Freiburg and München saying that a woman parachutist had been arrested in Freiburg as a result of a message she sent in English to a friend of hers working in a factory at Mannheim. The message was opened by a German foreman who reported it to the police, who promptly arrested two 'English parachutists'.[34]

Following the Gestapo's arrest of Heinrich Koenen, one of the Schulze-Boysen group, in Autumn 1942, he was 'turned' and transmitted messages to Moscow. Moscow told him – and the Gestapo – to expect Nikitina and Gorelov and to contact Heinrich Müller [Bruno Kühn] in Freiburg. The police knew the exact location of the dropzone and the estimated time of Nikitina and Gorelov's arrival.[35]

British interrogation of Horst Kopkow, the head of the *Sonderkommando Rote Kapelle,* revealed that the Gestapo had lured a Soviet agent called Anna Müller across the border from Switzerland and arrested her. She confessed to having worked for the Soviets for twenty years, acting as a courier and organising the escape of agents across the German border into Switzerland by befriending one of the border guards.[36]

Further light on their fate came in May 1945 following the American forces freeing women prisoners from Ravensbrück concentration camp, near Furstenburg in north Germany. A number of female SOE agents captured in France had been imprisoned there, most of whom were executed. 'Lise', one of the survivors of Ravensbrück, was debriefed when she was flown back to England. She stated that she had been very friendly with a woman named Helene Poska, who she believed was a British agent. The report written up by her interrogator stated:

This woman sends greetings to me and asked that, if possible, I would help her to obtain a British, French, Swiss or Spanish passport.

'Lise' said that Poska had been arrested in February 1943, whilst attempting to make her way to Vienna. The man she was with, who appears to have been Otto ULNOTI [Gorelov], was, according to 'Lise', 'un mauvais type'. Poska when she was arrested took her 'L' tablet, but this was remarked by the Gestapo and she was promptly treated, being given as well a glass of milk. She appears to have been reasonably well treated at Ravensbrück, and never consented to work for the Germans, though these latter tried hard to make her, by means of various third degree methods. She left Ravensbrück for an unknown destination, possibly Berlin, on 10th January, and this was the last that was seen of her. She asked me, via 'Lise', to inform 'her friends' of what had happened to her, so that they might tell her husband.

In the camp also was another German prisoner, who was a great friend of Poska's, a Fräulein FARRE, who was apparently released and was last heard of living in Berlin at an address which 'Lise' is going to give me (Berlin-Dahlem, Falkenreid 30). I was also asked to inform this latter person.

There seems little doubt that this woman is the one whom we referred to usually as Yelena NIKITINA, who was under our care from 29.9.42 to 24.2.43, and who was given the name of Kersti Poska during her stay in England. Should you agree, I propose sending the following telegram to Moscow for further transmission to our colleagues:

'Woman known as Yelena NIKITINA was for long period prisoner at Ravensbrück camp, whence she was removed 10th January this year for unknown destination. She asked us to inform Soviet colleagues and that they should tell her husband.'[37]

The final note in Tonic and Sodawater's file came from an interview with Odette Sansom, another female SOE agent and survivor of Ravensbrück. She had worked as a courier for Peter Churchill, who she subsequently married, and had convinced the Gestapo that she was married to Winston Churchill's nephew. She managed to escape execution when the Ravensbrück Commandant took her to the Americans, hoping to save himself. Her report claimed that the man known as Pyotr Koltsov, alias Juri Kruus and Hermann Koehler, was married to Yelena Nikitina alias Kersti Poska. He and Emilya Novikova had been picked up by the authorities immediately after landing and it was information they gave which led to the arrest of their colleagues two months later. Before that, they had had wireless contact with 'their friends', but SOE thought this unusual as they had lost all their equipment on landing.

I gathered the impression from Mlle. Sansom that Nikitina was somewhat jealous of Novikova, and that this latter might conceivably have been the cause of the leakage.

Mlle. Sansom had suggested to Nikitina that a letter been sent to him and they had been on the point of writing this when Nikitina had been taken away. The

Kalfaktor or person who was allowed to carry round trays to other prisoners and who did other menial jobs at Ravensbrück, was a certain Frau Hartmann; she informed Mlle. Sansom that she believed Nikitina had been shot. Mlle. Sansom further suggested that she considered Nikitina would have told us anything we wanted to know. She occasionally had a Polish woman planted on her in the prison, according to Mlle. Sansom. While she was in prison in Karlsruhe, Nikitina made great friends with a young woman known as 'Lise' who was very well educated and was believed to have worked for the Americans and was actually engaged to an American, who was also in the prison. Apart from this Mlle. Sansom knew little about this other woman, except that she was born in Strasbourg and her mother had been remarried to a lawyer.[38]

Additional light on the fate of the Tonic and Sodawater agents was shed by one of the documents in SOE's Russian file which included details obtained from 'PW', seemingly a defector from the SS, the elite Nazi regiment. Dated 24 August 1944, it included the following information on the German counter-intelligence:

In spring 1943, nr FREIBURG in Breisgau, a farmer found a suitcase attached to a parachute in his field. He was afraid to open it and summoned one of the local boys on furlough. This man called his Bn [Battalion] station in Alsace. The Bn sent an officer over who opened the suitcase. It contained a transmitter. A thorough search of the whole area yielded another suitcase, containing a man's and a woman's clothes.

At the same time a Russian agent was being grilled in VIENNA and under pressure revealed the address of an elderly couple living in FREIBURG. The Gestapo thoroughly investigated this couple but could not pin anything on them. As a matter of routine, however, Gestapo agents continued to drop in at the place. On such a routine call, Whitsunday 1943, a youngish woman opened the door when the Gestapo called. The moment she saw them, she put something into her mouth. She was rushed to a hospital and her stomach was pumped. She had tried to poison herself. [Written in the margin beside the elderly couple was written in pencil 'Koltsov' and beside the youngish woman was 'Nikitina'. This seems to have been a mistake as the earlier documents show that Koltsov went with Novikova.]

Upon interrogation she admitted being a Russian agent. She was the wife of a Hamburg communist and had fled to Russia in 1938. There she had been trained as an agent, mainly in operating a wireless set. The ship which was to take her to Germany sunk and she was rescued and brought to England. Here the British Secret Service (!) tried to buy her out but she had decided to go on with her mission. So the British provided her and her companion with a plane which flew her over Germany. After having been dropped, she could not find her male companion nor the two suitcases. But she went on with her mission and was caught. She confessed that she had instructions to stay in Germany even after the American army should enter that section of Germany. She had British, French, German, and even American money on her to provide for such an emergency.

The harmless old couple had a friend, a FREIBURG business man, who one day asked them for a favour. Would they put up in their apartment an old friend of his from COLOGNE. It was agreed that his friend would simply introduce herself as 'Tante Erna aus Köln.' On Whitsunday the woman appeared and was duly given a room. She had been there only one hour when the Gestapo called. During that short time she had already succeeded in ingratiating herself with the unsuspecting hosts and in passing RM 1,000.- upon them as an advance on the rent.

PW had the impression that the British agents were a dime a dozen but had never encountered or heard of any American agents.[39]

The participation of the Tonic and Sodawater agents in the *Funkspiel* was not mentioned in the Documentation Center of Austrian Resistance website. It describes Emilya Novikova as a fashion designer before the war, who was trained as a parachutist by the Soviets and jumped in February 1943. She was arrested by the Vienna Gestapo on 31 March, fingerprinted, charged with high treason and sent to Ravensbrück concentration camp. In early 1945, she was deported back to Vienna where, in May, she was identified as a traitor by Smersh, the counter-intelligence team, and deported to the Soviet Union where, presumably because of her collaboration with the Gestapo, she was sentenced to hard labour in the prison camps.[40]

Pyotr Koltsov's (Hermann Koehler's) biography on the Alfred Klahr Society website reveals that in the 1920s he was a carpenter who became important in the central committee of the communist party of Austria. When he was one of the delegates at the Seventh World Congress of the Comintern in Moscow, he agreed to be trained as an agent and was dropped by a plane over Austria to organise resistance, codenamed Hermes and known as George. Emilya Novikova was his radio operator. The Gestapo were aware of his arrival, he was arrested and tortured. He was then sent to Mauthausen concentration camp where he was shot in March 1945.[41]

Johann Sanitzer's 'confession', mentioned earlier, revealed that he was the Gestapo's expert on their *Funkspiel* operations. He said that Operation 'Lindwurm' involved Gregor Kersche and two female radio operators, Louise Soucek and Hildegard Nraz. They had been sent to Vienna having been parachuted into Poland in 1943. Operation 'Felixdorf' involved using Joseph Angermann and his wireless operator, Georg Kennerknecht, two NKVD agents who had been captured after being parachuted in in June 1943. These men, not infiltrated by the SOE, were 'coerced' into transmitting Nazi-inspired messages to Moscow. It was another radio game, Operation 'Burgenland', that shed light on Emilya Novikova (Emile Boretzky) and Pyotr Koltsov (Hermann Koehler).

In February 1943, a new group of NKVD agents was arrested. It consisted of KOEHLER, alias KNORAD [Pyotr Koltsov] and a woman Emile BORETZKY [Emilya Novikova], who was to operate the W/T set. KOEHLER had been chief organiser of the Communist Party of Austria between 1928 and 1938. He left for France after the Anschluss and from there finally emigrated to Russia.

The two agents of this group had left Russia over Mourmansk for England and had been, later, dropped from England by an RAF plane. (Subject explains that there were two such cases during all his activities with Russian agents.) KOEHLER was caught first. He had stored in one leg pocket of his jump clothes a bottle of cognac. The cognac had spilled during the drop and some blood-hounds used by Subject had picked up the trail. Later the parachutes were easily found. Actually the team was caught because of 'apartment trouble'. The Russians needed alternate current to operate their sets and, as there were very few quarters in Vienna which provided with this kind of current, it became relatively easy to supervise these quarters and arrest any suspicious person.

The team were 'persuaded' to co-operate with the Gestapo.[42]

Thomas Ampletzer, Sanitzer's boss, then had the latest British B Mark II wireless set. Weighing only 30 pounds and with a range of about 1,560 miles, it was far superior to the Soviet sets. Faced with the grim choice of execution or collaboration, Emilya Novikova (Emile Boretzky) handed over her crystals which provided the correct frequencies for transmitting to and receiving from Moscow, and declared her willingness to take part in 'Burgenland'. She and Koltsov (Hermann Koehler) provided Ampletzer with details of their preparation in the Pionerskaya camp near Moscow, the circumstances of their journey to Britain, and their treatment by SOE, even having farewell drinks at the airfield. Koltsov's information led to the Gestapo being able to catch Nikitina (Noffke) in Freiburg. Ampletzer sent what he found to Kopkow who built up a detailed report for his SS boss, Heinrich Himmler. Ampletzer was instructed by Kopkow to continue sending messages to the Moscow 'Direktor' pretending that the two agents had succeeded and that, as Novikova had lost her crystals, communication had to be made via Willi Börner, mentioned earlier. Thus began an elaborate deception scheme. Shortly afterwards, Moscow informed the Germans that two agents, 'Nikolaus' and 'Albrecht', would be dropped near Vienna bringing Boretzky's replacement crystals, and that Börner had to prepare safe houses for them. O'Sullivan claims that by February 1943, the Gestapo knew more about the Soviet agents than most of the British officers involved in the collaboration.[43]

OPERATIONS ARARAT AND ETNA

After Chichaev had been informed by General Marshall Cornwall that SOE could not drop Pickaxes into France without permission, he presented authorisation signed by General Cochet, one of the top officials in the French military. This was used to justify the sending of a further two agents without de Gaulle's knowledge and may explain why there is so little SOE documentation about them as compared to other parties.

Research by Nollau and Zindel reveals that between May and November 1943, two Soviet agents were dropped into France and two into Germany, all disappearing without trace. 20-year-old Igor Feldman, known as Ignace Fallieres and codenamed Ararat, was dropped with a wireless set in the Mantes area by the River Seine, west of Paris, on 12 May 1943.[1]

There appears to be no Ararat file in the National Archives. According to the SOE's Russian file, Igor was listed as one of the *Rote Kapelle* agents and described as 'probably Parisian, little idea of security; unlikely to last long'.[2]

On 16 August 1943, Peter Loxley, Private Secretary to the Permanent Under Secretary of State, created more tremors throughout SOE and the Russian Section in particular, when he informed them:

> ... the following statement has been made by a French agent [presumably ARARAT] who recently arrived in this country: - 'Many of the French people are surprised when they learn that the British are putting Russian agents into France. These agents appear to be acting as political agents, and not only for information.' This statement was called into question to try and elicit further information, and the reply was made that the fact that the British were putting Russian agents into France was well-known in de Gaullist circles, and frequently spoken of in critical terms.[3]

In early July 1942, the Russian Section was informed that two Pickaxes destined for Italy were being prepared, one of whom was unable to be parachuted. Various discussions took place about the practicalities of sending them by the southern route via Teheran and Egypt or the northern route in one of the 'Grey Funnel

Line' (Merchant Navy) convoys.[4] In fact, they did not arrive until six months later, disembarking at Greenock from HMS *Beagle* on 9 January 1943, and reaching London by train the following morning. In a memorandum two days later, it was stated:

> ...the following are the details of these agents cover story for this country: Andrei KALIAIEV, now known as Alberto ROSSI, an Italian Swiss, born at Bellinzona, Ticino, on 16 May 1898, a single man and an engineer by profession (this last is genuine). Alexandre FILIPOV, now known as Alessandro FLORO, born at Capolago, Ticino, Italian Swiss and date of birth, 4 November 1910, a single man and an engineer by trade. Both these men will enter Italy as engineers. They are both at present accommodated at 25 Cropthorne Court, Maida Vale.[5]

They were described as fully documented and only awaiting transport facilities. Once Major C. Roseberry, the head of the Italian Section, codenamed 'J', was provided with all their details, the Russian Section proposed the project officially to D/Plans, Colonel R. H. Barry, 'with the request that all assistance should be given to the N.K.V.D. in infiltrating these bodies via Gibraltar or Massingham'.[6]

In November 1942, following the Allies' success in North Africa, SOE had set up a headquarters at le Club le Pines, a former luxury resort outside Guyotville, west of Algiers. Known officially as Inter-Services Signal Unit 6, its codename was Massingham.

The SOE's official history of their agreement with the NKVD states:

> In a note to Gubbins, C.D. [Hambro] said that Pickaxes who were to be infiltrated into North Italy should come via Gibraltar and not by the 'American soil'. C.D. had consulted CADOGAN privately who thought it would be better not to inform O.S.S. [American Office of Strategic Services] of our infiltration work for the Russians at present though it might later become necessary to put them wise.[7]

The Russian Section was informed that the operation codename was Etna and that, should they have to use this word with other services, they had to use the prefix 'Leafmould', it being the generic word for SOE operations. It was the second 'mountain party', operations named after famous mountains. The men were to be provided with uniforms and documents showing that they were privates in the Royal Pioneer Corps, a group of engineers who undertook labouring work for the military. The original plan was to land them by felucca, a 40-foot-long, narrow beamed, 20-tonne wooden sailing boat on the Mediterranean coast of France. The Gibraltar smuggling fleet, manned by tough Polish crews, had clandestinely landed numerous SOE agents on the French Riviera and returned with agents, VIPs, downed pilots, and compromised resistance members.

From France, the men were to make their way overland into northern Italy. However, when the Germans took over the unoccupied part of France during the autumn and winter of 1942, the plan had to be revised and a decision was made to fly them to Massingham. It was acknowledged that, as Soviet agents, there might be an issue in providing them with accommodation as they 'should not meet "J" chaps,' other SOE agents that were being infiltrated into southern Europe. From Massingham, it was hoped that the Royal Navy would be able to send them by submarine and drop them by night on a remote beach on the Italian Riviera. In retrospect, one of the Russian Section officers commented:

> The whole operation was viewed with disfavour by all concerned in view of past trouble with these nationals, but the matter being on the highest level it was proceeded with and the two agents were despatched by air to Massingham on 20th March 1943 by submarine or felucca, the greatest possible security conditions being requested at Massingham which was then in an embryo stage.[8]

Captain Kempthorne, codenamed AMO, was the conducting officer appointed to escort them to Italy, despite the fact he could speak neither Russian nor Italian. All agreements were made by 4 March when a message was sent from Massingham to the Air Liaison Officer with the following reminder:

> These nationals always entail particularly careful handling from the security point of view and it is, therefore, impossible that they should arrive via Lisbon; it would be advantageous if they could be flown direct to Algiers without disembarking en route.
>   ...D/Plans [Colonel R. H. Barry] informed me that there is no likelihood of obtaining passenger space in the Halifaxes proceeding to Cairo and suggest that, if ordinary transport application is impossible, it may be necessary to ask AL [Air Liaison] to assist with a special aircraft from Tempsford.[9]

In a telegram dated 7 March, Captain Osborn, SOE's man at Massingham, acknowledged receipt of the order but expressed concerns: 'Please amplify quote absurd and impossible unquote with definite decision.' When queried about his cryptic comment, he responded that the difficulties of using a felucca would be 'unsurmountable' and that, being short of aircraft and submarines, they could only do the operation 'at the expense of their own operations'. He sent two telegrams, the second with the codes to understand the first:

> Consider movement by E [felucca] most hazardous ... I will on no account allow your men proceed that method even if freeze up in nautical relations eliminates use of A [submarine] in future.[10]

Winston Churchill and Josef Stalin in Moscow, 1942.

Photographs of some of the Soviet Pickaxes. Top row (L to R): Ivan Botsevitch (alias Otto Bach, 'Rigi'), -?-; Second row: -?-, Pyetr Kousnetsov (alias Bruno Kühn/Ivan Roberts, 'Sauterne') Eugen Nesper (alias Georg Schmidt, Eiger); Third row: Pyetr Koltsov (Juri Kruus/Hermann Koehler, 'Sodawater'), Alexandre Filipov (alias Alessandro Florio, 'Etna'), -?-; Bottom row: Stepan Sidorov (alias Siegrfried Schmidt, 'Rigi') Josef Zettler (alias Nicolas Kessler/Nicholas Kharlamov, 'Everest'), Ivan Roussakov (alias Jean Roussel, 'Orange'). (*TNA KV2 2827*)

Left to right: Colonel Ivan Chichaev, the head of the NKVD mission in London, 1941-44; Gaik B. Ovakimyan, known to the SOE and OSS as 'General Ossipov', their main NKVD contact in Moscow; George Hill, head of the SAM (SOE) Mission in Moscow from 1941-1944; Major Manderstam, head of SOE's Russian Section from May 1944. (*All pictures courtesy of Donal O'Sullivan*)

Left to right: Pyetr Kousnetsov (alias Bruno Kühn/Ivan Roberts, 'Sauterne'), parachuted into Holland on 30 November 1942; 'Grand Chef' Leopold Trepper, head of the 'Red Orchestra', the Soviet network in Western Europe; Willi Kruyt (alias Willi von Krumin/Frederik Schmidt, 'Barsac'), parachuted into Belgium on 24 June 1942; Niko Kruyt (Nikolai Kravets/Jean Philippe Castaigne, 'Burgundy'), parachuted into Holland on 21 June 1942. (*TNA KV 2/2827*)

Left to right: Raymond Guyot (alias Georges Robigot/Grigory Rodionov, 'Rum') parachuted into France on 3 March 1942; Francine Fromont, married to Raymond Guyot, parachuted into France with her husband. Executed by the Germans for espionage in August 1944; Georg Tietze (Henrik Gorelov/Otto Ulnoti, 'Tonic'), parachuted into Germany on 24 February 1943; Else Noffke (alias Elena Nikitina/Kersti Poska, 'Tonic'), parachuted into Germany on 24 February 1943. (*TNA KV 2/2827*)

Clockwise from top: Pyetr Kousnetsov's SOE-forged identity card; Lorenz Mraz (Peter Staritsky/Peter Schulenburg, 'Whiskey'), killed in plane crash in Bavaria on 20 April 1942 with Franz Löschl (alias Vasselod Troussevitch/Maschinentechniker Franz Mayer/Donner Franz, 'Whiskey'); Homeward bound, a Liberty Ship in convoy RA64 sails through heavy seas in the Arctic Ocean. The Pickaxes were brought to Scotland in ships like these belonging to the Merchant Navy. (*Courtesy of ww2today.com*)

Control Tower at RAF Tempsford, codename BRASSTRAY. (*Courtesy of Squadron Leader K. A. Merrick*)

Looking north over RAF Tempsford, 1943. The administration area is in the foreground and the Gibraltar Farm buildings are in the upper right. (*Courtesy of Hugh Verity*)

Undated photograph of Squadron Leader Richard Wilkin, his crew, and ground staff in front of a 138 Squadron Handley Page Halifax bomber. The aircraft was modified to carry containers and agents to be parachuted into occupied Europe. (*Courtesy of Squadron Leader K. A. Merrick*)

Above: Recent photograph of Dunham House, near Altrincham, Cheshire, where agents were accommodated during their parachute training at nearby Ringway aerodrome. (*Courtesy of walten/panoramio.com*)

Below: Recent photograph of Chicheley Hall, near Chicheley, Buckinghamshire, where the Coffee party, Barsac, and Burgundy were accommodated in 1942. (*Courtesy of Chicheley Hall*)

Having been told that the mission was of major importance and authorised by the Foreign Office, Kaliaiev and Rossi had to wait for the next moon period. On 29 March, when they were told their mission was on, they requested one of their compatriots to see them off. Colonel Graur was allocated the task. After being searched, Kempthorne, who had been entrusted with the agents' false Italian papers, took them by train to Pembroke Dock in south-west Wales. The commander-in-chief in Gibraltar had been informed of their arrival and was 'requested to arrange their reception with the fullest possible security arrangements'.[11]

They arrived in Gibraltar on 3 April and were transferred by plane to Massingham on the 8th. Immediately upon their arrival, they had their uniforms, military documentation and dog tags removed to be returned to England; they were then issued with civilian clothing and their Italian papers.

When they were told they were to be taken to Italy by felucca, they adamantly refused, claiming that they had been promised a submarine in London. Maybe they were concerned about the nationality of the crews and whether they could be relied upon not to talk about carrying Soviet agents. As a felucca had been earmarked for their trip and purposely held back ready for them, the naval authorities in Algiers were 'considerably inconvenienced'. They claimed that they had been forced to cancel another operation because of the wait.

The importance of operation Etna was evident from the numerous telegrams that were sent between London, Massingham, Malta, Cairo, and Tehran. In one of Massingham's early messages back to London about Etna they added: 'If in meantime Navy can do operation by submarine result would be of inestimable value to our relations with Soviet.' It was then suggested that a submarine be laid on from Gibraltar or from Malta, but with no prospect of one for three weeks, Peter Murray Lee, the security officer, had the difficult job of arranging to keep two Italian agents separate from the others based at Massingham. Little did Major Hewitt, the operations officer, know what a difficult task it would be dealing with the new arrivals, but in a telegram from Massingham dated 9 April he commented: 'Do not feel we can accept responsibility or devote necessary time and officer personnel to that.'[12]

On the following day authority was given through the Russian Section for the bodies to 'be infiltrated at any repeat any point on X [Italian] mainland by any available craft on which you can persuade them to embark.'[13] The correspondence does not reveal what additional work went on behind the scenes between the different departments to ensure this operation went ahead. On 12 April, news came through that 'Malta reports can do job by submarine and can cope with security ... hope this ends story.'[14]

Conscious of the trouble Massingham was put to, the Russian Section telegrammed, 'Thank you very much for all your exertions and efforts on behalf of these bodies. Consider latest arrangements excellent and Soviet colleagues most grateful.' Tactfully, a copy was sent to SOE's naval liaison officer.[15]

Malta suggested providing the two agents with cover as French officers on a liaison visit but Massingham's response was:

> Suggested cover not repeat not suitable. BRUNOT and MARVIN dressed as British lieutenants in battledress. Cover should not be necessary. HEWITT has papers which will enable journey to be completed without interrogation. Essential questions should not be asked during stay in MALTA.[16]

Kempthorne accompanied them on their flight to Malta on 16 April where they were provided with separate accommodation. There was no indication in the documents about how they had spent the previous fortnight. On the same day they left, London received the following coded telegram:

> Most immediate
> ETNA boys left for A. [Malta] with AMO 14th repeat 14th
> A. has B. [SOE's man in Malta] leaving for C. [Calabria] about 28th
> Boys agreed this method of transport and stated preferred it to D. [felucca] from E. [North Africa].
> Just before leaving for A. they again expressed doubts whether C. suitable.
> It is apparent that they are doing all possible to postpone departure for F. [North Italy].
> Please arrange with owners to send definite orders that they will leave B for C on 28th.
> Last message from owners made considerable effect consider another in same tone will do trick.
> Essential this be done if boys not to be on our hands indefinitely repeat indefinitely.[17]

Although there was not a copy of the encouraging telegram from the Russian Section in the Etna folder, other documents suggest it was sent. However, on 19 April, there was an objection at the very highest level to their men landing in Calabria, stating that they had to be landed further north. The next day, the NKVD, described by staff at Massingham as the agents' 'owners', stipulated that any point north of latitude 40° N would be acceptable, but as there was going to be no submarine available for another four weeks they were flown back to Massingham.

On 21 April, the owners insisted they had to be landed at any latitude north of 42° N and on either the west or east coast. Revised plans were made as shown in the following telegram from Malta:

> Any locality north of 40 repeat 40 means that A. [Submarine Captain S] will have to cancel a patrol which he does not want to do and cannot do without special sanction.

B. [Captain Submarine B] has some C. [Submarines] on D. [West coast] all controlled by E. [Submarine Captain S.8].

F. [Gulf Policastro] not repeat not popular with G. [another code for submarine] suggest north end H. [Italy] which might be done on patrol or alternatively J. [uncertain].

If J. sanctioned from K. [Submarine Captain S] in L. [Adriatic] suggest any locality suitable to owners except near tigers.[18]

The Navy in both Massingham and Malta were understandably upset that the agents had changed their minds three times about where they should be landed. In fact, the latter stated that 'Proposals for future operations if accepted here will be subject to complete divorce of owners control from date of acceptance.'[19] London welcomed the strong language.

On 25 April, there was news that a submarine might be available at Tripoli in Libya, leaving on 30 April to despatch the men to the Gulf of Genoa. The men were therefore flown to Castel Bonito airfield on 28 April and were reportedly 'in good heart' when they left on 2 May, to which London replied to Massingham: 'Thank you. Well done.'[20]

Over a week later, London was informed that Etna had failed due to bad weather, and as the men had been returned to Massingham on 14 May, the query was for how long they might have to be kept. Massingham were worried that it might be up to six weeks. All London could tell them was that 'Owners will be pleased if boys can be sent at next available opportunity.'[21]

A pinpoint was allocated between Ventimiglia and Bordighera, just over the border from Nice, but before transport could be arranged, another problem arose. London was informed on 22 May:

Following medical report by throat specialist on ROSSI quote there is TB laryngitis involving mostly the arytenoid regions which are infiltrated pale and swollen treatment required is sanatorium treatment with rest of voice he should whisper only. He is quite fit to fly to UNITED KINGDOM unquote.

Military situation now such that any operations for us from NORTH AFRICA highly improbable next few months.

In view of above suggest we return bodies on next convoy with one of returning officers.[22]

The NKVD's response was to ignore Rossi's medical condition and insist that the men be sent as a matter of urgency. SAM reported:

Colleague most incensed and at loss to understand our volte face. NKVD request most strongly we should carry out operation and state they do not wish men returned to U.S.S.R. or UNITED KINGDOM.

Colleague stressed point that he regretted having to make very emphatic protest on day of first anniversary of Anglo-Soviet pact and asked most pointedly whether this was S.O.E. idea of co-operation. He repeatedly enquired what was political reason for our refusal, for he did not believe true explanation could be due to military, operational or weather difficulties.[23]

A comment in one of London's replies was that the NKVD ought to realise that SOE 'are not able to give the same guarantee of arrival as those shown in our railway timetable. Equo mortuo, vivat flagella.' (The horse is dead, long live the whip).[21]

As Massingham had received no reply from London, tickets were bought and cabins booked for a boat leaving for England on 27 May. The initial response was to cancel the trip as the USSR wanted them back in Moscow, but the next day came the message:

> Owners now state that they are anxious for boys to be delivered to destination at first possible opportunity and request that they be retained with MASSINGHAM until this is feasible.
>
> We realise inconvenience caused and shall be grateful if we may be informed when this operation can reasonably be accepted.
>
> As regards ROSSI's health they showed not slightest interest is there any possibility of local recuperation?[24]

On being informed that their return to the UK had been cancelled, the agents argued that the documentation they were carrying was now out-of-date but refused to let their papers be examined. The NKVD in London confirmed that they were in order and that the mission had to proceed regardless.

A submarine eventually arrived and picked them up. There is then a marked absence of telegrams in the file; whereas before there had been two or three messages sent a day, there was a sudden gap. Massingham waited. London waited, and the NKVD waited. There was no news about what happened to them for several days. Then, the following telegram arrived in London:

> Most Important
>
> Preliminary report from submarine says 1 repeat 1 body landed safely other body returning with submarine and due back within the next few days.
>
> Will advise full details as soon as available. In meantime require your disposal instructions for one still on our hands as considered extremely unwise expect S to undertake again. Unquote.[25]

Prior to Operation Husky, the Allied invasion of Sicily, Major Manderstam was attached to the SOE in Algiers which used the cover name, Fifth Special Signals.

In his autobiography, *From the Red Army to SOE*, Manderstam admits receiving reports that there were Russians in Italy, some of them serving with the Axis forces. He was instructed to try and infiltrate a Soviet agent – Rossi – into Italy in the hope that he could make contact and organise subversive activity. The Royal Navy went to great lengths to place a submarine at his disposal, which was used to pick up the agent in Algiers.

> He was white as a sheet when he clambered aboard, but I did not regard his pallor as significant since all landlubbers were apprehensive about travelling in submarines.
>
> We nosed into the Mediterranean and dived and I noticed that the further we went the more agitated our Russian friend became. At last we surfaced in pitch darkness off Naples, where the Russian adamantly refused to be landed. I spent some time trying to persuade him but he would not be budged. Finally, the skipper, in terse Naval fashion, said he could hang about no longer and we returned to Algiers.[26]

For whatever reason, there was no mention of there being two agents. Two days later, after the submarine's captain and the returned agent were interviewed, London was told:

> ROSSIE [sic] repeat ROSSIE has returned and represents usual security problems. He gave point blank refusal to land to submarine captain.
>
> 3 attempts made in all. ROSSIE refused every night. 1st night FLORIO refused also. 2nd night FLORIO agreed to go alone but upset folbot apparently deliberately and landing postponed. 3rd night FLORIO landed alone without incident. Folbot stood off-shore 15 repeat 15 minutes and all seemed well.
>
> ROSSI assures us FLORIO took w/t set and money.
>
> ROSSIE [sic] gives illness as grounds for refusal. He is unquestionably a sick man but not worse than any time since his arrival own observation throughout last three months convince us ROSSI never intended land. FLORIO naturally unwilling to go alone in rear got frontal extremely annoyed. Submarine was endangered three consecutive nights apparently with nothing achieved. He refused to carry again quote so-and-so's who do not intend to land unquote.[27]

The folbot mentioned was a specially designed folding boat covered in canvas which was used by submarine crews to get personnel onto the shore. In the telegram informing SAM of the incident, it was added:

> In view of above and P's refusal to attempt operation again, and since this is N's third refusal to carry out plans, we have now classed him as bad agent and must demand his immediate return to U.S.S.R. as we cannot further jeopardise our relations with operational staff.

> We will inform DPR.1 [Chichaev] this evening. Please cable urgently decision with regard to N and whether in your opinion it would be better return him via southern route. [28]

The response from the Russian Section was swift. They requested Massingham to pass an urgent message to Rossi.

> Your friends have been informed that you refused to land at appointed place and that you have returned to base. They ask you to inform them immediately of your reasons for not obeying instructions and why you have returned, and they request you to explain to them the state of your health. [29]

Whether Florio met up with other communist agents and completed his mission was not revealed in the Etna file. Rossi, after further negotiations, was accompanied by Colonel Sweet-Escott and Lieutenant Morris on 14 July to Cairo under the cover name, Second Lieutenant Brurot. From there he was flown to Tehran for repatriation to Moscow. What happened to him there was not documented. Massingham was informed that NKVD

> Expressed sincere regret at N's refusal to land and underline their appreciation of great risk run by Q, on each of three nights. He conveyed N.K.V.D's thanks for all services rendered by S.O.E. and X.N. [30]

The affair was not closed by Rossi's departure. There was a need for some delicate diplomacy as, on 8 August 1943, London was informed that Admiral Sir Andrew Cunningham, the Commander-in-Chief of the Mediterranean, demanded

> A written explanation as to why he was called upon to jeopardise a submarine and crew for a man of this calibre. He has told his staff that he expects to be informed who was responsible for insisting that these bodies be delivered and who owned them. [31]

In the official 'Notes on the Russian Section of S.O.E.', the commander-in-chief was reported as having responded to the question of what else could have been done with Rossi with, 'He [the Captain] should have thrown the man overboard and reported "Mission Accomplished."'[32]

Having not received the expected immediate response from London, two more demands for an explanation were sent. Liaison between Captain McLaughlin and the Foreign Office 'to pacify the indignant queries' resulted in the following reply: 'This man and another who was landed were Russian agents. The bodies were delivered pursuant to an agreement signed by us and the Russians, with the knowledge and approval of Z.P. [the Foreign Office].'[33]

A more detailed response followed which provided a summary of the Pickaxe operations.

Nearly two years ago we made an arrangement with X [NKVD] defining the respective territories in which we would work and providing for mutual assistance in certain respects.

Agreement was made with approval of Z.P. [the Foreign Office] who have on various occasions emphasised importance of helping Y [Russia] whenever political considerations allowed because in absence of recognised second front gesture of help is valuable.

In spite of constant pressure from X, we have resisted requests to infiltrate their agents into Z [Occupied Allied Countries] because of grave complications which would arise if it became known to the governments of Z.

Consequently our help to X has been virtually limited to operations into enemy repeat enemy countries and even there our shortage of transport has limited results to bare minimum.

X had pressed us for months past to introduce ETNA party as matter of urgency and we had explored all possibilities including air transport felucca from GIBRALTAR both of which for various reasons proved impossible.

X persistently refuse to accept our statements about shortage of transport and insist that there is political motive. Z.P. attach importance to dispelling such suspicion on the part of X.

For these reasons and in view of urgency of request from X which recent events have proved justified we felt bound as last resort to ask for help from C-in-C Mediterranean.

We did so reluctantly knowing how precious such facilities are. We would far rather have reserved our request for the benefit of our own operations but felt in this case that other considerations had to prevail.

ETNA party were sponsored by X on behalf of Y government, we regret that one of them proved yellow but had no reason to suspect it.

You may show this telegram to C-in-C if you think fit. [34]

OPERATION ORANGE

Like Operation Ararat, Operation Orange is hardly documented in the SOE files. In the SOE's official history of their agreement with the NKVD, it mentions that SAM cabled the Russian Section on 3 October 1942 asking SOE to infiltrate four fully trained Pickaxes in the Marseilles district. What happened in the meantime was not revealed, but the party didn't arrive until 17 June 1943.[1]

Circumstances must have changed as the *Rote Kapelle* file identified only three agents: 27-year-old Mikhail Belov, who travelled under the names 'Michel Belfort', 'Miguel Gonzalez', and 'Belfort Gonzalez', and was described as 'Sp. French with marked Spanish accent; prob. Basque; cheerful, loquacious'; 28-year-old Anton Marsov, codenamed Antoine Martin, who was described as 'prob. Spanish, but spoke French well and had relatives in France, cheery, sociable'; and 30-year-old Ivan Roussakov, codenamed Jean Roussel, described as 'small, dark, Spanish looking; spoke little either French or Russian.'[2]

There was concern about whether SOE was authorised to send them into Vichy France without the consent of the French authorities. FSO.1, an unidentified officer in SOE's F section, wrote a memo to Colonel Sheridan (AD.4) at 64 Baker Street, 'We must therefore drop them, and if the matter comes up, we shall have to say that we understood they were destined for Spain.'[3] This suggestion caused Sheridan some disquiet.

It will be seen that D/PR.1 [Chichaev] asked whether we would still dispatch the three agents destined for France who arrived in this country two and three months ago (April/May 1943) and have been awaiting longer nights, and that he was assured by General Marshall Cornwall that we would fulfil our obligations. This places us in a very difficult position. D/P.4 [McLaughlin] is of opinion that if we decline to send these men, after giving our word that we would do so, it will further weaken our relations with Russia. On the other hand in view of V/CD's [Hambro's deputy, Lieutenant Colonel Harry Sporberg] conversations with Massigili [sic] [de Gaulle's Foreign Minister] it seems to me impossible to dispatch them without Massigili's assent, and it appears unlikely that we will get it.

Can considerations please be weighed and can I please be instructed as to what decision is to be conveyed to D/PR.1?

D/P.4 is of opinion the men are Spaniards and that they are really destined for Spain. They are to be dropped near Avignon.[4]

SOE Operations would not accept the undertaking because it had not been authorised by André Philip, the Commissioner of the French Committee for National Liberation (CFNL) in Algiers. As Chichaev claimed that he had written proof of this agreement, the Foreign Office told D/P to ask him to provide them with a copy. On 13 September 1943, Chichaev produced a letter signed by Georges Boris of de Gaulle's Free French in London which conveyed Philip's authorisation for the infiltration of three agents. When Gabriel Cochet, one of de Gaulle's generals based in London also gave his go-ahead, a flight was arranged for the following day.[5] Their dropzone was in the Malemont/Murs area near Avignon. Clark mentions a number of sorties on the night of 14 September but provides no details of the Orange operation. Three days later, SAM was informed that the mission had been successfully carried out.[6] What became of the agents is unknown.

Aware that the NKVD wanted to send in more bodies, Sir Charles Hambro expressed concern that he had not been shown Philip's warrant and considered Georges Boris's signature insufficient. He argued that it ought to have been sanctioned by the CFNL. On 21 September, a telegram was sent to Algiers asking for assurance from the committee that Boris had been a duly authorised signatory.[7] It was duly given.

OPERATIONS RIGI AND JUNGFRAU

Some in the Russian Section recommended in April 1943 that they suspend the Pickaxe operations until it could be proved that the agents were engaged in sabotage missions behind enemy lines. However, Moscow wired London saying that the NKVD wanted to send one trained man into Germany via Holland. SOE refused to help, using the Foreign Office's ban on sending agents into occupied Allied countires as an excuse. However, they told the NKVD that they were prepared to drop two agents into Germany close to the Dutch border, but because of accommodation issues, they did not want them to arrive in Britain with other NKVD agents whose arrival had already been planned.

Forty-year-old Ivan M. Botsevitch from Estonia, who spoke Russian and German, and 33-year old Stepan Sidorov, a fully trained parachutist from Saratov, arrived in London on 7 August 1943. Their proposed destination was the Duren region in the triangle between Gressenich, Roetgen, and Heinbach, south of Aachen and close to the Belgian border.

Botsevitch was known as 'Otto Bach' and described as a 'working-class German, tough and discreet'. His mission's name was Rigi. Sidorov, alias 'Siegrfried Schmidt', was described as a 'working-class German, pleasant, placid; round-shouldered' and his mission's name was Jungfrau.[1] They were the third and fourth mountain parties.

Envisaging that they may have to travel overland before they reached a safe house, emergency rations – food for ten days – were issued.[2] Operation Rigi, planned for 20 August 1943, was postponed at the last minute. A memo from the Russian Section to Moscow informed them:

> RIGI got as far as aerodrome on 20th August take-off being scheduled for 10.10 pm. At 10 pm operation cancelled through sudden illness of pilot.
>
> Today which is last day of this period have just been informed that no operations will be possible in respect of RIGI and JUNFRAU [sic] or ORANGE owing to bad weather conditions.
>
> Am already experiencing back-blast but considerable amount of blame for this lack of success is due to vacillations of our colleagues whose last minute request made it impossible offer these operations until half period had elapsed.[3]

Bad weather postponed the next flight until the next moon period, which did not begin until 8 September. It was not until 19/20 September that another flight was planned but this attempt was thwarted when heavy ground mist over the dropzone forced the plane to return to Tempsford. Chichaev's angry reaction led SAM to be told to brace themselves for an NKVD onslaught. In fact, SOE thought the liaison would be terminated as a result.

Another opportunity arose before the end of the September moon period but it was again unsuccessful. SAM was sent a telegram:

> Much regret report that RIGI and JUNGFRAU were not carried out this period owing to continued bad weather and will stand for October period.
>
> Colleague much upset (as are we) and has again questioned our ability to deliver goods.
>
> Please express fact that we have done our best but are entirely in ZA [Air Ministry] hands operationally.[4]

On 3 November, Moscow informed the SOE that they were being given a last chance to send Rigi and Jungfrau to South Germany, and another operation, Everest, to Vienna. They also told them that they had five agents still in the Soviet Union who were ready to be sent into Italy and three ready for France. All they needed was the relevant permissions to be given. In the meantime, Air Liaison at Tempsford was told that the Pickaxes had to be given three-star priority for the November moon period.

It worked. Botsevitch (Bach) was taken to Tempsford on 5 November for the fifth time and successfully parachuted near the Eifel town of Schleiden, north of Schmidtheim in south-western Germany, a lot closer to Belgium than to Holland.[5] Clark reported Squadron Leader Cooke finished 'the outstanding operation Rigi to Germany, dropping agent blind, his parachute was seen to open.'[6]

The following day there was both good and bad news. SAM was informed that Rigi had been dropped successfully, but:

> JUNGFRAU was accepted for last night but after waiting on aerodrome operation had to be called off owing to very bad weather conditions. He is still at 61 hoping to go tonight.[7]

The NKVD expressed hope that Sidorov (Schmidt) would go during the current moon period as, should there be a delay, landing in snow would make it difficult for the agent to avoid leaving a trail. Three weeks later, at the beginning of the December moon period, SAM was sent a telegram with bad news:

> JUNGFRAU attempted last night and although it reached target area was unable to off-load owing to wind velocity. No operations today owing weather conditions.[8]

Another telegram a few days later stated:

> We will do utmost get bodies referred ... to away as soon as possible after arrival
> and in order expedite arrangements will be grateful from dropping area selected
> by Y.M.C.A. [NKVD] so that we can get to work at once on pin-point.[9]

Sidorov's dropzone was at Stadtkyll, just over 6 miles south of Botsevitch's, but
the NKVD expressed concern that he might be more easily detected in the snow.
A white jump suit may well have been suggested. An attempt was made to drop
Sidorov on 11 December but it was called off due to heavy winds. The rescheduled
flight was on 4 January 1944 when, carrying newly produced ration cards, a
wireless set, and a 'Welbike' (a folding motorcycle), he made a successful jump.[10]

> The appalling weather continued into January. Of the twelve Halifax sorties
> launched by No. 138 Squadron on 4/5th January to start the new year's operation
> only four succeeded. F/Lt Stiles flying Tybalt 9 to Belgium a target some 22 km
> SW of Givet, found no reception. From thence he flew to Gerolstein and made a
> DR to JUNGFRAU a target in Germany near Koblenz. Here in clear visibility he
> dropped blind from 600 feet a NKVD agent with a package (said to be a folding
> bicycle) which was delayed a second or two since it became 'caught in the hole'.
> This operation had been outstanding since 10th December.[11]

The Gestapo knew exactly where they were due to land and arrested them
immediately. Horst Kopkow, head of the *Rote Kapelle*, attempted a playback
scheme with them, but when the Soviets asked them to supply military information
about the Rhine-Ruhr area, the Gestapo refused to provide it. They abandoned
the scheme and executed Sidorov and Botsevitch.[12]

On 6 November 1943, around the time that Operation Jungfrau was successfully
completed, the Russian Section was informed of the death of Lieutenant Colonel
Milnes-Gaskell. He was one of ten passengers and nine crew of a Short-Sunderland
flying boat that crashed about 75 miles south-southwest of Sollum during a flight
from Cairo to London. Numerous obituaries appeared in the national press and
even General Ossipov sent a letter giving his organisation's 'sincere and deep
condolences on the occasion of the great sorrow which has overtaken you in
connection with ... the death of our mutual friend.'[13] A few days later Colonel
Chichaev wrote a similar letter to Seddon, asking him to convey to Milnes-
Gaskell's family his condolences in their bereavement.

OPERATION EVEREST

On 10 November 1942, the Russian Section was informed that two more Pickaxes were due to leave the Soviet Union. They arrived on 19 January 1943 at Thurso on the north coast of Scotland where they were met and escorted by train down to London. Their file gives their names as 41-year-old 'Nicholas Kharlamov', codenamed Everest, and 33-year-old 'Alexandre Jacoubov', codenamed Atlas. Although the names on the Swiss passports they used in Britain were Nicolas Kessler and Alexandre Jeannin, subsequent documents revealed that their real names were Josef Zettler and Albrecht Huttary. Although it was originally planned to send them to northern France in a party of four, when they met the NKVD, they were told they were to go to Austria. Jacoubov was to be known instead as Albrecht Klein and both were to be known as the Everest party.[1]

Klein and Kessler were accommodated initially in the Bedford Hotel, on Southampton Row in the Bloomsbury district of London. Having been provided with official papers, a ration book, sweet rations, and clothing coupons, they were given suitable attire for the English winter and taken to Hansteads, where previous Pickaxes had been accommodated. Once settled in, Lance Corporal Wild, their conducting officer, made notes:

[Klein] told me that he has not been very long in the organisation [NKVD], and that he did not particularly want to join it, but on hearing that it would take him to Austria he agreed. He is only interested in fighting for Austria against the Germans, and considers himself an Austrian Nationalist.

He has a wife and two children in Austria, but considers that it would be too dangerous to see them until after the war. He last saw them three years ago.

He says that he has plenty of friends among the anti Nazis in Germany, also that he is not a Communist and does not think much of Communists.

When I asked him how he came to go to Russia, he shrugged his shoulders and said that it was stupidness.

He said that if he had been in England instead of Russia at the outbreak of war he would have joined the British Army voluntarily (on a previous occasion he asked as if there were any Austrians in the British Army). He would not like to

see the Red Army occupy Austria, far better for the British to do it, as then there
would at least be a free Austria after the war.

He said he would never dream of returning to Russia after the war.

Has not known companion N.K. long, and does not know much about him.[2]

The dropzone they were allocated, 19½ km north-west of Wiener Neustadt and
8 km south-west of Berndorf, was exactly the same as the one the Coffee party
were going to use. Their flight was planned for the March moon period but
Air Liaison suggested that the proposed site was too far up in the hills and that
pinpoints in the area ought to be either nearer the river Danube 'or near the lake
[Constance] in the area of the Sodawater pin point'. Any point within a 10-km
radius was agreed, as long as it was not south of the River Piesting. There was an
intimation that Kessler and Klein had been told that they were the replacements
for the Coffee party and were aware of what had happened to them.

On 18 February 1943, Major E. K. Saunders, the commandant at Hansteads,
wrote to Major Seddon saying that Chichaev had asked Lance Corporal Wild
whether Kessler and Klein could have automatic pistols and earphones so that
they could do some shooting. He also asked if they could do some night marching
and practice in concealing parachutes.

> I submit with respect, that any such activities here would evoke the greatest
> curiosity locally, and that one of the schools would provide all that is wanted.
> The two new recruits here appear to dislike one another very cordially based on
> a mutual distrust![3]

On Thursday 11 March, they were taken to 25 Cropthorne Court and told to stand
by for their flight from Tempsford. As with many of the previous Pickaxe missions,
it was cancelled due to adverse weather conditions in both the March and April
moon periods. Consequently, the men were returned to Hansteads to wait.

The only documented additional training they were provided was of avoiding
detection once they arrived. One of the trainers wrote to D.S.R., an officer in
SOE's scientific section, with advice that presumably was acted upon, not just by
the Everest agents.

> Recently I have for the second time instructed some men in the use of the dog
> drag. I am very glad to have done so because, dealing with the actual users of the
> drag in this way, has brought home to me their needs and difficulties.
>
> One of the things these men have to do is to bury a store (of explosives
> presumably) and to return to it from time to time. They have also to move about
> from one place to the other after reaching their first destination and they asked
> how they were to elude being tracked on these other journeys. Now the way of
> eluding dogs, apart from the use of special drags, is to ensure leaving no scent

trail on hard ground – on soft ground or grass one always leaves a scent trail because of the disturbed earth or crushed vegetation – and the easiest and most practical way of leaving no scent or trail on hard ground is the use of stilts or clean wooden shoes, or the wearing of clean rubber boots or galoshes. The latter will serve very well indeed for our people because at the end of a track the galoshes can be picked up and put in a bag. Therefore I think that all men who are going about and who are likely to be tracked by dogs should be provided with rubber galoshes. If it is going to be impossible to get ordinary galoshes, then I suggest that serviceable galoshes for our purpose be made from some artificial rubber-like substance or from calico impregnated with such a substance. We do not need a hard wearing galosh, but only one sufficient to last for a total of say 10 miles on a hard road. In use, the galoshes would not be worn continuously, but only at the beginning of a journey to ensure the dog not being able to find the track. A clean waterproof bag would be provided for the galoshes and the inside of the bag would be thoroughly cleaned.... To ensure a good fit with the galosh firmly gripping the shoe, I suggest that cloth or canvas bags be provided for the sole or heel of the galosh only, leaving an elastic rim to grip the shoe firmly. Failing galoshes, a pair of gymnasium shoes with a lip of rubber right round the shoe along the edges of the sole and heel would serve. The men would land in these – then later, when well on their journey at dawn, change to ordinary shoes. They will act in the same way in other journeys.[4]

When the Russian Section was told that there could be no flights to Vienna until the nights got longer in the autumn, Major Seddon passed his concerns upwards to Hambro, head of the SOE:

This has placed us in a very unfortunate position with our Soviet colleagues as we had already informed them that the April period would be at our disposal and postponement until October would be highly prejudicial to our relations and to the morale of the agents in question.

We have already in the past had this unfortunate situation and it would be most undesirable if more agents had to be removed to Russia by the Soviet on the plea that we were incapable of carrying our commitments....

These Pickaxe operations, although a source of embarrassment to SOE – and to D/P Section in particular – have as their basic importance the retension [sic] of the NKVD goodwill in Moscow and as higher authority has already ruled that Moscow Mission constitutes an important item of our policy, it would obviously be inadvisable to give the NKVD an excuse to terminate its function on the grounds that we were lukewarm in our handling of the Pickaxe operations.[5]

It took some explaining by Sir Charles Hambro to convince Chichaev that the Everest mission had been given high priority. The Air Ministry had, since early

1942, stopped long-range flights after the April moon due to there not being enough night-time hours to undertake operations and return safely to base. They also argued that the movement of German night fighter defences in south-east Europe had occurred due to the RAF bombing raids on Munich and similar areas. This necessitated a greater flying time to Austria and there were not enough hours of darkness after April. It was added that weather conditions in the more mountainous south-eastern Germany made flights impossible even though flights to lowland Poland went ahead.

> There is no intention of our being 'lukewarm in our handling of the Pickaxe operations'. Operations to this part of Europe are inevitably more difficult to carry out than to anywhere else owing to the great extent of defended land that has to be traversed and to the generally unsuitable weather prevailing over the mountains en route. It is inevitable that only on very few nights will operations to Austria be feasible.[6]

A copy of this response was forwarded to Chichaev in the hope that he would understand. However, when he came back suggesting a drop near Augsburg, Klein and Kessler refused, arguing that it would entail them carrying their wireless set 300 miles across Germany to Vienna. When they were offered an adequately camouflaged set 'they were adamant that the dangers were too great and that the whole of the operation would be jeopardised'.[7] Travelling that distance would involve yet more time waiting as the documentation would have to be redone. A query was made as to whether a flight by a de Haviland Mosquito could be arranged, but Air Liaison said it was impossible. There was only room for the aircraft's crew, but they were not experienced in low-level night flying without lights. Also the plane's safe slow speed was faster than the maximum for parachute drops. As Toropchenko refused SOE's conditions, the men had no alternative; they had to wait.[8]

On 27 August, to give the Hansteads staff a holiday, Klein and Kessler were moved to the Victorian Bailey's Hotel in South Kensington, returning on 12 September. During their time at SOE's expense, there were plenty of opportunities for Sergeant Kratzoff to find out more about them. His handwritten accounts were found in their file.

Maurice Klein.
Austrian, aged 34 years, married, strong Roman Catholic.
Personal Characteristics:–
   Easy going, good natured, sociable, intelligent, very patriotic towards Austria. Inclined to be talkative. Fond of England and the English. Despised Kessler, & secretly, all Russians, so does not intend to go back to Russia after the war. Is keen on keeping fit, & not afraid of work. Has a good deal of the dreamer and idealist in him.

Very confident of success in this work. A decent sort of person, has ambitions of becoming a schoolmaster in Vienna after the war.

Political Activities :–

Was a member of the Social Democrat Party before the German occupation. Well acquainted with an Austrian General who was also a leader of the party (This man was later arrested and sent to Dachau for two months. When he returned home he would say nothing to his wife and son of the treatment to which he was subjected there, but died two weeks later). A member of the party was killed by the Gestapo (of which there were 5,000 in Vienna). The party retaliated by sending the Gestapo a printed pamphlet informing them that two of their members would die for this outrage. They did! A fortnight later the Germans occupied Austria, and on the same evening came to Klein's house to arrest him. He escaped and lived for 3 months under cover trying to cross the Czech border.

He eventually succeeded by boldly walking through with stolen papers. Spent some time in the Balkans, heading towards Russia all the time. He has since regretted the route he took, saying he could have made his way to England instead. Wishes to cease all political activities when once Austria is freed.

When invited to take on this job he at once accepted, but at the same time he knew he had no alternative but to agree. All his history has been closely examined by the HKBD [sic] and during his stay in Russia was watched, especially after accepting the work. He was rather impressed by their thoroughness. He realises that he cannot escape his obligations to Russia once he is in Austria, because his family & relations are all in Austria.

All these people seem to be kept under a pretty tight rein even in Vienna, probably by direct radio communication with Moscow. Although he is literally going home, he is not to visit his family until permission is given. This will be granted according to existing conditions. Was told that his own discretion was the best guide in the matter. If the Gestapo became weak, then he could visit his family.

The part in the scheme originally was to find accommodation for Kessler * (see note at end). Made an arrangement in Moscow that he would be liberated from the organisation when 1/ the war is over, 2/ the Germans are beaten, 3/ Austria is free. The commanding officer has promised to come to Austria after the war, to explain to his family. Asserts he is not a proper agent, so will have no connection with Kessler.

Domestic Life:–

Married, has a daughter 8½ years of age. He made enquiries in Moscow thro' Colonel C. [Chichaev] as to the present whereabouts of his wife and was told: She left Vienna and is now with parents in Salzburg; will return to Vienna in September (They are both actually from Salzburg). His parents are both in Salzburg. Father aged 60, mother 58. Younger brother was in a crack regiment,

43rd division Austrian Army. When Klein left, his brother was a senior NCO & is now most probably an officer. His div. was one of those in Stalingrad. Klein is trying to trace him.

Occupation was mainly a jack-of-all trades. Was a teacher of the zither.

General Notes :–

Languages, Russian fairly good; English, good; Czech, good; German, good; French, good; has a smattering of others.... Is fully aware that Kessler was, & probably still is a Polit Commissar & is held back from really expressing his opinion of him by the fear of being sent back to Moscow.

The original part of the job is probably to be larger now. He is learning Morse Code, & everything necessary in that respect, & not merely as a pastime. He has had two recent interviews with Colonel C. & his progress was remarked upon. Will be capable operator within a month.[9]

Barry McLoughlin was a little more circumspect. In his article he suggested that Klein convinced the SOE that he was a good Catholic Austrian Social Democrat, and like the Coffee party and Hermann Koehler (Pyotr Koltsov), did not mention his membership of the Austrian Communist Party.[10] Max Kessler on the other hand was described as:

Soviet citizen of Bavarian origin. Aged 41 years; married. Is an atheist. This is his life story as volunteered by him to me:–

He was left an orphan at a very early age. At eight years of age was put to work on a farm, working very hard & receiving no money. Was then sent to work in a coal-mine, where he stayed until the age of 19-20 years, at a very poor wage. His health then became very bad, so the doctors gave him until 28 years to live at the most.

At about this time he came to Russia. In Moscow he underwent treatment which proved very successful. Naturally he felt greatly indebted to the Soviet Union. He then joined the Red Army, serving in both the Infantry & tanks. After some time he was assigned to his present work. Just before boarding ship for England at Murmansk, he slipped [and] ruptured himself. He is still in practically the same condition, but looks to under-go an operation for it in Moscow after the war.

General Characteristics:–

Dislikes strenuous exertion, frivolity, & 'unimportant things'. Has a good appetite for learning & 'culture', but most of his learning is parrot-fashion, without a deeper understanding of the subjects.

Is in the habit of doing various things, mostly because he thinks it is 'cultured' to do so, but spoils himself immediately by numerous exhibitions of ill manners. Has a one-track mind, enormously pro-Soviet, about his every thought is reddish in colour. Appears to be a man who will blindly do as he is told by his superiors,

& has always done so. Now that he is in England is indulging in independent thought for the first time, therefore when involved in any discussion, if he quotes statistics and figures etc he is to be relied on, but his own opinions are frequently childish. Then if getting the worst of an argument, will fall back on personal attack, because he detests to be proven wrong.

His political perception generally is quite sound, albeit slightly tinged with red. For him the Comintern still exists & holds rather optimistic views on post-war Russian foreign policy; namely of expansion and introduction of Soviet methods abroad.

Favourite topic of conversation is Russia, & what a splendid country it is etc. Is strong-willed & very confident in his own abilities.

Capabilities :–

Is a trained radio operator. Has travelled extensively (for the Party) in France, N & S Americas, Spain, Italy, Poland, & the Balkans. He has a smattering at least, of these languages. Actually speaks – German, well; Austrian dialect, well; Russian, fair; English, fair; the rest not known.

He served in the Spanish Civil War with the International Brigade as a Polit Commissar. Also in this war in the same capacity. Is considered a 'very big number' in Moscow.

The choice of a companion for this work was left to him, & out of a number of applicants he picked Klein. That was a year ago. There was some hesitation in Moscow regarding Klein's suitability but Kessler vouched for him, & a General carried the suggestion. Since leaving Russia Kessler is not quite so pleased with his choice, & at one time almost had Klein returned.

When taking on this work, a Colonel suggested to Kessler that he be sent alone, being supplied with addresses etc. He consigned the Colonel and his idea to the devil, saying he would choose a man who knew the district as a guide. This of course was done.

It may be that he has no such influence because of his friendship with Voroshilov's secretary. He receives letters & telegrams from his family via the Embassy, a very unusual concession. He was a German Communist & took part in the Spartacus movement. Been tested and tried by the Russians & not found wanting. Completely forsaken the land of his birth, & considers himself a Russian.

Domestic Life :–

Was legally married to a woman, who afterwards left him. He is married to a widow, who already had one child, a boy. Now has a son of his own. At present they are living in Omsk.

In my opinion he is being sent to Vienna as a Commissar to 'keep in touch' with the others already there. He hopes to stay there after the war, directing the political interests of the USSR.[11]

Major Saunders, the commandant at Hansteads, wrote a covering letter in which he suggested that Sergeant Kratzoff's account was somewhat biased against Kessler, adding that he 'would rather be in a tight place with him than with Klein'.[12]

On 23 September, in the hope of a flight the next moon period, Chichaev put in a request for a small wireless set capable of reaching Moscow from Vienna. Because of Everest's delay, their original set had been given to another group who had lost theirs in transit. When the date of 10 October 1943 was given, one of the conducting officers reported:

> Captain Darton and I today went down to Little Hansteads in order to pick up Klein and Kessler's luggage & bring same up to London. On arrival at the house Major Saunders told us that (Max) Kessler had told him at 6.30 pm that on Saturday that his wireless set was out of sorts, and that he wanted an expert to come out and put it right. We spoke to Kessler and he told us that he was not sure what was wrong, but the receiver did not work and he thought that it was probably the valves or condenser which were faulty. He also told us that he needed to take with him 4 spare valves.
>
> In view of the shortness of notice, it being necessary to get the luggage in the same evening for packing, if the operation was to take place on Wed the 13th, we formed the opinion that Kessler was trying to be 'difficult'.
>
> Whilst at Bricket Wood, Klein told me that if Kessler's w set might [be] delaying the operation, then he would like to go by himself.
> Klein expressed satisfaction with the W/T set supplied by us, this set was handed to him on Friday 8/10/43 and the working of it was explained to him at Bryanston, he took it back with him to L. Hansteads in order to study it, and it was in view of his refusal to part with it that we were unable to take it for packing before Sunday 10/10/43.[13]

It is possible that the problem with the wireless set was responsible for them missing the October moon. However, the telegram sent to SAM on 22 October did not mention it.

> Regret inform you that impossibility of carrying out PICKAXE operations today brings moon period to inconclusive end, and these operations will not be possible until Novmeber period. We had hoped that further two days would be available in this period but, for operational reasons, period has been cut short. DPR.1 is depressed as are we all.[14]

On 26 October, they were moved to Alderton where the Tonic and Sodawater parties had stayed. It was not for a change, but because Klein had got into trouble.

He had quite a pleasant character and was keen on the good things of life, i.e. beer, music and on one or two instances, the local 'ladies'; it was due to the latter that it was decided to move the party to Loughton from Bricket Wood.[15]

Whether the incidents with the local 'ladies' was used to put pressure on Klein is not known, but on 2 November, Major Krassowski, DPR.5, one of the NKVD mission, went down to Loughton 'and told these two that they would probably be going back to the USSR. D/P.6 [Captain Wild] who saw them immediately afterwards noticed that both of them were rather pale and were breathing hard.'[16]

A few days later they were taken to Gaynes Hall to prepare for their flight. However, for an unspecified reason, at 2330 hours on 7 November 1943, the station commander refused to carry the Everest mission, suggesting instead that it should be flown into Austria from the Allies' advance base in the boot of Italy. As the British, American, and Canadian forces had gained a foothold in Italy, the SOE set up a forward base, codenamed Maryland, in a castle at Monopoli, near Bari on the Adriatic coast. Its tasks included liaising with Italian partisans and infiltrating guerrilla fighters into Rome ahead of the Allied troops, and over the Alps into German-occupied territory.[17] However, as permission was needed from Bomber Command for a mission into Austria, there were delays.

Three days later, London was informed that another two agents, 'Georg Schmidt' and 'Johann Gerbert', had just left Murmansk on the Grey Funnel Line. These men were to be the Eiger party, dealt with in detail in the next chapter. The Russian Section passed on Air Liaison's message to Chichaev that the latest time for flights to Germany and Austria west of longitude 14° E would be the middle of the April moon period.

> However in view of the intense flak and increased night fighter defence operations from home base to AUSTRIA and central GERMANY have become very hazardous and costly. To overcome this difficulty plans are under consideration to operate to these areas from Mediterranean base and we will advise you immediately definite scheme emerges.[18]

After Bomber Command's suggestion that the agents be sent from Italy, the NKVD queried whether it might be possible to drop Everest during the December moon on the most northern boundary of Austria with Yugoslavia. To reassure the Russian Section, SAM pointed out that this was not subterfuge to get them into partisan territory.

The southern route was not acted upon immediately as an alternative solution was found. On 15 November, there were instructions that Klein and Kessler were to be dropped separately with one container each, 3-5 kms apart. The dropzone had been changed to about 5 miles south-south-east of St Pölten, just over 3 miles north-north-east of Wilhelmsburg, about 50 miles west of Vienna. They were provided with Reichmarken, rations for meat, and lightweight sleeping bags.

A series of telegrams followed between London and Massingham:

An operation code name EVEREST repeat EVEREST is being attempted from LONDON on behalf of the Russians to deliver 2 repeat 2 Austrians into AUSTRIA.

If operation is not successful pilot may make for BRINDISI.

London say these men are well behaved speak English and are not likely to cause any trouble. They ask that you take them under their wing.

First attempt will be made November 18th repeat 18 and attempts may be made on succeeding days until further notice.

If aircraft lands at BRINDISI it might attempt operation on return journey.

London please inform us when operation is either successful or cancelled so that we may tell DRIZZLE.[19]

They telegrammed 'DRIZZLE', the codename for Brindisi, to be prepared, but the mission did not happen during the November moon. On 19 November, SAM was informed:

Neither JUNGFRAU nor EVEREST were possible on night 18/19th although EVEREST had been accepted in morning and proceeded to aerodrome.

Fog and cloud conditions over whole of Europe caused failure and same conditions still exist with the result that neither repeat neither operation is scheduled for today.

We now have only one day left.[20]

It was not to be so. Georg Schmidt, Kessler, and Klein had to wait for the December moon period. It came and went, so did Christmas and New Year. How they celebrated was not documented. Then, on 6 January 1944, they were taken again to Gaynes Hall, given a good meal with drinks, and having had their equipment checked, they were described as being 'in the best of spirits' when they got to Tempsford. Kessler's last words to Captain Wild before he climbed on board the Whitley bomber were said to have amazed him: 'Thank you very much for all you have done – you have been very good.'[21]

Clark details seven successful sorties that night. Flight Lieutenant Perrins, with Wireless Officer Thomas acting as his despatcher, flew an NKVD sortie Everest 1 to Austria.

A remarkable flight by any standards, taking off at 20.03 hours he went via Bognor–Cabourg–Loire (isles) Never–Lake Bourget (east of Lyon)–Châttilon (some 25 km east of Aosta, Italy)–Lake Como (north of Milan, Italy)–Lake

Ossiacher (west of Klagenfurt, Austria) –St Polten–EVEREST 1 (48°08' 30" E)
position 44°10' N, 15°02' E-Viesta (?)–Ptealice (?)–Malta.[22]

The plane touched down, not in Brindisi, but in Malta at 0700 hours. Confirmation
of the flight's success was not officially reported to SOE until four days later.
Perrins' report stated:

> Weather good at vicinity of target when heavy storm cloud was encountered. On
> exact pinpoint was what appeared to be a prisoner-of-war camp so agents dropped
> about 5 miles east of pinpoint. Agents dropped about 8 miles apart since despatcher
> had to let Captain know when he was ready for the second agent to drop & then a
> clear space found for the drop. 1st agent dropped from 800 ft above ground heading
> 180° at 135 mph. 2nd dropped from same height & at same speed heading 185°.
> Agents jumped OK. Packages OK in each case. Parachutes seen to open.[23]

Details about what happened to the Everest party were not revealed until after
the war. In the SOE's *Rote Kapelle* file was an entry for Kessler stating that he was
'arrested and agreed "play-back" but eventually did not.' [24]

Nollau and Zindel's research reveals that Kessler and Klein were arrested
when they arrived. Kessler turned out to be Josef Zettler, a Bavarian Communist
who had fought in Spain and then settled in the USSR. Klein, real name Huttary,
immediately told his captors that he had only volunteered for the mission to get
out of the USSR and was prepared to assist in a *Funkspiel*.

Zettler,worried initially about his family in Omsk, reluctantly gave in, but
fooled the Gestapo by managing to insert a coded warning in the messages to the
'Direktor' in Moscow, who broke off contact with the group. Zettler was sent to
a concentration camp in Theresienstadt but he survived, eventually becoming a
colonel in the East German Army.[25]

The SOE folder on Everest also contained an extract from a report on Johann
Sanitzer's interrogation. The account, dated July 1945, shed light on the fate of
captured NKVD agents dropped from both RAF and Soviet planes who agreed or
were forced to transmit Gestapo-inspired messages back to Moscow.

In his 'debrief', Sanitzer mentioned capturing two NKVD agents, Huttary and
Zettler, who had their wireless sets played back in what he called *Funkspiel Rote
Mauer*.

> This concerned another NKVD group, transported over MOURMANSK to
> England and finally dropped by a RAF plane, around February 1944. It consisted
> of a former Viennese communist called HUTTARY and his W/T operator,
> ZETTLER, from Bavaria. HUTTARY was a soldier in the German Army who
> had deserted and was recruited by the NKVD. ZETTLER had fought in the
> Spanish Civil War and had left for Russia afterwards.

They had been partially equipped in England where they had to wait nine months before being dropped. Their sets were Russian. They had received previously some jump training (two or three jumps). Curiously enough HUTTARY had, as usual with these agents, a complete set of papers but instead of using a false name, these were made out in his own real name. While they waited for their drop in England, HUTTARY had learned how to send and had been equipped with a signal plan.

Their drop was rather unfortunate as they landed about 200m away from a German airfield in Greater Vienna. They got away and managed to hide in town.

HUTTARY was already in subject's files, which contained at this time several hundred names and descriptions. They were arrested because of 'apartment trouble' (having to look for an apartment that was sufficiently high up to enable them to send and that also had AC , [Alternating Current for the wireless set], of which there was very little in Vienna.)

They were arrested and were 'willing' to begin a play for Subject. First Subject tried with ZETTLER, who apparently had lost his signal plan and said that he had memorized it, but that never worked out well. Then Subject began with HUTTARY and his written signal plan and that went all right. The usual military and political information was fed to the NKVD; Subject received it through the same channels. Weather reports at that time were not demanded anymore.[26]

Sanitzer admitted during lengthy interrogations in Moscow that he had arrested sixty British, thirty Soviet, five US and three French agents. These included the Sodawater and Everest parties. Most had been tortured and forced to participate in over twenty playback schemes. He had also arrested over 500 people who had offered accommodation to the agents, and had executed about 300 foreign agents.[27]

O'Sullivan comments that one effect the Pickaxe scheme had on the Gestapo was to make them seriously worried about their future. Kopkow claimed that senior Gestapo officers favoured a compromise with the Allied forces but deeply distrusted the Soviets. When they realised that the RAF were dropping Soviet agents with instructions to engage in activities far beyond military espionage, they suffered a 'severe ideological blow'. They had not expected Anglo-Soviet co-operation to include sending both men and women with long-term political ambitions. This dampened their hopes for a separate peace between Germany, the United States and Britain.[28]

OPERATION EIGER

In a telegram dated 1 October 1943, Colonel Graur asked SAM if the Russian Section would accept two more agents destined for Central Germany who were able to travel almost at once. The following day, SAM informed the Russian Section that the two agents would soon be leaving on a British destroyer, which prompted an urgent request to the security officers at all northern ports to expect them. Their names were given as 42-year-old Eugen Nesper travelling as Georg Schmidt, and 35-year-old Herman Kramer, travelling as Ivan Johann Gerbert. Both men were said to be originally from south-west Germany and were travelling via Sweden with Swiss passports. The codename for their operation was Brood, but for some unknown reason, it was changed the following day to Eiger, the last of the mountain parties.[1]

Two days later, the Russian Section was asked by Colonel Graur whether the four Pickaxes still in England – I. M. Botsevitch (Otto Bach), Stepan Sidorov (Siegfried Schmidt), Nicolai Kharlamov (Josef Zettler), and Alexandre Jacoubov (Alexandre Jeannin) – would be sent that month. Having been told that the weather factor was always incalculable, Graur told the Russian Section that the NKVD required a written reply from London. If there was to be any further delay, he said, NKVD intended 'to distribute these bodies and take other measures.' London's reply was that they could not make any promises but pointed out that they had been given high priority.

When two Russians got off a train at Euston Station on 13 October 1943 after being escorted down from Scotland, they were taken aback by their welcome. After a brief discussion with the Russian Section, it was discovered that they were Soviet diplomatic couriers, not Pickaxes. 'They were somewhat surprised at the special attention paid to them ... the arrangements for the wrong party had gone without a hitch!' Consequently, there was an awkward moment when the Russian Section officer, accompanied by one of the NKVD team, eventually met Nesper and Kramer. As there was no office car available, they had to be taken by taxi. A note was made in the file to ensure that future arrivals might receive a better reception.[2]

As with the other Pickaxes, Nesper and Kramer were provided with appropriate clothing and ration cards. To help them in their mission, a request was made to D/FIN, Group Captain John Venner, head of the Finance Section, for 5,000 reichsmarks, which they were told Chichaev would repay in sterling.

Air Liaison was asked to determine which of the following dropzones was more suitable: Schwänbische Gmünd in Weissenstein, or Göppingen in Geislinger, east of Stuttgart. They suggested dropping them in the Basle area, but the men refused, arguing that they could not possibly travel 150 miles across country with their wireless sets with any degree of safety. Their plan was to bury the sets on landing and return to pick them up later. Instead they asked for a dropzone in the Aaln, Gerstetten, Blaubeuren, Reutlingen, Eszlingen, or Welzheim area, or anywhere in the immediate vicinity of the Schwäbischer Jura, south-east of Stuttgart. Air Liaison informed them on 24 November that their pinpoint would be about 5 miles east of Hechingen and 12½ miles south-south-west of Reutlingen.[3]

A request was made that they be sent on the next moon with two 'A' type containers. To help the packers at Holme know which luggage to pack, they were told Eiger's included one black leather suitcase with two shiny nickel locks, with leather corner pieces and nickel studs underneath, a light tan leather suitcase with brass studs underneath and two brass locks and a brown crocodile suitcase, marked EIGER-G, with one brass lock and two brass clasps.

Two days before Christmas, in anticipation of a winter drop, they were issued with long pants, long-sleeve vests, long shirts and boots. On 4 January 1944, Nesper and Kramer were driven up to Tempsford with newly forged German meat rations. According to the Air Transport report, the plane took off at 1947 hours but Pilot Officer Cole commented that 'icing was experienced up to 9,000 & operation abandoned owing to weather conditions. Load returned to base'. They arrived back at 0344 hours.[4]

A flight was arranged for 5/6 January, which had to be cancelled due to fog at Tempsford, but two days later another attempt was made. Nesper and Kramer were taken up to the airfield, prepared and left at 2030 hours.

The flight report stated that 'Pin-point found and identified by ground detail. Agents dropped slightly N. of point in a good clear space from 800 ft. above ground, heading 360° at 150 miles per hour. Dropping area appeared very flat and lonely without houses or trees.' The despatcher reported that 'Agents jumped well. Package O.K. Parachutes seen to open.' He reported leaving the Wartenburg area at 0119 hours, returning to base at 0525.[5] The conducting officer noted the following day:

> On saying goodbye to SCHMIDT [Nesper], I expressed my hope that we might be seeing each other again one of these days and said that I was looking forward greatly to hearing from him, through the usual channels, of his safe arrival. I said that undoubtedly he would communicate with his people as soon as he could. He replied, 'Naturally, you will be able to find out all about us from our people here.' The implication is that undoubtedly they have got means in their possession of communicating with either Moscow or even perhaps London.[6]

Whether their message got through is undocumented in the SOE file. The telegram informing SAM of the success of the Everest and Eiger operations ended with the comment: 'Colleagues are delighted and grateful for assistance from our operations department.'[7]

A week later, the SOE received a telegram from Switzerland stating that 'Charles' had heard a story from Rhine bargees of parachutists being caught by villagers at Odernheim am Glan, south-west of Mainz, but that they had managed to escape by jumping onto a train moving out of the station. The British Embassy in Basle sent a copy of a newspaper report to the SOE in London, which stated that British parachutists dropped in Alsace, south of Baden and the Black Forest on the night of 7 January had set the whole district into a state of alarm. Two parachutists wearing German-made uniforms and having full papers were arrested in Mulhouse. These were the Eiger party. A pencilled comment on the top of the telegram read 'Mothball Pickaxes as there was a BUP [British United Press] report in Daily Tel[egraph] 10/1 saying Brit parachutists landed near German frontier in Baden and Alsace.'[8]

Nesper, from Stuttgart, trained as a wireless operator in the German army before defecting to the Soviets in August 1942. Described as a German officer 'of the Prussian type, with good manners and a sense of security', Nesper offered his services to the NKVD to obtain his release from a prisoner-of-war camp. The German Communists who interviewed him convinced them that he was suitable for the mission.

Kramer had been a long-term communist and fought in the Spanish Civil War on the Republican side and then underwent parachute training in the USSR. The Gestapo knew exactly when and where the agents were going to be dropped and waited for the low-flying British aircraft. Once they landed there was a struggle during which the local police fired several shots. Both men were arrested, Kramer after being shot in the head and losing his eyesight.[9]

Nesper managed to flee and attempted to contact one of the addresses the NKVD had given him. However, the list of safe houses was quite old as NKVD had great difficulty in maintaining a network of communist supporters in Nazi Germany. Most known communists were under surveillance, and as the *Funkspiel* developed, the Gestapo knew Nesper was bound to contact someone for help. He met Friedrich Schlotterbeck, a communist who had just been released after spending ten years in a concentration camp. Schlotterbeck immediately suspected Nesper of being an agent provocateur. Later, he remembered their conversation:

'Who sent you?' Schlotterbeck asked the stranger.
'The party.'
'Who is that, the party?'
'I do not know any names.'
'How did you get here?'

'By parachute.'

'From Russia? Impossible. No Russian plane can get here.'

'I came on an English bomber.'

'So you come from the English and not from Moscow?'

'I don't have anything to do with the English. They just dropped me.'

'Well, you don't pretend that the English do this for free. In particular the English.'

'No, the English just had to transport us and do not even know our names.'[10]

In an attempt to prove his credentials, Nesper showed him his 'L' pills, his pistol, ration cards, and forged Swiss papers and told Schlotterbeck that Moscow needed information about the military and economic situation in Germany and the strength of the anti-Nazi groups. Despite Schlotterbeck having to report to the Gestapo every two weeks, he managed to supply Nesper with information that Moscow would find of interest. Schlotterbeck had been asked by the Gestapo if he knew anything about parachuted agents, but he claimed he did not. However, he was afraid that they knew what Nesper was doing. Schlotterbeck confronted Nesper, and Nesper confessed that both he and Kramer had been arrested by the Gestapo and that he had agreed to participate in their playback scheme. He claimed, however, to have used the agreed security checks.

Schlotterbeck fled to Switzerland and the Gestapo arrested nine of his relatives, executing them for treason on 30 November 1944. Nesper managed to escape as well, but whether he was able to inform Moscow about the *Funkspiel* is unknown.[11]

The next note in the Eiger file was not made until 21 June 1944, regarding a Soviet agent who was in a Swiss police station. The agent claimed to be called Nagel and said he had been dropped in Wartenburg on 11 January 1944. Notes taken during his 'interrogation' revealed:

Schaffhausen Police have arrested and detained a deserter from Germany who makes the following statement.

His real name is EUGEN NES (grp.mut.): mechanic; born 1913; resident Schwabischgmund near Stuttgart. He further states that on January 7th 1944 he was parachuted into Germany (Wuertemburg) by the R.A.F. with W/T sender with which he was to transmit to Russia. After some time he was captured by the Gestapo, together with another Soviet agent on similar work. Both were forced to continue to transmit false information to Russia.

The man states that when he was sent from England he was in possession of forged identity papers in the name of NAGEL, an engineer. He had served with the German Army on the East Front until the Autumn of 1943, when he deserted to the Russians on the strength of being a former member of the German Communist Party at Stuttgart. He had been trained by the Russians as an intelligence agent for infiltration into Germany.

He has announced all the above to the Swiss Police and added the request
that he should have an interview with some member of the British Legation in
Berne.[12]

The advice given to the Russian Section was, 'It is desirable I think, to ask 'C'
[Sir Stewart Menzies] to approach the Swiss police to whom this man has given
himself up and to request that the matter be kept on a low level and not become
a subject for diplomacy.'[13] The Foreign Office advised the Russian Section to get
a message through to the Swiss telling them not to allow the man to contact the
British Legation, arguing that he might be a German or Soviet double-agent. A
telegram was sent to SAM on 24 June, detailing the above but adding, 'We have
every reason presume subject is SCHMIDT or EIGER. Propose inform DPR.1
concerning above but make it clear we cannot help extricate or assist agent in any
way.'[14]

After discussions about what to do about him, the Russian Section sent the
following telegram to Berne informing them that:

> It is most undesirable we should have anything further to do with this man. He
> should therefore make his own arrangements.[15]

What proved interesting was the response from Air Commodore Boyle (A/CD), at
Baker Street. Chichaev was told verbally of Nagel's arrival in Switzerland and that
he had claimed to have been captured by the Germans, escaped, and captured by
the Swiss Police. No suggestion that he was forced to 'playback' to Moscow was
mentioned. Chichaev's reaction was to request that Nagel be asked the date of
when he was arrested. Perhaps he suspected something was amiss.

Berne's next telegram in response added some pertinent points.

> In order to facilitate probe could you not wire us urgently leading questions on
> trivial matters connected to +'s stay in and departure from U.K. which imposter
> could not answer.
>   Await your reply, but can assure you that in any case all precautions will be
> taken to avoid uncovering ourselves in any way.[16]

In a subsequent communication, an SOE officer at Baker Street, codenamed
V.C.S.S., noted that the man claimed that he came to England with a Soviet
passport in the name of George Ivanovich Pocopa (sic) and that he was born 2
October 1910 at Engels.

> On landing they were immediately caught by the Gestapo who were apparently
> expecting them. He maintains that various other Soviet agents have been caught
> immediately on arrival and then forced to transmit to Russia under German

control. He infers from this that there must be some leakage from the secret
agent training headquarters in Moscow.

His own transmissions took place every Thursday morning and Sunday
evening. His call sign was O.T.B. The Gestapo blended correct news with
misleading.

I am very loath to get further into this matter because the latest indications in
my mind are that the man has probably been sent out by the Germans. I spoke
with Loxley at the Foreign Office about two days ago on this matter and it was
agreed that it was very undesirable for any British to show any interest in the
man.[17]

It seemed that the SOE was more concerned with the fact that the Gestapo had
successfully infiltrated opposition groups in Germany than the man's fate. A few
days later they received a more detailed report:

A German named Eugen NESPER alias Georg Ivanowitsch SCHMID [sic] called
here and told the following story.

He was very unwilling to give the details mentioned, and admitted that he
could tell a lot more, but that he would only tell it to his Russian bosses, he also
admitted that he had made a fairly full statement to the Swiss, on the same lines
as the following.

Part or all of this is I believe already known to you. In 1943 Nesper deserted
from the German army to the Russians. After he had stated that he was a
communist, and wishes to help the Russians, and his statements had been
checked, he was sent to Moskau, where he was more or less free for 5 months
during the time of his training. The Russian official in charge of him was called
Iwan Petrowitsch of the N.K.W.D. [sic] On the 11th Nov, 1943 he landed in
Scapa Flow, and was received by the British and taken to London. He then had
Russian papers on the name of Georg Ivanowitsch SCHMID, with him was
another colleague, whose name he has forgotten. In London he was taken over
by a British Officer and a member of the Russian legation.

He was more or less free in London, but was always accompanied by a British
officer named Webb, who he described as a small man with specs, age about 28.
His address in London he had forgotten, but it was somewhere in Maida Vale
near Sunderland Av. Later he stayed on a farm in Loughton near London, with a
former sailor of the navy who had seen 27 years service named Chief (phonetical
spelling).

On the 4th Jan. 1944 he left England in a plane to be parachuted, the plane
reached the target area, but it did not go down for parachuting owing to the
danger of iceing. Another successful attempt was made on the 7th. Jan, and
Nesper landed in the Schäwbische Alp somewhere near Stuttgart. He then had
German papers, of a 'Kriegswichtige Persönlichkeit' which had been made in

Russia. He would not say in which name. (I forgot to say that during his stay in London he had papers from Scotland Yard, as Georg Schmid born 2.10.10 in Winterthur Switzerland.)

In Germany he did several things, but would not say what, he only let slip that he had WT connection with Russia, and that he was unlucky, owing to inefficiency of the Secret Service. After 5 months in Germany he fled to Switzerland, crossed the frontier near Schaffhausen on 11th June 1944. He was able to get in touch with Bringolf in Schaffhausen, who later confirmed that his message had been checked and proved correct.[18]

The Russian Section decided not to get involved and on 12 July sent a memo to 'X', Lieutenant Colonel Ronald Thornley, head of the German and Austrian Section, which stated:

> The reply must be that it is our policy not to take part at all in this case; in view of the unknown possibilities of double-crossing, we feel that it is better that NAGEL should be safely held by the Swiss federal Police and that we should not attempt to follow up or probe in any way.[19]

Berne's reaction on 14 July was that they were getting some very interesting information out of him:

> He has already mentioned 'CHARLES' by name in connection with contact CHARLES once had with STUTTGART Gestapo agent MARIE LUISE FUCHS. His work with Gestapo STUTTGART may throw interesting light on what they do or do not know of our S.I.S. work. Unless you have special reasons against, propose 500 should interview him member of YM's.[20]

In the *Rote Kapelle* list in the SOE's Russian file it noted that Nesper was living at Arbeitslager Hohlin, Switzerland, in May 1945 and expressed a wish to go to the Soviet zone in Germany. He was reported living there on 24 January 1946 and in August 1950 was mentioned in an SIS memo suggesting he was involved in arms trafficking in Tangier.[21]

What happened to Kramer, whose name Nesper could not remember or was not prepared to divulge, is unknown. In the transcription of a 'confession' obtained from Walter Habecker, a captured German Kriminal Kommissar who had been employed in tracing radio operators, the name Kramer was crossed out and beside it was written 'presumably Ivan Gerbert.'[22]

THE RISING TENSION OF 1943

Less than a fortnight after British, Canadian and American forces landed in Sicily on 10 July 1943, as part of their plan to force the Germans out of Italy, the NKVD requested that SOE drop a party of five Soviet agents into the Turin district. There was consideration into sending them by plane to Massingham via Tehran and Cairo, or via the Arctic Ocean to Scotland by the 'Grey Funnel Line'.

Although the Russian Section agreed in principle, Sir Charles Hambro and the Foreign Office had to be contacted. The SOE agreed but the gist of the Foreign Office's response was that they would have no political objection if they were dropped into German-occupied territory. They also considered that General Eisenhower should be consulted in some form before full acceptance was given, and suggested that the Russian Section or NKVD should approach him themselves. This proved a stumbling block as both were wary of letting the Americans know that SOE had an agreement with the NKVD. They wanted the approach to be made by Hambro.

In August 1943, Chichaev provided the Russian Section with a summary of the Pickaxe operations. It stated that five had been sent into France, four into Austria, two into Germany, two into Holland, one into Belgium, and one into Italy. He went on to tell them that five Italian-speaking Soviet agents were ready to be sent into Italy and were awaiting transport in the USSR. Their names were given as 'P. I. Feodorof', born in Irkuski, 1917; 'K. N. Voronov', born in Ulianovsk, 1911; 'N. Chernov', born in Buorkast, 1913; 'F. K. Zernov', born in Kazan, 1903; and 'A. H. Gribov', born in Kazan. All were described as Italian-speaking Russians.[1]

There were also eight Pickaxes waiting to be sent into France, including five not yet arrived in the UK, two waiting to be sent to Germany and two waiting for the longer nights so they could be sent to Austria. In addition, four for Austria and one for Italy had been returned and one destined for Germany was killed when his aircraft crashed. Chichaev omitted mentioning the two members of the Whiskey party who were killed when their aircraft crashed into the mountains of Bavaria.

Sending five more Pickaxes into Italy caused concern for some in SOE as they thought that their mission was not likely to help the war effort. In a memo, Lieutenant Colonel Ronald Thornley, head of the German and Austrian Section, admitted to knowing nothing about the briefing of Soviet agents that had been infiltrated into Germany and Austria.

> I can only say that, judging from the way in which Russia appears to be stimulating and penetrating the more Nationalistic émigré groups, both German and Austrian, it is reasonable to suppose that any Agents they are despatching into these two countries are intended to prepare the ground for post-war Russian activities inside Germany rather than for active subversive work during the war.
>
> In my opinion, it is unlikely that these Agents are intended to be of any use to us in our conduct of the war.
>
> This is my personal opinion and, for obvious reasons, I cannot substantiate it with proof.
>
> If the practice of infiltrating these agents into Germany does continue, I recommend strongly that there should be an understanding that they should arrive in this country with complete documents etc. as we do not like supplying any of our forged papers to Russian Agents.
>
> Clearly this is a matter of high policy and officially we know nothing about the infiltrating of Russian Agents.[2]

In O'Sullivan's words, SOE was afraid it was becoming an accomplice in the 'communisation' of post-war Europe. On the same day, 17 August, the Russian Section wrote to Colonel Macdonald, Assistant Director of Operations at Baker Street, expressing concern that a minute had been circulated from Eric Mockler-Ferryman, SOE's Director of Operations, North-West Europe, codenamed AD/E, to other departments when it should only have been sent to the Russian Section. In response Hambro ruled:

> The security aspect of our relations with the N.K.V.D. demanded that secrecy should be maintained as regards the Pickaxe operations governed by our Charter.
>
> It is true that for certain operational reasons we had had to consult with other departments of the organisation but the ban on broadcasting still exists and I am most unwilling to discuss Pickaxe matters with anyone without C/D's [Hambro] approval.[3]

When Major Roseberry, the head of the Italian Section, was informed of the plan, he wrote to Mockler-Ferryman commenting that they should only provide assistance when it was demanded by a higher authority and that such operations had to have a war-winning aim.

> So long as Fascism existed, it could be argued that assistance to Communist elements could help to embarrass the Fascists and consequently hinder the Italian war effort, even though the agents were instructed primarily to nurse

Communism with anti-war efforts a mere accidental sequel. Now that fascism has gone, it cannot be in our interests to have extreme Left elements subjected to stimulation. The average Italian Communist is merely a subscriber to the Communist ideal and is inclined to a nationalistic outlook. I do not consider that we should assist the entry of agents whose object will be doubtless to harness this form of Communism on to the Moscow wagon thereby increasing the difficulty of civil administration.[4]

The Russian Section's response went through the history of SOE/NVKD relations, but added that refusing to send in any more Pickaxes would result in SAM's mission being asked to leave Moscow.

Although this suppression of liaison with N.K.V.D. would not materially embarrass S.O.E., at the same time, the arguments in favour of keeping the Mission in Moscow from a general point of view are most important. The Foreign Office and 'C' [Sir Stewart Menzies] on the advice of H.B.M. [His Britannic Majesty] Ambassador in Moscow have informed us that they do not desire any action to be taken which would jeopardise the Mission's position and our policy therefore at present is to give the maximum assistance to the N.K.V.D. in the infiltration of their agents. As long as the Charter exists I cannot see that we could do otherwise.[5]

SAM was considered vital as a source of valuable intelligence about the USSR's political and military intentions. As Hill had been in place for several years, he had built up good relationships with important figures in the Soviet military and intelligence hierarchy. However, the Russian Section was conscious of the arguments against dropping communists into occupied Allied countries.

The ordinary security objection to starting a separate réseau in any territory. This I am fully ready to overrule.

    The odium incurred with our opposite numbers in the relevant Allied government when we are found out. As the Russian agents concerned are of a very poor type, very badly trained and equipped and inadequately briefed, this in the end is almost inevitable.[6]

Hill argued that the consent of sovereign governments was needed. This explained the ban on sending further Pickaxes into Belgium and Holland. The situation in France was explained where there had been a long delay in obtaining such permission from the French Committee for National Liberation (CFNL). In response, Captain Macdonald conceded to Lieutenant Colonel Sporberg, Sir Charles Hambro's deputy, that, 'having put our hand to this particular plough we cannot turn back.'[7] However, in Sporberg's memo to Hambro, he made the following point:

... there is absolutely nothing to be got out of putting in Russians. I doubt whether they are intended to further the war effort, but are intended for preparing the post-war ground. Their security is a danger, they take up our aircraft and, naturally, the ordinary Frenchman does not thank us for it. I hope it can be stopped.[8]

Events in Italy threw the plans of all parties into the air. On 8 September 1943, the Italians surrendered and shortly afterwards, when Sir Charles Hambro resigned over the Government's Middle East policy, his replacement, Sir Colin Gubbins, ruled that the operation should be stalled until events in Italy had crystallised. An indication of the Russian Section's attitude was found in a letter to Colonel Sheridan, dated 9 September:

With reference to the five Italians now held in Moscow and offered to us by the N.K.V.D., I presume that in the light of recent events a new policy will have to be defined. I should be grateful if I could be instructed what line to take with my Soviet colleague, as I think we should inform him at once of the possibilities or otherwise of infiltrating these agents. I presume that the answer will be 'Make you own way on a holiday ticket.'[9]

SAM was getting pressure put on him to get details of what arrangements the Russian Section was making. In a telegram the following day, 10 September, he stressed that 'the Russians are still anxious to send these persons, because they have been specially trained for the purpose.'[10]

In a memo dated 16 September, Colonel Sheridan queried with F.S.O.2, an unnamed officer in the French Section, 'What does not appear to have been settled, and what I feel we should have a ruling on from CD [Sir Colin Gubbins], is when we have "stalled" until we can "stall" no longer, what is our policy to be?'[11]

When SAM told Colonel Graur on 18 September 1943 that bad weather meant the departure of the two Pickaxes (Rigi and Jungfrau) had to be postponed until the October moon, his reaction was one of disappointment.

More in sorrow than in anger he asked me why it was that with such an excellent arrangement we had made virtually no progress during past two years. Once again I recounted what had been done and explained difficulties both here and in LONDON.

I feel that if our work is to prosper (or even to continue) in coming year D/P.101 [Hill] should bring back with him some positive proposals for cooperation in various fields of activity. As you will remember, last winter 'O' [an unnamed officer in SOE's overseas section] was not in favour of continuing collaboration unless we can enlarge scope of our work during next few months and show some concrete improvements. We shall have no reprieve when next the situation is reviewed.[12]

SAM had to tell Chichaev that the infiltration of the men into Italy had to be postponed. Also, as a delaying tactic, he was told that Massingham had asked to be shown a copy of the signed authorisation from André Philip, the Commissioner of the French Committee for National Liberation (CFNL) in Algiers, authorising the mission. He was also told that the final decision had to be taken at a meeting between the Foreign Office, SIS, SOE and the Russian Section. This response irritated Chichaev who expressed concern about SOE not keeping their part of their agreement. However, the letter was obtained and a copy duly sent to Massingham.

It did not resolve the problem though. Graur stated that he was 'thoroughly dissatisfied' with the 'interminable delay', not understanding why so few people had to stay in London month after month. He was referring to Rigi, Everest and Jungfrau. In the meantime, on 22 September, the NKVD had managed to drop four men and a woman from one of their own planes into Yugoslavia. Not part of the Pickaxe operation, Cairo thought that these five Soviet agents were Yugoslavs who the NKVD were sending back from Moscow to join Tito's HQ. [13]

When the NKVD was told on 25 September that bad weather had stopped the dropping of Rigi and Jungfrau and that the next opportunity would not be until October, their concerns intensified. The Russian Section was questioned as to their ability to 'deliver goods'. SAM commented to the Russian Section:

> Much of course depends upon successful completion of pickaxe problems. N.K.V.D. without doubt attach great importance to this work and at present they feel that they are not receiving a square deal. Our + [Russian counterparts, NKVD] are unable to justify themselves to their own authorities. [14]

Two days later, in a long memo to George Taylor, director of SOE's overseas groups and missions, Colonel Sheridan stated:

> Recent telegrams received from Moscow and a long conversation I have had with D/P.101 [Hill] show that the future of our Russian Mission is nearing a crisis. This is a matter of concern, not merely to S.O.E. but also to ZP [the Foreign Office], S.I.S, and H.M.G. as a whole. [15] [The rest of the memorandum can be found in Appendix B].

The following day D/Plans, Colonel R. H. Barry, suggested to Gubbins, the new CD, the line they should take with NKVD:

> [We have] now entered a phase in which our efforts are concentrated upon preparing resistance groups to give the maximum support to forthcoming military operations, and it is essential for us to justify to the Supreme Commander that any allocation of aircraft for operations would have a direct bearing on this object.

We must warn N.K.V.D of the difficulties with which we are faced in this respect; since however, such agents as they wish to deliver to Europe are presumably charged with missions designed to assist in the defeat of Germany, our hand would be strengthened if N.K.V.D. could indicate to us: -

    a. in very general terms the type of mission on which each party is engaged;

    b. the methods by which the activities of these parties would be co-ordinated with military requirements.

We should then be in a position to point out to the Supreme Commander that these operations are designed as much as any others, to assist his plans.[16]

There was then a break in the correspondence until Massingham was told on 19 October 1943 that five Italians were to be sent to the Turin area and that they needed to obtain Eisenhower's agreement as soon a possible. As SAM was to have a meeting with General Ossipov on 21 October, he desperately needed an update of what was happening. In his telegram he commented: 'Our colleagues are extremely worried. We are more than ever convinced that much depends upon the immediate and successful completion of these operations.'[17] He was told that the Russian Section was just as worried. Rigi and Jungfrau were ready and waiting for an available plane but unfavourable meteorological conditions had curtailed all Special Duties Squadrons' activities across Western Europe.

    In his feedback from his meeting, SAM described Ossipov and Graur's attitude as sullen and hostile. They were bitter about what they saw as difficulties that had deliberately been put in front of these operations. Another issue arose when Massingham told SAM that the Allied Forces Headquarters refused the proposed infiltration to Italy, arguing that they 'could not tolerate any uncoordinated action.' An added complication was identified – the Americans.

We prepared draft stating that operation would be controlled by S.O.E. LONDON and that we would keep them fully informed. This however has not beeen passed and matter has been referred by AD/E back to ZP.

    Very much regret this and have stated our objections to inevitable delay which this will cause at an unfortunate time. We were however overruled by fear that, should Americans find out our control of these agents extends to granting of transport facilities only, they would accuse us of double-crossing them.

    We will do our best to press matter and will keep you informed. [18]

In a letter dated 26 October, addressed to C. F. A. 'Frederick' Warner in the Foreign Office with a copy to Mockler-Ferryman, SOE's director of operations, North-West Europe, Major Seddon asked for help in what appeared to be an intractable problem.

We are in disfavour with NKVD because of our lack of success in dropping various of their agents recently. Our efforts on their behalf (which have been very genuine) have been dogged by bad luck and bad weather, and I am afraid that, in spite of our explanations, they believe we are deliberately holding up the despatch of their people. This feeling has been increased by difficulties there have been about sending three of their agents into France. Sir Alexander Cadogan very naturally ruled that these men were not to be dropped into France without the consent of the French Committee of National Liberation and this has caused most vexatious delays and uncertainties, due in part to a difference of opinion between various sections of the Committee.

You will remember that in the case of the five men for Italy we were instructed to approach General Eisenhower. As a result we have had a telegram from our people in North Africa asking whether we shall control the activities of these agents after they are in Italy. The telegram states that it is AFHQ's [Allied Forces Headquarters] policy not to tolerate any uncoordinated action in their theatre of operations and they are obviously afraid that these men might form resistance groups or otherwise take para-military action conflicting with our own. The latter is, of course, entirely under the control of AFHQ.

I am afraid our answer to AFHQ's question must be negative, so, from the time the Russians reach Italy, we never expect to hear from them again. In these circumstances it would, I think, be useless for us to argue the point with AFHQ. The only course would be for the matter to be referred to the Combined Chiefs of Staff in Washington with a request that they should instruct General Eisenhower to allow the operation to take place. In fact I do not think there would be any danger of the five Russians accomplishing anything which could cause confusion or embarrassment to AFHQ.

The first question to be decided is whether the matter is politically of sufficient importance to be referred to the Combined Chiefs of Staff. If we tell the Russians that we cannot infiltrate these five men because AFHQ will not allow us to do so unless we control their activities after arrival, I am afraid the Russians will certainly regard this as a further instance of procrastination and non-cooperation on our part. In the present state of our relations with them such a reply would be likely to lead to an open breach and this would be extremely unfortunate, particularly at the present juncture.

Perhaps you will be good enough to consider the problem and give me your advice.[19]

George Taylor, director of SOE's overseas groups and missions, asked for a list of those Pickaxes not sent. Three members of the Orange party had been sent on 14 September, which left nine bodies waiting in the UK, the Rigi, Jungfrau and Eiger parties for Germany, the Everest party for Austria, and the Apache party for France. Those earmarked for Italy had not yet arrived.

SOE decided to place the responsibility on the NKVD to approach the French, but this led to the NKVD starting to suspect SOE's motives. A note dated 26 October stated:

As matter stands NKVD are nursing a bitter grievance which is likely to breed more general distrust of us in even higher quarters. It looks moreover as though the Russians will now invite the French Committee of Liberation, who will presumably comply, to transport their agents from Africa in this and future cases. We shall then lose control of all operations.

I have explained the position to the Secretary of State who entirely approves my view that we should at once inform the Russians that we are ready to transport these three agents [Apache] provided that it is understood that no precedent is established.[20]

It is worth noting that the whole of the last paragraph was underlined in blue pencil. While it was later pointed out that SOE had received no specific dividend from its collaboration with the NKVD, it was felt that they should continue their co-operation as best they could. A memorandum on the situation, dated 1 November 1943 (Appendix C), outlines the political complications of getting permission from the right quarters.

All this was happening during the thwarted attempts to get Rigi, Jungfrau and Everest missions off the ground which made matters extremely tense for the Russian Section. It can hardly have been a coincidence that, at the end of the Three Powers Conference between Churchill, Stalin, and Roosevelt in the Soviet Embassy in Tehran, SAM was given the following report by the Russian Section:

DPR.1 [Chichaev] has just informed me that he is instructed by Moscow to return all PICKAXES to USSR. He has asked for our assistance in effecting this.

I asked him if this meant no more PICKAXES would be sent and he stated that he presumed so.

He then stated that soviet was unfortunately unable to provide visa for D/P.4 [McLaughlin].

To straight question whether this all meant cessation of collaboration he said he presumed so but was not yet fully informed.

Please cable urgently exact situation.[21]

A carefully worded telegram was sent to the resident minister's office in Algiers on the same day asking him to speak with the SOE representative who would show the minister the correspondence regarding five men destined for Turin. There was a plea at the end, 'Please press General Eisenhower strongly to agree to SOE being authorised to make arrangements for dropping the five Soviet agents as requested by NKVD. Matter is urgent as there has been some delay in meeting request.'[22]

Hill's attempts to explain SOE's relative impotence as compared with the NKVD fell on deaf ears. In his *Reminiscences* he comments that the SOE was not as all-powerful as their Soviet counterparts, who automatically gave themselves any facilities they required without consulting anyone: 'Ossipov thinks the SOE has the same power in England, poor mut!'[23]

Christopher Warner, Under-Secretary at the Foreign Office with responsibility for Northern Europe, wrote a report the same day, seemingly for Churchill, outlining the above and adding:

> Our belief has been amply confirmed this morning. Our N.K.V.D. contact in this country, who is a member of the Embassy staff called Tchitchaev [Chichaev], sent for the head of our Russian section this morning and informed him that he had instructions from Moscow to say that, as we seemed incapable of sending their agents to Europe, they proposed to discontinue their attempts to use a method of infiltration which was obviously valueless. He asked for our co-operation in winding up the arrangements and in returning to Russia those agents who are still waiting to go.
>
> He added that he had instructions to say that the visa we had applied for in respect of a new member of our Moscow Mission due to go out to take the place of a man recently returned to this country would not be granted, and that for his own part his work with us would come to an end and he would in the future confine himself entirely to his diplomatic functions.
>
> This seems to us to be a particular unfortunate development at the present juncture, and I am anxious that you should know about it immediately. We telegraphed at once to our people in Russia informing them, and it will be interesting to see whether on the next few days they are asked to withdraw.
>
> There does not seem to be any action which we can usefully take at this end, but you may think it well to address a telegram to H.M. Ambassador on the subject. Doubtless George Hill will have communicated with him immediately he received our telegram.[24]

Given the urgency of the situation, a telegram was sent off at 2200 hours to the Ambassador in Algiers, requesting him to get permission from Eisenhower and the French to allow SOE to drop the five agents into Italy. There was also the comment that they were prepared to drop another three into France without permission.

Advice was sent to SAM to help in his meeting with Ossipov, which stated:

> We accept without condition all agents destined for GERMANY and AUSTRIA.
>
> All operations entailing dropping Soviet agents in occupied countries which are represented by properly constituted governments outside native soil must, prior to acceptance by us, have been agreed to by governments concerned after direct repeat direct consultation between them and Soviet.
>
> Close co-operation in all areas of mutual interest is ardently desired by us and we should if possible take advantage of present favourable political atmosphere to urge as strongly as possible for collaboration in BALKAN countries.[25]

Sir A. Clark Kerr, the British Ambassador in Moscow, wrote a memo to Loxley in the Foreign Office informing him that, after four hours of discussion with his counterparts, SAM had persuaded the NKVD to postpone for a month their decision about withdrawing their agents.

> As matters stand Hill's mission must inevitably come to an end unless we can convince the Russians that we are ready to give them a square deal. This would not only involve the loss of important contact established for our observers over the past two years but would leave aftermath of bitterness on the Russian side at a time when solid support should be given in practical ways to the agreement which the Three Powers Conference has reached on general principles.
>
> May I therefore strongly urge that everything possible should be done to deliver those Russian agents whom S.O.E. has already accepted for various destinations?[26]

Within days of this communication, the Russian Section received notification from the NKVD that they desired 'to terminate collaboration in respect of those clauses which relate to the infiltration of their agents, which may be taken in general to presage a total breakdown of SOE/NKVD collaboration.'[27]

Harold Macmillan, the British government's representative in the Mediterranean, felt that with the Lebanon crisis, the Soviet's approach was 'not opportune'. The Resident Minister in Algiers and the CFNL were both against any operations on behalf of the NKVD. They felt that that the Soviet Mission in North Africa was more favourable to the British than the French.[28]

On 4 November, London was informed that the CNFL had stated that André Philip was no longer concerned with SOE business and that General Cochet had been appointed as his replacement 'with full powers to act'. They were instructed to arrange personal contact with him to obtain permission to send in the three agents. When Seddon met Chichaev to tell him, they both had a good laugh over the situation as it had brought matters back to where they were several months before. SAM got to hear of it a few days later but did not think it funny.

> HILL sent a message to SEDDON via C.D. saying that he regretted that SEDDON had been so frank with CHICHAEV on this occasion. CHICHAEV might be sufficiently westernised to laugh with S.O.E. but HILL's chief contacts in Moscow who had heard the news when he had seen them the day before had been very sour about it, and would clearly remain so until authorisation had been given. This particular matter had been taken up on the highest level by the Foreign Office in the midst of the strain of the Moscow Conference in the hope that it would improve not only S.O.E./N.K.V.D. relations but Anglo-Russian relations generally.

It was useless to cry over spilt milk but HILL ventured to suggest that SEDDON should have endeavoured to arrange for a very senior official of S.O.E. to negotiate with General COCHET, and not to have taken CHICHAEV into his confidence until a decision had been made one way or the other.[29]

Circumstances changed quickly. Warner sent a memo to Gubbins stating his position and asked for his views.

We have heard from our people in Algiers that there seems to be no hope in extracting any decision from the French Committee of National Liberation at the moment upon the dropping of the three unfortunate N.K.V.D. agents in France. The Lebanon crisis has naturally left a difficult atmosphere, in addition to which there has been another upheaval in the French Special Services as a result of which our friend, General Cochet, has been forced to resign and things are somewhat in a state of flux. [30]

As the NKVD were suspicious of SOE's motives telling them to approach the French directly, Warner went on to say:

I feel strongly that the most practical step to take now would be to ask the Russians themselves to approach the French direct in Algiers and try to get a favourable decision. This will at least serve to remove any Russian suspicion that we are using the French complications as a mere excuse and are not really pressing the matter with the French at all.[31]

At the beginning of December, the Russian Section was informed by Gubbins that:

...no N.K.V.D. agents should be introduced into Allied countries whose governments were refugee, without the full knowledge and consent of these governments.[31]

This ruling, added to unavoidable delays in producing documents and obtaining air priorities, nearly brought about a rupture of SOE/NKVD relations at the end of 1943. Given the pressure from Moscow, the Foreign Office took an executive decision and resolved the matter a few days later, informing SAM that:

All efforts having failed to extract reply from French Committee I [Lord Cadogan] am informing S.O.E. that they may inform N.K.V.D. that they will deliver party on the understanding that no parties will in future be delivered to France except at the request of the French Committee with whom N.K.V.D. should take up the matter direct.[32]

THE END OF THE PICKAXE OPERATIONS

Operation Apache

On 5 January 1944, three more Pickaxes arrived in Britain after a two-and-a-half-day voyage on a cruiser. Unlike the earlier operations, none of their personal files have come to light. Also unlike other missions, their stay in Britain only lasted a month. The Apache party was made up of three men, M. S. Simonov, alias 'Marcel Simon', born in Rostov in 1914 and codenamed Stepan; A. A. Livanov, alias 'Antoine Laurier', born in Tiflis in 1914 and codenamed Aristide; and S. Rosov, alias 'Simon Rogiere', born in Voronezh in 1912.

As the Everest and Eiger parties were dispatched successfully on the 6 and 8 January, the Russian Section told SAM that if Apache went according to plan, they would be set for a record. It was not to be. When their flight was scheduled for 18 January, they were taken to Gaynes Hall, only to be told two hours after they arrived that it had been cancelled.

On the same day, news came through confirming that the CNFL had accepted the Soviet plan of infiltrating agents into France. A telegram to SAM informed him that:

> Since we have already accepted APACHE without reference to French, it is presumed that this present authorisation will cover further operations to the limit of five bodies, and we recommend that in your conversations with your colleague you should emphasise fact that any request entailing numbers in excess of five must be made subject of fresh approach to C.F.L.N.[1]

Without losing any time, a flight was arranged for that evening and Apache II took off from Tempsford. Marcel Simon and Antoine Laurier were successfully parachuted onto a dropzone near Lyon/Heyrieux in southern France. Clark made no mention of the Apache party in his book. It was not one of the more memorable missions; the *Bomber Command Diaries* reported that forty-seven Stirlings and seventeen Halifaxes were flying resistance flights that night.[2]

Apache III, the dropping of Simon Rogiere, was attempted on 8/9 February, but it was forced to return owing to bad weather over the dropzone. A second attempt on 11/12 February also returned without making the drop, owing to bad weather. When the third attempt failed on the 16th for the same reason, the operation had to be postponed until the March moon period. Despite all this, 'the agent stood up well to the strain'.

SAM was informed by the Russian Section that they very much regretted the unfortunate anti-climax. However, the attempt on 5/6 March was successful. Although there was no mention of it in Clark's book, Simon Rogiere successfully parachuted into the Lodovec area, near Clermont de L'Herault.[3]

Details of what became of the Apache party were revealed in a letter from Colonel Vivian to Roger Hollis, the head of MI5's F Division, who had responsibility for 'supervising' the country's Communist and other political groups. It read:

> With reference to Iscot 202 in Service 168 :
>
> We have just heard from [Air Commodore] Archie Boyle that a young French student was dropped in the neighbourhood of Lodeve/Clermont de l'Herault on 5.3.44, being one of a number whose parachuting into Europe was arranged through their organisation at the request of the Foreign Office.
>
> This young student was one of three others who arrived in this country on 5.1.44. The others were dropped in the region of Lyon/Heyrieux on 5.2.44. This student, who was dropped on 5.3.44, went by the name of S.V. ROZOW when he arrived in this country and D/P.4 [Captain McLaughlin] of your office will presumably have traces of him. When he was parachuted he was furnished with papers in the name of Simon Valanian ROSIERE of Swiss nationality, born 6.12.1912 in Geneva.
>
> We have no other information about him, but Boyle's records describe all three as young French students of the lower classes much the same as a previous group of very young Frenchmen who were described as politically-minded of the student class and obviously looking upon their trip from the adventurous point of view.[4]

On 17 March 1946, Kim Philby, who was secretly working for the NKVD, wrote to Hollis informing him that there were a number of answer stations in France manned by NKVD agents dropped by SOE between March 1942 and March 1944.

> It would seem however, that Moscow had previously had wireless communication with Occupied France for we know that the first agent sent to London under the S.O.E. and N.K.V.D. agreement – one Anna Ouspenskaia by alias – was charged 'to reach Paris at all costs and there to visit certain Soviet agents, with one object – re-establishing the wireless communications between Occupied France and the U.S.S.R.' She was landed at Lannion Bay, North France on 10.1.42 and took no wireless equipment with her.

Incidentally 11 N.K.V.D. agents were put into France by S.O.E. Ouspenkaia was probably Polish – at any rate not French, three others were obviously Spaniards, the remaining 7, six men and a woman were French Communists who escaped to Russia at the beginning of the war.

All these agents were put into France without the knowledge of the French authorities although by 5.2.44 the French National Committee had agreed on the landing of 5 agents for purely military purposes.

...The material is not in itself particularly interesting, but the analysis does prove that the N.K.V.D., in wartime were working in close cooperation with elements of the dissolved Comintern. It also proves that the N.K.V.D. agents parachuted into France were given political rather than intelligence assignments – a conclusion which S.O.E. had themselves arrived at.[5]

What became of the Apache party remains unknown.

Operation Bologna

By the beginning of 1944, events on the Eastern Front were changing rapidly. As the Red Army advanced into south-east Europe, the Foreign Office and SIS began to worry that their intelligence networks in Bulgaria, Hungary, and Austria might be jeopardised. Despite the volte face, offering to send Soviet agents into Germany and Austria from Italy now seemed politically advantageous, especially if British agents could be flown out of Hungary and military intelligence and plans exchanged. With the Allied successes in the Mediterranean, agents destined for the Balkans and south-eastern Europe could safely be flown in from Massingham or Maryland, near Bari on the Adriatic coast, rather than from Tempsford.

On 4 January 1944, the same day that Jungfrau was sent, plans were put in place to fly four 'Italians' from Moscow direct to Massingham for training before being transferred to Maryland for infiltration into northern Italy. A note in the file suggested the NKVD had learned lessons; the agents were described as 'fully documented and equipped parachutists.'[6]

Towards the end of January 1944, SAM was sent a memo confirming that Emanuel D'Astier (a French Resistance leader who had joined de Gaulle's government-in-exile in Algiers) had provided Chichaev with permission to infiltrate five agents ready to be sent into France. A week later D'Astier sent London a telegram stating that Cochet's original authorisation had been supported by the CFLN.

With this qualification QUOTE you have confirmed to me that if agents in question intend to enter into relations with subversive political movements or organisations in France, these relations will be regularised in the first place with

C.F.L.N. which is recognised by your government as sole representative of all French patriots engaged in fighting against Hitlerism UNQUOTE.[7]

A week later, Major Manderstam, who was attached to the SOE in Algiers, flew to Bari with XA.2, an unknown officer in SOE's German and Austrian Section, to discuss the problems in handling Etna with Major J. H. Darton, SOE's representative at Maryland. The plan was also to discuss the potential for sending other agents that SOE might be asked to infiltrate through Mediterranean bases. On 21 January, the Russian Section sent X, Lieutenant Colonel Ronald Thornley, head of the German and Austrian Section, a memo outlining SOE's policy.

INFILTRATION OF SOVIET AGENTS FROM MARYLAND
The principle of assisting N.K.V.D. to infiltrate agents into occupied Italy and Austria has been accepted by S.O.E. and certain bodies are already trained and waiting in the U.S.S.R. for completion of arrangements.

The S.O.E. operational department have been instructed by the Air Ministry that such operations shall be carried out from our advanced base in Southern Italy.

At present the D/P [Russian] Section has no representation in Maryland and in order to deal with Pickaxe operations it would be necessary to arrange for this. It is to be anticipated that the D/P Section will be called upon to provide a Conducting Officer and a representative of the N.K.V.D. to carry out all the details of these operations.

Since there is at present no detailed information upon which to gauge the possible period during which such an officer might be fully employed, it would seem uneconomical to appoint a representative to Maryland solely for Russian affairs. It appears though that the problem might be solved if the D/P Section representative could be attached to X [German and Austrian] Section's Mission and when not engaged with Pickaxe duties should work for X.

The question of the Soviet representative is more difficult but as there are I understand both military and civil Soviet Missions in Italy, arrangements might be made for such an officer to be attached to one or the other. Possibly they might only ask for one of their representatives from U.K. to go there for such operation, but the problem of his entry into and sojourn in Italy would, however, remain the same.

I believe that we shall have to ask Maryland to obtain a holding house for us there, somewhere within easy reach of our headquarters and naturally also near the Russian Mission concerned. But I should recommend that such an establishment should come directly under the control of X/A.3's [an unknown officer in SOE's German and Austrian Section] Mission, to whom all orders and directives from London headquarters would go.

X/A.2 [an unknown officer in SOE's German and Austrian Section] is fully trained in Pickaxe duties and aware of the situation, and he would be an ideal chief representative, since he could deal with all questions affecting both the Conducting Officer and the local Soviet representative.

I am giving you these details, therefore, in the hope that you may be able, after discussion with S/A.e [an unknown SOE officer] to accept the principle of his acting on our behalf.

I should be grateful if you will obtain his comments on this proposal, based on the experience he has lately had in Italy, and I shall welcome any scheme which he may suggest for the proper solution of this problem.[8]

Lieutenant Colonel Thornley's opinion was to accept the proposal with the proviso that the NKVD were told that they would not be offered the same facilities as in London and that, as Maryland would be a transport agency only, all agents had to arrive fully equipped, otherwise they would be sent straight back to the USSR. Aware that the NKVD had a policy of not allowing the Pickaxes to mix with other agents, he pointed out that they might need a number of houses to accommodate them. SOE agreed to make the necessary arrangements with the Allied Forces Headquarters for any operations out of Maryland.

I think there is no doubt that our arrangement with the N.K.V.D. binds us to make the necessary arrangements for them with our own military authorities – i.e. the position is that they come to us with bodies to infiltrate and we make all the arrangements to infiltrate them from our bases. In doing so we are just as much obliged to square A.F.H.Q [Allied Forces Headquarters] in regard to the use of Italian bases as we should be to square any relevant authorities in ENGLAND for using TEMPSFORD.[9]

On 11 February 1944, Victor Cannon-Brookes (AD/S.1), private secretary to Lord Selborne, wrote a memo informing Gubbins that Roundell Palmer, the Earl of Selbourne who had taken over from Dalton as Head of Economic Warfare, had overheard Comte de Chevigny, one of the CFNL in Algiers, mentioning that the Vichy government was making out that the Soviets were dropping parachutists into France. He suggested that he may have seen an article in the *Evening Standard* on or before 11 January which mentioned it. While the Comte poured scorn on the idea, arguing that it was impossible for the Soviets to undertake such operations, the SOE's Special Operations Section wasn't sure whether it was Vichy propaganda or whether they had actually caught one or more of the Pickaxes. The response was that they had no evidence that a recently dropped agent had been captured, but they had learned that a Russian woman (Anna Ouspenskaya) had been captured almost immediately on landing eighteen months earlier.[10]

When worry was expressed that not having visas might delay the departure of the agents into Italy, they were reassured that none were needed, 'provided military authorities are in agreement'.

On 15 February, SAM informed the Russian Section that two more Pickaxes were ready to be sent to Britain and dropped into northern Italy, either flown direct from the UK or infiltrated by the southern route. They were 38-year-old M. V. Aliev, alias Alberti Valentino, born in Odessa, and 40-year-old I. P. Kourakine, alias Cortona Pietro, born in Gorki. Both were reported to have been trained parachutists and 'fully documented', but that assistance might be needed in bringing their documents up to date. They were to be flown from Cairo to Bari, arriving in the third or fourth week of April, and from there, dropped in the Forli – Faenza – Modegliano area, south-east of Bologna. When the Air Ministry investigated, they considered the area unsuitable for blind drops and suggested extending the triangle north-west to the Forli – Firenze – Bologna area.[11]

The Bologna agents were described as a 'party of high importance for political reasons'. The plan was for D/P 103, Captain J. D. Killick, sometimes spelt Gillick, to accompany them.[12] There was also the matter of a signal from Massingham to London with an instruction from C.3 Special Operations, which stated, underlined in red pencil:

Commander-in-Chief has directed that all agencies shall avoid scrupulously taking sides in current Italian political situation. Please see to it that all concerned are so informed.... Any activity involving Italian politics have always been most carefully co-ordinated. Commander-in-Chief's local political advisors both American and British.

I bring this to your attention in case the PICKAXE landing advocating for MANDERSTAM could be destined for work which would conflict with this order.

The Sir ANDREW CUNNINGHAM/ETNA episode is not forgotten. Therefore please direct me whether or not I am to inform Commander-in-Chief of MARYLAND's new commitment in this parish.[13]

The matter had to be taken up by higher quarters but Gubbins pointed out that General Harold Alexander, Deputy Commander-in-Chief, North Africa, and General Henry Wilson, Commander-in-Chief, Near East, would probably object if they knew Soviet agents had already been put into Italy. He acknowledged that the agents could have been nothing more than political agitators and that the matter had best be dealt with by Harold Macmillan and the Allied Commander-in-Chief in Algiers.[14] Following their discussions with the 15 Army Group, they decided in favour and authorised their immediate despatch.

The difficulties this created for the Russian Section were aptly put to A.D., George Taylor, director of SOE's overseas groups and missions:

The understandings we have with the N.K.V.D. is that all their agents are destined for active sabotage against the enemy and officially we have accepted this, though there may be reasons for doubt on occasions. The specific bodies destined for Italy have been accepted on this same understanding but it would be impossible for us to guarantee that they are not associated with political intentions, since they go as representatives of a government which deals almost exclusively with the communist element in the areas in which they operate.

In answering this we shall have to take our stand by the assurance given us by the N.K.V.D., but since these Italian bodies were proposed and accepted at a time before the Italian surrender, it is almost certain that they are not connected with the new Italian political set-up.[15]

By 26 February, London was told that Maryland had made all the arrangements and had got clearance for the agents to be delivered. It was not until a month later that Lieutenant Colonel Sporberg forwarded a letter to British commanders abroad regarding the proposed dropping of Soviet agents into Northern Italy.

Major-General Commanding S.O. Mediterranean Theatre.
Commander, Force 133, Cairo.
Commander, Force 266.
Commander, Maryland.
Commander, Massingham.

As you are probably aware, an agreement exists between S.O.E. and its Russian counterpart for mutual assistance in the fulfilment of their respective roles.

This agreement had, of course, the approval of the Foreign Office when it was negotiated and its implementation by us is agreed with that Department at every step.

The principal way in which the agreement operates on our side is the offer, from time to time, by S.O.E. of its facilities for the infiltration of Russian agents into various areas of Europe.

The policy decisions involved in any such arrangements are made by the appropriate authorities in London, principally the Foreign Office, and are by no means merely the decisions of S.O.E. When therefore the facilities available to any S.O.E. force are required for the carrying out of the operation, there is no question of such assistance being asked merely as a favour to a section of S.O.E. On the contrary, S.O.E. in carrying out such operations, is executing the policy of H.M.G., under the immediate guidance of the Foreign Office.

Similarly, no operation will ever be authorised by this Headquarters unless and until it has been properly cleared with any local authority with a legitimate interest in it.

Once therefore, a decision to carry out such an operation has been taken, the Section of S.O.E. responsible for its implementation has the right to expect from any Commander and his staff such assistance as is within their scope and can reasonably be given with due regard to the carrying out of their other duties.

I cannot too strongly emphasise that I expect this assistance to be given loyally and ungrudgingly without regard to private views, political prejudice or anxiety as to consequences. Commanders can rest assured that they considerations have been fully weighed before the decision to provide the facilities in question for the Russians was taken.

The Commanders, moreover, entertain no doubt that real importance is attached to this work and it is essential that it should be in no way prejudiced by lack of enthusiasm and support.

I do not intend to suggest that this necessary cooperation has been lacking in the past, but I would ask Commanders to ensure that the position as outlined above is fully understood by all concerned and to see that a fully co-operative attitude is adopted by all under their command towards the D/P Section or its representatives in the execution of their duties.[16]

Despite all the intense negotiations on their behalf, the four agents of Operation Bologna never left the Soviet Union. The SOE prevaricated by telling the NKVD that the delay had been caused by their inability to find suitable conducting officers, fluent in Italian.

On 3 May, London was told that 'the principal agent had a serious operation which meant they would not be able to leave for between four and six weeks while he recuperated.' When Massingham commented that they didn't want Killick unemployed in Cairo for six weeks, arrangements were made for him to return to London.[17] NKVD expressed their regret for the inconvenience caused. A fortnight later, SAM reported that NKVD had decided to abandon the operation.

The Red Army's Intercession

When Hill returned to Moscow in April 1944, after an absence of fifty days, he sensed that the agreement reached by the Allies at the Three Powers Conference (28 November – 1 December 1943) had diminished slightly. The previous December, Hill had been optimistic about the future, but the deterioration in relations over what should happen in Poland and over the Italian shipping controversy made him worried. There was also another important factor. Russian nerves were being stretched to the limit. Despite their military successes, the Russians were aware of the great risks they were taking and the heavy costs they were incurring. According to SOE's official 'Notes on the Russian Section of S.O.E.':

They now needed time to reorganise their forces and consolidate their gains. To do so successfully they must depend for the next few months on Allied action in the West. Despite these problems, however, HILL thought that things could be much worse. So far, the Russians had been reasonable over Roumania, and in other ways had manifested their desire to behave as a major Power and to maintain the understanding reached at the Moscow and Teheran Conferences.[18]

On 17 April 1944, Chichaev informed SAM that the NKVD was able to do the job on its own. This left Hill with little to do except wait for his recall to London. A week later, SOE entertained Chichaev for dinner; after his third cocktail, he was reported by Major Manderstam as saying:

> On the whole we are most dissatisfied with the three years of our cooperation with your organisation. There was a time when we needed you and needed you badly, the results however were poor.... The necessity for it has now passed. We are doing very well without it, the Red Army sees to it.[19]

The Red Army's successful advances on the Eastern Front extended south-west into Ukraine and had pushed the German army out of Sevastopol, the Black Sea port. More than five million troops massed along the front lines ready to start Operation Bagration. As the generals were confident of reaching Warsaw, Bucharest, and Budapest by the end of the year, they would be able to recapture airfields, repair them and then use their own planes to infiltrate their agents into south-east Europe. On 7 May, SOE learned that several Soviet agents had already been dropped into Bulgaria.

In early May, London informed SAM that the question had been raised whether there was any need to maintain the safe houses used in the past to accommodate the Pickaxes. Hill was told to ask the NKVD whether they 'envisaged any further traffic'. The reply was 'not at present'. Chichaev informed SOE that he had been advised by Moscow that there would be no further Pickaxes in 'the foreseeable future'.[20]

There was an event earlier in the year which may have been a trigger to the ending of the SAM mission. In early February 1944, Erich Vermehren, a German member of the Abwehr, the equivalent of the NKVD and SOE, defected with his wife to the British in Istanbul. To avoid recriminations against his extended family, the BBC and British press announced that they had captured him and the Abwehr's secret codes. The latter disinformation so convinced Hitler that he abolished the organisation, ordering Heinrich Himmler, the head of the SS, to take over its intelligence function. NKVD was very keen to find out what information the British had extracted from Vermehren in relation to the Soviets, and made a request to the Russian Section in London.

A telegram from SAM, dated 14 May, stated:

> Contents of Z.P. telegram 497 March 4th to Moscow was duly communicated to MOLOTOV but this was after story had broken sensationally in world's press and after D/PR.1 [Chichaev] had asked that his organisation should have

sight of VER+REN's statements. In particular they wish for such information as impinged in any way on solution German-Turkish exchange of intelligence concerning Red Army and matters appertaining to espionage on Turkish-Soviet frontier.

This request was passed to C [Sir Stewart Menzies].

C's organisation in due course stated that VER+REN had not repeat not dealt with Russian Intelligence and that no information concerns VER+REN's statement could be passed to NKVD. In this communication name of German official in Turkey who dealt with Russian was given but S.O.E. were instructed not to pass this N.K.V.D. This agreement has of course been observed.[21]

While the end of the Pickaxe agreement might have been a weight off the Russian Section's shoulders, they made enquiries about whether the NKVD were willing to share the dropzones in Bulgaria as they were doing already in Yugoslavia. In the meantime, the SAM mission in Moscow was expected to be closed immediately and Hill ordered to return to London. In the final paragraph of the earlier telegram SAM commented that

D/PR.1 on being informed on morning of my departure expressed keen disappointment and regret. I was so impressed by his sincerity that I ventured to telegraph D/4 [an unknown officer at Baker Street] from CAIRO urging C. should be asked to reconsider matter. But C. remained adamant.[22]

At the end of May 1944, Major Seddon left the organisation and was replaced as Section Head by Major Manderstam. The following month, he invited General Ossipov to come to London to discuss the possibility of redrafting the SOE/NKVD charter. The offer was never accepted.

MAJOR MANDERSTAM'S
ENDEAVOURS

With the Allied advance through France, Belgium, and Holland being thwarted by the German counter-offensive in the winter of 1944, SOE was keen to strike back. The French Resistance reported being harassed by Russians, Ukrainians, Georgians, and other Soviet nationalities in German uniforms. From interviews with hundreds of captured former Red Army soldiers held in POW camps in Normandy and Britain, SOE estimated that there were over a million Soviet POWs who had been forced to fight in the Wehrmacht and up to five million working as slave labourers in German factories. In Nikolai Tolstoy's *Victims of Yalta,* he noted how in early August 1944, SOE planned with General de Gaulle's Free French and SHAEF Headquarters to recruit selected prisoners, train them and infiltrate them back into France to try to encourage other anti-partisan Russians to defect. Major Manderstam, who interviewed many of the POWs, found several who were keen to be dropped in Germany where they would establish active resistance to the Nazis who, they argued, had cheated and betrayed their cause.[1]

Creating a viable resistance in Germany was thought a valuable contribution to the Allied efforts. However, one day Manderstam was called to the office of General Gerald Templer, the head of SOE's German Section. He relates the conversation in his book, *From the Red Army to the SOE:*

> 'Mandy, from now on there will be no operations into Germany, because the C [SIS] people think we are a lot of amateurs and decreasing the chances of their men. It's an order – no operations into Germany.' This ban from the Foreign Office ... appeared counter-productive and I said, 'But surely, sir, our objective is to tax the German security forces?'
>
> 'Yes,' he replied. He then asked me if, during one of my fits of mental diarrhoea I had come up with anything useful, and I put to him a scheme which became known as Operation Periwig.
>
> First of all I enquired of the general if he was familiar with the sayings of Voltaire. He blew a cloud of smoke from his inevitable cigarette, gave me a look of an indulgent uncle who was humouring an exasperating nephew, and he boomed, 'Voltaire? No! Why should I? What has he got to do with it?'

Voltaire, I explained, had said that if God did not exist it would be necessary to invent Him.

'Since our operations into Germany are stopped, why not invent them?' I suggested. 'What about building up an image that we are still dropping people and are continuing our operations, so the Germans will be chasing their own tails?'

'Damned good idea,' Templer responded enthusiastically.[2]

With the assistance of Flying Officer Ken Potter, SOE set up a completely bogus organisation of German agents operating within the Third Reich. Manderstam had interviewed captured SS officers at the tented POW camp on the racecourse at Kempton Park, near Sunbury on Thames in Surrey. They all vehemently denied being Nazis and argued that they had been only 'acting under orders'. He identified half-a-dozen rabid Nazis, two of whom assured him that that they would do anything to speed Hitler's downfall. If the RAF could drop them back inside Germany, they would work for the Allies.

After a severe grilling by Manderstam, they were convinced that he trusted them and believed their protestations of innocence of war crimes and hatred of the Nazis. Despite knowing that one of them, called Schiller, had acted as a double agent and was responsible for the death of many agents on both sides, Manderstam briefed them as if they were going on a genuine mission. They were given 'messages in easily-breakable codes, including the names of loyal Nazis, leading members of the Gestapo, who were identified as Allied agents.'[3]

A map was prepared identifying thirty-two dropzones across Germany, close to the fighting areas, and papers were created suggesting that containers packed with false information could be parachuted, ostensibly for the German agents, but in reality to deceive the enemy. Leo Marks, the head of SOE's code section was involved in their signals training. They were provided with small silk sheets on which were specially printed secret four-figure radio codes of hundreds of imaginary resistance groups. The plan was for the BBC in London to start broadcasting messages using these codes informing the imaginary groups to keep silent until orders to take action were received.[4]

In order for the enemy to believe this plan, the agents would have to have an 'accident'. Enquiries were made at Ringway to develop a parachute that would not open. This proved difficult, as the parachutist would normally check it before the drop. The dispatcher could take action to stop the ripcord opening, but that would involve him being in the know. Yet another option was to drop the agents below 150 feet, so that the chute would have no time to open. According to Manderstam,

The two German 'agents' were flown separately from Tempsford airfield, near Cambridge. One can imagine the thoughts that went through their heads as they passed over the English coast and roared towards Germany – how they had fooled the imbecile British and how they would be welcomed back to the Fatherland when their story was known. I'm certain they had no suspicion their parachutes were defective.

They were dropped at widely different locations over Germany and were picked up dead, the apparent victims of unfortunate accidents. Later on, we received reports that the phoney documents found on the bodies had caused quite a stir. Gestapo faithful were arrested, protesting the German equivalent 'we've been framed', and Himmler's men were chasing round in circles for months.[5]

A special radio station was set up to broadcast programmes in German with the aim of accelerating the corruption of Germany. Listeners' attention was guided to the pleasures and benefits of avarice, crime, greed, and lust. It sought to foment envy, suspicion, and hatred by spreading rumours of the sexual depravity of influential military and government figures.[6]

Dead carrier pigeons were dropped with containers attached to their legs. The RAF dropped thousands of live pigeons in specially adapted boxes with the intention that people would find them, open the container and fill in the enclosed questionnaire with details about German troop dispositions etc. Manderstam claimed that he arranged to send some with the questionnaires already completed. In this way the Mayor of a German town was suggested to be providing a safe house for British agents. He was arrested and shot. 'The Gestapo thinking that they had been very clever in liquidating Allied agents with Teutonic efficiency. I was delighted by this little caper and the deaths of the Nazis had to be weighed against the number of lives saved by keeping the Gestapo otherwise engaged.'[7]

Manderstam had discovered that the Allies were planning to repatriate several million Russians from France and Germany. Knowing that they would face execution or the gulag, he endeavoured, without success, to pressure the government to change its mind. He identified a group of about forty Russian POWs who were willing to go on commando missions, sabotage Germany industry and encourage their compatriots to surrender. His plan was to train them to be real Pickaxes, drop them into Germany to link up with fellow countrymen in factories and organise sabotage and subversion. He believed that a party of Russians trained in England would create a tremendous impact by promising their compatriots fair treatment if they surrendered. He supervised their training, organised uniforms for them, provided them with parachute training at Ringway and 'safe houses' near Kempton Park.

The first mission, using four men, was all set up and ready to go when I was informed by General Gubbins that we must obtain Foreign Office consent. There was a further complication. SOE and NKVD had reciprocal missions in Moscow and London. Our man in Moscow was a shady character, Brigadier George Hill, who must have been consulted by the Foreign Office and who sent a message, saying clearance from the Soviet representatives was imperative before we went any further.

This gave me no choice but to approach the head of the NKVD Mission in London, Colonel Ivan Chichaev, who said that he would pass my request to Moscow, which in all probability meant the chief of the Soviet secret police and spy networks, L. P. Beria. The next I knew, after a lapse of several weeks, was a stern warning from our Foreign Office not to proceed with the operation.

I was furious and, completely against all the rules of protocol, I sent a signal to Brigadier Hill, whom I blamed for this turn of events. If the NKVD had been looking for an efficient representative they could not have found a better one than him, I told Hill.

Gubbins tore a strip off me when he heard about it. 'You can't do that sort of thing,' he said. 'I understand how you feel, and to some extent I agree with you, but you should know better.'

Hill, during a visit to London, confirmed he had used his influence to stop my Russian parachutists. He sent for me and said with a sneer, 'So you are Manderstam. If there is one man I would like to see shot at dawn it's you.'

I told him the feeling was fully reciprocated.

I made it clear I thought he was taking the Foreign Office for a ride and we parted the best of enemies....

I was sure George Hill was a triple agent. There was, in my opinion, no other explanation for his conduct and for the subsequent events other than he was feeding information to the British, the Russians and the Germans. Even when he was liaising with the NKVD on an official basis, I believe Hill supplied to them a great deal of important information and received little in return.

...Ivan Chichaev and I also had a friendly, if guarded relationship. The analogy of a game of chess is often used to describe negotiations with Soviet representatives and that was how it was whenever I met Chichaev. He would make a move. I made a counter move. We each conceded a pawn or two and the exchanges invariably ended in stalemate.

Our negotiations over the forty Russians were typical. Some time after the operations into Germany had been aborted, Chichaev asked if he could be allowed to interview the men. I pointed out that his own superiors had torpedoed the plan and there seemed little to be gained from his proposed interview. In any case, the men would be returned to the POW camp, where he could apply through the normal channels to see them.[8]

When Manderstam was unable to delay Chichaev from seeing the POWs, he told them of his proposed visit. He claimed that they bowed their heads and promised never to go back to Russia. When one jumped out of a three-storey window rather than return, Manderstam made plans to help the prisoners 'disappear'. When Chichaev was informed that they had 'escaped', he nearly had a heart attack.

'It's you, Manderstam. You did it. I'll report you for this.'

'All right,' I replied. 'Go and see the General.'

He did, and he told Gubbins, 'Manderstam engineered the escape of forty prisoners to prevent me interviewing them.'

Gubbins put on his best display of indignation. 'How dare you accuse one of my officers! What evidence have you got? I can assure you we do not go in for that sort of thing.'

Chichaev, when he calmed down, accepted the episode as just another nuance in the fortunes of war. We remained on friendly terms and, as a gesture of goodwill, I took him to the theatre to see a performance of James Bridie's comedy *Storm in a Teacup*, which was made into a film starring Rex Harrison and Vivien Leigh. The sophisticated dialogue completely flummoxed the Russian. 'Where is the moral?' he kept asking, as he could not understand how Westerners could go to the theatre merely to be entertained and not instructed.

Chichaev was also perplexed by the way in which I was able to contradict the official line, especially as the Foreign Office appeared to be intent on pleasing the Russians at all costs. He protested to Gubbins. 'Manderstam is a nice person, but he argues too much. If you would order him not to argue with me, then he would be a really first rate man.' Gubbins laughed, but otherwise paid no attention to the request. He and Chichaev got on well together socially, and Gubbins gave a party in Chichaev's honour.[9]

During the party a drinking competition between Gubbins and Chichaev ensued with them matching each other, drink for drink, mixing vodka, whisky, gin and wine. Chichaev was left standing, albeit with a silly grin on his face and wobbling a little, while Gubbins was slumped over the table.[10]

O'Sullivan relates an occasion when Manderstam told Chichaev that he had been disappointed by the NKVD's lack of support for his scheme to send Russian POWs on commando missions in Germany. He noted that, despite a 'very friendly atmosphere' existing between Hill and Ossipov in Moscow, there had been no results. Chichaev responded,

Why not? Brigadier Hill keeps an open house. He gives extremely good dinners. He is not a nuisance in any way. Why should not General Ossipov be very friendly with your Brigadier? They will go on patting each other on the back for the rest of their natural lives![11]

Manderstam identified for Chichaev the differences between their two organisations.

You are part and parcel of NKVD which concerns itself with matters of internal security, collecting intelligence, propaganda, counter-espionage, meting out justice, enforcing sentences, such as sending people to Siberia, shooting them etc. we are different – we are purely and simply a military organisation which was called into existence to support the Army by dealing with targets of importance to the conduct of the war, under the direction of the military command.[12]

THE YALTA CONFERENCE AND THE
END OF THE SOE/NKVD AGREEMENT

In January 1945, Geberal Gubbins, with Lord Selborne's support, recommended that Manderstam should visit Moscow to replace Hill. The plan was to consolidate his work and to negotiate a new agreement between the SOE and NKVD by which they could work together in the countries surrounding Germany, and later in Germany itself. Manderstam stated that they were not informed why Hill returned but suggested the most likely reason was that 'he had done his worst and lost interest.' The Foreign Office vetoed Manderstam's appointment, sending instead Colonel Anthony Benham, who, according to Manderstam, had been a regular soldier, spoke no Russian, and had a drink problem.[1]

The NKVD in Moscow expressed interest in the talks but demanded to see a full agenda, which after vetting by the Foreign Office, was sent in March.

> The Soviet reaction was that the whole matter concerned only the present and had no bearing on the future....
>
> On 12th September, 1945, a letter was circulated by V/CD [Sporberg], stating that C.D. [General Gubbins] had ruled, in agreement with the Foreign Office that the Mission should be withdrawn, the date of closing to coincide with the winding up of the Military Mission, i.e. 1st October.[2]

After attending the Yalta Conference in February 1945, Hill returned in Churchill's plane to London where he reported to Gubbins at SOE's headquarters on Baker Street. In his memoirs he commented that

> The purpose of my being called home was to try and clear up a number of serious difficulties between SOE and NKVD. A tricky task indeed. Both sides were about equally to blame for the strained relations. SOE perhaps a bit more to blame, for the dropping of the saboteurs had been a farce from the word go; on the other hand NKVD had many sins and omissions to answer for. Sir Colin [Gubbins] was frank and broad-minded. Keen to right matters if possible.[3]

In March 1945, SOE prepared a draft revision of the 'Charter'. They suggested that foreign workers in Germany and Austria should be recruited to sabotage industrial production and target road, rail, and water transport as well as the personnel engaged in U-boat production. They also suggested that attacks should be made on an underground Nazi organisation in Czechoslovakia and that the SOE and NKVD should focus on supplying resistance groups for a potential uprising.

Vyacheslav Molotov, the Soviet Foreign Commissar, received SAM's proposals on 22 March. Vsevolod Merkulov, the head of the Soviet secret police, intelligence, and counter intelligence, recommended rejecting them, commenting that, 'During the period of cooperation the agreement has achieved no significant results. On the contrary, in several cases the British have acted in an illoyal fashion. We propose to reject General [sic] Hill's proposal to sign a new agreement.' Molotov agreed with him, and despite the early enthusiasm for Soviet-British relations, Stalin agreed to reject them as well.[4]

Hill returned to Moscow with newly promoted Major Graham of the Intelligence Corps, and during a dinner at the Aragvi restaurant, Direktor Fitin told him that there was no need for a new agreement if Britain acted openly and honestly to fight the common enemy. Chichaev was to be recalled and subsequent talks would only be held in Moscow. In response, London withdrew Hill on 11 May. After a farewell dinner, he later commented that,

> I was conscious of the honour that was being accorded to me. We looked back over the four years between October 1941 and May 1945, dwelling more on the successes than the failure of liaison between SOE and NKVD. Towards the end of the evening, I asked Ossipov (Ovakimyan) to give me an address where I could send letters, for over the four years our only link, when apart, had been his telephone number.
>
> 'An address?' asked Ossipov, looking genuinely puzzled. 'What for?'
>
> 'For letters. You and I have worked together for years, faced dangers side by side, so, naturally, I'd like to keep contact, even if only to send you a seasonal greeting once a year.'
>
> Ossipov shook his head firmly. 'Quite unnecessary. If our respective organisations wish to keep contact or work together, communications will be arranged through the official channels. Otherwise there can be no question of contact between us, or call for letters!'
>
> Verily, the cold war had started.[5]

Hill left Moscow and was flown to Berlin where he took up a position in the British administration of the occupied city. He was present at the German surrender ceremony on 9 May 1945 at Karlhorst. Soviet researchers suggest his wife tried to commit suicide when he asked for a divorce. He returned to Moscow in October 1945 and saw his mistress before taking up employment as Regional

Controller of British European Airways in Prague in August 1946. In December 1947, he became director of Appolinaris Brunnen, a British-owned mineral water company in Bad Neuenahr.[6]

Chichaev left the U.K. in April 1945, with his family, to return to Moscow. Colonel GRAUR told Brigadier Hill that he had arrived safely, and although Brigadier Hill repeatedly said that he would like to see him, he never showed his face at the SAM Mission. Graur said that Chichaev was severing his connection with the Soviet organisation and was going into the Diplomatic Service, having obtained a post in the Balkans.[7]

Foot commented that the NKVD gave Hill no advice and that no fragment of the experiences of the party-dominated partisan groups was ever passed officially to SOE. Although SOE provided the NKVD with some data about explosive devices, they got nothing in return except, according to O'Sullivan, complaints when a few agents were quite unavoidably delayed by the vagaries of western European weather and the unavailability of suitable aircraft.[8]

From 1943 Chichaev was said to have acted as NKVD's liaison with other governments-in-exile in London, and he is said to have run an agent network of émigré officials from Eastern Europe. Manderstam claimed that he was invited to defect by Chichaev with the offer of being promoted to a general. His response was,

'Where – in the Lubianka? And how long will it last, twenty-four hours?'
'I give my word of honour.'
I told him not to take me for a fool.[9]

When the war ended in May 1945, Chichaev was sent to Prague where he became NKVD's station chief with the cover of Ambassador-at-large before taking up a post in Finland as political adviser to the Soviet Embassy. In 1947 he returned to Moscow and became department head, then deputy chairman of the newly created Committee of Information, intended to unite military and political intelligence.[10]

Chichaev's role in London was taken over in March 1945 by Philip Kislitsin, who is thought to have organised Burgess and Maclean's flight to the Soviet Union in 1951. In a letter addressed to Evelyn MacBarnet of MI5, with the signature blanked out, questions were asked about whether the two British agents might have been recruited by Chichaev.[11]

The NKVD provided London with valuable information about the 'German oil dumps, the defences around the port of Le Havre, details of factories in France, blockade-running ships as well as information on the partisan movement in the USSR. They also provided documents, uniforms and insignia of German, Hungarian, and Romanian troops. In exchange, London provided NKVD with information on the German defences around Kirkenes in Norway, escaped Soviet POWs, 'events in Poland' and Romanian shipping. In the hope of gaining reciprocal information, they also provided them with what were called 'Patriarchs'. These contained details obtained from captured Germans and British/American agents about the fate of some of the Pickaxes.[12]

SOE documents show that the NKVD were provided with thirty-six 'Welbikes' (collapsible motorbikes that could be dropped by parachute), twelve wireless sets and two field sets. Their request for SOE's top-secret 'Welmans', one-, two-, and three-man submarines, was met with the polite response from the Navy that they were still undergoing trials. In their attempts to foil German counter-intelligence plans, NKVD and SOE ran agents together and manufactured a range of false documents. Both sides also exchanged 'large sums' of foreign currency.[13]

Hill visited a Soviet parachute and partisan school, a collective farm and the front line at Leningrad from where he sent a detailed report. Chichaev and Krassowski were taken round The Thatched Barn at Borehamwood, SOE's camouflage section, and The Frythe, near Old Welwyn, their wireless and weapons research and development. Of particular interest were the latest developments in camouflage, silent arms and underwater craft.[14]

Chichaev asked Major Manderstam whether he could be provided with

...a list of our 'toys', the special devices used by SOE agents, which Brigadier Hill had promised to him? These 'toys' included gas pistols, pencil guns and a poison which gave the symptoms of syphilis.... Fine, I told Chichaev, but could I have a similar list of the NKVD's toys? He said he would need clearance from Moscow. 'All right,' I replied, 'Get me clearance in writing and we will be in business.'

'That's an insult', he protested. 'Why in writing? I give my word of honour. No one has ever doubted my word.'

Despite his assurances that he wanted to co-operate he did not produce a list and so he did not receive ours, at least from me.[15]

THE LEGACY OF THE SAM MISSION

With the Anglo-Soviet Pact, Winston Churchill valued having not just an Embassy in Moscow, but also the SOE Mission. Foot commented that

> 'Our gallant Soviet ally', that phrase, reiterated from countless platforms and in countless broadcasts during 1942-3, was a great deal more than a phrase. It was only this solidly tyrannous lifebelt that kept the grand alliance of free peoples afloat through those two terrible years. Stalin's and Beria's iniquities have now become journalists' commonplaces, and were iniquitous indeed; yet hindsight, though sometimes it clarifies, can also distort. Had it not been for Stalin and Beria and their iron grip on the Soviet empire, no British reader of this book aged under forty would (in all probability) have been born at all, because his or her father would have been deported to work in a Nazi labour camp in eastern Europe, with no chance to beget a child. Without Russian help Great Britain would have lost the war against Nazi Germany.[1]

It is worth noting that when the Americans joined the war, their Office of Strategic Services, what became the CIA, established links with the NKVD. Although the American public remained suspicious of Communism during the early 1940s, the Soviet Union received a 'highly favourable wartime press'. In March 1943, a special edition of *LIFE* magazine called Lenin, 'perhaps the greatest man of modern times', the NKVD, 'roughly analogous to the FBI,' and said that Russians 'look like Americans, dress like Americans, and think like Americans.'[2]

The Moscow mission allowed the British direct communication liaison with Lavrenty Beria, the head of the NKVD. Other positive aspects of the SOE–NKVD agreement were noted by O'Sullivan as being,

> ...the exchange of currencies, espionage devices, German uniforms, German documents and the defence plans of Le Havre; information on Bulgaria, shipping dates and SOE officers visits to Russian training schools. The negatives were the refusals to co-operate in Yugoslavia, Turkey or Rumania, to transfer arms to resistance groups in Poland and Czechoslovakia, to give information on NKVD

activities in Germany or to employ Soviet prisoners-of-war in German camps in joint operations.[3]

Hill's *Reminiscences* mention a visit he made with Ossipov to partisan units in 1942 which helped him to write the official NKVD handbook on partisan warfare. In effect, the NKVD did a similar job to SOE in supplying arms, ammunition, and training men and women in Morse code, signalling, and sabotaging the German forces in Russia.

> ...apart from the Partisan Handbook, we tackled a further problem, which was to condition the Red Army Command to work with and make full use of the Partisans. Soviet Generals, Red Army high ranking officers, the regulars on the General Staff, had a similar distaste for Partisans and Guerrilla riff-raff as has their British counterparts. How the activities of SOE were disliked! What enormous opposition its efforts met, and what ruthless persecution it had to contend with in the first two or even three years of World War II![4]

Aware that the future of the SOE/NKVD agreement and his position in Moscow was in the balance, Hill submitted a longer report attempting to assuage SOE about the Soviet Union's post-war intentions.[5] A shorter report outlining the progress of the SAM mission since 1941 reads:

> It may be an opportune moment to put on record some of the more outstanding achievements of the Sam Mission.
>
> For the whole period it has kept in contact with the N.K.V.D. and, in spite of every kind of difficulty, has maintained friendly relations with this very important body.
>
> It has acted as an observation unit which had had better facilities for doing so than any other British or American organisation that is at present in the U.S.S.R. Much intelligence has been sent back to the Head Office for distribution to the British Military Mission and very close contact has been kept with the British Ambassador and his staff.
>
> Possibly for the joint war effort as far as collaboration with Russia is concerned, the Sam Mission has been in the matter of the Bagat Rum case. Unfortunately it did not directly concern S.O.E. and has been very badly handled by C; I.P.E> and the Government of India.
>
> We have recently received unexpectedly from the N.K.V.D. a report on Le Havre, which the War Office have appreciated, and we hope to get some further information.
>
> Various visits, such as to Gorki – Prisoner-of-War camps – and recently to Leningrad, have been of great intelligence value.
>
> Through our work with the N.K.V.D. Sam has been able to get in a great deal about the Partisan movement, all of which has been sent back to London.[6]

O'Sullivan, having examined the relevant documents relating to Hill's work for both the SOE and SIS, commented that Hill was 'ineffective, out of touch and easily neutralised by the Soviets.' Gubbins remarked in a letter to Sir Orme Sargent at the Foreign Office that the Moscow Mission was a waste of time, money, and effort and he suggested that London ought to take the firm line and order Hill back permanently. Sheridan, another SOE officer, complained that Hill's work had not helped the SOE in any substantial way and that he had been 'a bloody obstructionist'. He referred to Hill's 'habit of life' and indicated that 'a lady finds sanctuary in his flat'. He also mentioned Chichaev's comment that Hill 'keeps an open house, he gives extremely good dinners and he is not a nuisance in any way.' 'Ina', a ballerina, 'Xenia', 'Tamara', 'Kiri Vassilevna' and 'Natasha Petrovna' were names mentioned as Russian girls who attended SAM's parties. Indicating just how little power Gubbins had over others in the intelligence service, Hill's connections with Clark Kerr, the British Ambassador in Moscow, saved him his job. Sargent asked Gubbins for patience.[7]

In response to the SOE organising several visits to their special training schools for the DPR Mission, Hill was taken on a four-day tour of a prisoner-of-war camp in Oranski, a parachute training centre, partisan training camp and flying school near Gorki, followed by a visit to a collective farm. He pressured Baker Street to give the Pickaxe missions higher priority and encouraged them to take up NKVD's proposal to co-operate on subversive propaganda in enemy occupied countries. Although the SOE and the Political Warfare Executive felt this was highly desirable, nothing came of it.[8]

Hill's replacement, Major John Elliot Benham, arrived in Moscow on 3 June 1945 with the full rank of Colonel. His position in the Russian Section was taken by the newly promoted Major McLaughlin, who had returned to London in March. In August, the war against Japan ended. There was little for SOE to do so the mission was closed. Captain Wild, one of the original members of the SAM mission, returned in July. In early September, Colonel Graur, having arrived back in Moscow, met Benham, who reported him as saying:

I have been instructed by General Fitin to say that looking back upon our cooperation during the war period it would seem that not a bad job had been done. True it might have been better, but results which seemed to us at the time as insignificant have now proved their value. On the whole our cooperation has not produced bad results. It is true there have been some mistakes, but I am inclined to blame these on the clash of personalities concerned (he named himself, Chichaev, Major Seddon). It is true that when people are more interested in small side issues, they lose sight of the main objective. In our case the main objective (I am not sure whether he meant winning the war or cooperation) was never lost sight of. We have achieved a great thing in opening a new path to cooperation between our two nations and it is a path down which we shall have to walk during the next 20 years.[9]

Although the meeting was 'very cordial and friendly', when asked about future cooperation, Benham met a 'stony silence' from the Soviets. While the Pickaxes may have broken some ice with some of the SOE officers they came into contact with, there was a breakdown in SOE's relations with the NKVD. Along with the negative attitudes of many in the SIS and the Foreign Office, this contributed towards what became known as 'The Cold War'.

CONCLUSION

For decades after the war, details of the Pickaxe operations were classified in both the East and the West until the recent release of material by the National Archives. Together with official Soviet publications, these sources have allowed a glimpse into SOE and NKVD operational matters and have shed light on the human tragedies involved.

As has been mentioned, after the war, SIS started investigating the Pickaxes. They were interested in whether those that might have survived the war were still active. In the SOE's Russian file there was a memo from Miss P. M. Small to Mr Philby commenting that

> It has occurred to us that there may be other Russian agents who were trained by S.O.E. for work on the continent about whom you have full particulars. These people, being thoroughly trained agents, might, we feel, at any time be used again, perhaps even for work against this country. We should like therefore to have some record of them.[1]

It was not until 23 January 1947 that she determined that thirty-four agents had arrived from the USSR. Analysis of the Pickaxe files reveals that of the thirty-four Pickaxes who arrived in Britain between November 1941 and January 1944, four were returned to Moscow for refusing to undertake the mission and one was sent back for medical reasons. SOE sent twenty-nine. Of those, three were killed in air crashes and one refused to land and was returned to Moscow. A detailed list was drawn up of suspected *Rote Kapelle* agents and a copy of the list was sent to the CIA and the French Sûreté. In fact, NKVD had planned to send 170 agents, but the majority were refused due to objections by the Foreign Office and various governments-in-exile.

The SOE managed thirteen successful Pickaxe missions: four to Germany (Tonic, Rigi, and Eiger), five to France (Pickaxe 1, Rum, Ararat, Orange, and Apache), two to Holland (Barsac, Sauterne), one to Belgium (Burgundy), one to Austria (Sodawater), and one to Italy (Etna). The Whiskey party for Austria was killed and the Coffee party for Austria was returned to the Soviet Union. One party was sent within three weeks of landing, two waited six weeks, three waited two months, two waited three months, two waited four months, two waited five months, one waited six months, and two had to wait for a year.

The Pickaxes were émigrés from Germany, Austria, the Netherlands, and France, or Soviet citizens who had previously acted as agents for the NKVD. While most were committed communists, some had held high positions in their countries' communist parties.[2] McLoughlin claimed that their political background was given greater consideration than physical fitness, enthusiasm, and sound military training. From looking through the Pickaxes' personnel files, it is apparent that for some it was their military background that the NKVD valued; for others it was their political background rather than their training or enthusiasm to be infiltrated into enemy territory.

A Pickaxe's life expectancy once landed was short; most survived only between four days and eight months. From the available evidence, only two followed their instructions to take their 'L' pill, Else Noffke (Elena Nikitina) and Willi Kruyt (Willi von Krumin). It appears that they swallowed rather than chewed them. The cyanide did not work as quickly as they had been informed, and the Germans managed to get them to hospital where they were resuscitated. Few managed to dispose of their wireless crystals, which allowed the Germans to identify their transmitting frequencies. Of those who did, some were forced to reveal where they had hidden them.

Most Pickaxes were unable to withstand the Gestapo's severe interrogation and torture techniques, and they revealed the locations of other Soviet agents. As they were often trained together, the Pickaxes were able to identify other Soviet agents. It quickly became clear that they had either fought in the Spanish Civil War, were members of the Austrian *Schutzbund*, or were German deserters. How many collaborated in various playback schemes is difficult to ascertain. Needless to say, the Gestapo's success with their *Funkspiel* led to the arrest of not just other Pickaxes, but also many existing communist agents, their families, and friends. Exactly when Moscow first learnt about *Funkspiel* is unknown, nor is it known how effective the disinformation they were fed by the Gestapo was.

Only six Pickaxes survived the war. Eugen Nesper escaped to Switzerland, Daniel Georges and Raymond Guyot survived in France, Niko Kruyt survived in Holland, and Albert Huttary and Josef Zettler survived in Austria. What happened to Alexandre Filipov in Italy is unknown. The eleven Pickaxes sent to France are said by O'Sullivan not to have made a significant contribution to the Soviet network, and to have only aroused deep suspicion among the Free French that Britain had sent communists in without consulting them.

Bad weather and poor visibility explained, to some degree, RAF Tempsford's inability to parachute Pickaxes in as planned, but the Special Duties Squadrons also had difficulty getting hold of planes from the RAF. While delaying tactics may have explained why some Pickaxes spent many months waiting, it must be remembered that SOE had responsibility for infiltrating about 1,400 other agents into occupied Europe. These included men and women for the SIS, SAS, and OSS, the American Office of Strategic Services, forerunner of the CIA.

Guy Liddell, the head of the Security Service's 'B' Section, wrote that the British performance was 'less than perfect', that 'our efforts to get [the Pickaxes] dropped have on the whole been somewhat disastrous', and the Pickaxes were of 'a pretty low mentality'.[3] The NKVD's attitude to human life was hardly advantageous.

Instead of investing time to prepare the agents and their cover stories, Moscow's disregard for human life turned many missions into suicide missions. As an Austrian agent (not part of the 'Pickaxe' scheme) Gregor Kersche, put it succinctly, 'If the party has decided that I should die, then I will just die'.[4]

There were errors based on inexact intelligence in the preparation of the Pickaxe missions. Forged *Soldbucher,* military pass books, were easily detected as they omitted a faint pencil mark from the military inspector. Some agents were arrested for carrying a full set of papers when most citizens did not. It was common for the Pickaxes' forged papers to be made out in the agent's real name and, as many were on the Gestapo's wanted list for previous communist activities, they were easily identified. The British carefully removed any maker's identification marks from agents' clothes, toiletries, and batteries, but in some cases, clear white labels had been glued over the originals.

The radio operators' signal plan was usually on microfilm, half the size of a postage stamp. It was usually hidden by being own into clothing, and it could easily be disposed of if necessary. O'Sullivan reports one Pickaxe calmly taking his signal plan out of his tie and flushing it down the toilet.

The suspicions of the German police were sometimes raised when they discovered anyone carrying a large number of cards. One agent was reported as having been given ration cards for 180 kgs of meat, 120 kgs of butter, and 200 kgs of bread. Learning from this 'oversight', Moscow gave the Pickaxes large amounts of money instead, so that they could buy food on the black market. However, some notes that had been taken from wounded or dead German soldiers had bloodstains on them, and this also raised suspicions if noticed by the police.

There is no evidence of the Pickaxes receiving any training in withstanding torture during interrogation. While it may have been part of their training in the Soviet Union before they left for Britain, it appears that many of them were 'turned' when they were caught and forced to participate in German playback schemes. SOE's training regime included having armed men dressed in Gestapo uniforms waking agents up in the early hours of the morning. The trainee agents were shouted at in the language of the country they were being sent to, they were hauled out of bed and dragged downstairs, pushed onto a chair and had spotlights shone into their faces. If they protested they were hit and abused. Some agents referred to being given internal searches, being stripped and given harsh interrogation. If an agent was destined for France and spoke in English they would fail the course. One trick played on them when the mock interrogation session finished was to give them a cigarette and say in English, 'Pass me the ashtray.' If they did, they failed.[5]

The SOE had been expecting 'trained, highly disciplined and reliable' agents who would be able to contribute to the war effort. However, many in SOE came to believe that committing acts of sabotage in Western Europe was low on the list of Soviet priorities. The NKVD was thought not to believe that the German advances into the Soviet Union would be stopped by a few agents blowing up a few bridges or disrupting railway communications. A delay of a few days while the Germans made repairs was considered too insignificant to have an impact on the Eastern Front.

Considered as expendable assets by the NKVD, the Pickaxes were not expected to organise a network themselves, only to make contact with existing Communist agents already in the field. Apart from those assigned to the Coffee party, the SOE's conducting officers were unable to identify exactly what the Pickaxes' missions were. SOE's Russian Section was not fully informed of the instructions the Pickaxes had been issued, but in some cases they suspected political goals that were unrelated to sabotage. On their journey from the Soviet Union to Scotland, the Pickaxes, or 'bodies' as the SOE called them, travelled under assumed Russian names. Sometimes, Estonian names were given to Germans or Austrians, probably because they were not fluent Russian speakers and did not look particularly Slavic. Sometimes, they posed as Volga Germans. The NKVD also issued them with another identity and a cover story, depending on their ethnic background and the country they were being infiltrated into.[6]

Shortly after the war, someone, possibly Seddon's secretary, was given the task of typing up the history of Russian Section. In 'Notes on the Russian Section of S.O.E.', it stated:

> In general, Pickaxes ... caused a great deal of trouble, waste of time and energy on our part – a fact which never seemed to be properly appreciated by our Russian colleagues, who were forever carping at our slowness and inefficiency. This complaint, though perhaps in some cases well founded, seems nevertheless rather unfair, in view of stories which have since reached us on Russian organisation and dropping of agents – all of which tend to prove that the Soviet methods are, to say the least of it, very rough and ready.[7]

There was only one attempt by the NKVD to drop a British agent into Eastern Europe. Operation Blunderhead was described as 'an abject failure'. It involved dropping William Seth, alias John de Witt, an SOE officer, into Estonia in 1942. After being captured by the Germans, he was 'turned' by the SD, the Nazi Security Service, for a mission to Britain that never transpired. He spent most of the war in

OFLAG 79, a German prisoner-of-war camp for Allied officers in Waggum, near Braunsweig in Germany.[8] In fact, Mackenzie, author of *The Secret History of the S.O.E.*, questioned how seriously the Russians regarded the Pickaxe operations; whether they were really part of the Soviet plans or merely to test Britain's good faith.[9]

In *Churchill and the Secret Service*, David Stafford describes the SOE/NKVD agreement as having been at the least important level, and the operations that took place as 'little more than a gesture.' Hampered by their inability to acquire planes for the missions, SOE was heavily reliant on RAF's Bomber Command, which at the time had greater priority.[10]

On the National Archives website, an introduction to the SOE/NKVD catalogue states that

> The Special Operations Executive's dealings with its Russian counterpart, the NKVD, proved, from a SOE point of view, both unproductive and frustrating in the extreme. All attempts to achieve some positive and productive agreement with the Russians came to nought and while the NKVD were quite happy to enjoy SOE cooperation, they themselves were reluctant to reciprocate. SOE undertook, with mixed success, the infiltration of Russian agents into occupied Europe (Operation PICKAXE) on the NKVD's behalf but met with a total lack of cooperation when it, in its turn, sought the NKVD's assistance in the suborning of Russian prisoners of war who had been forced to serve in the German Army.[11]

The Pickaxe chapter of the Second World War is a story of politically motivated individuals caught up in a web of political and diplomatic intrigue. For the NKVD, the Pickaxes offered a chance of re-establishing links with Soviet agents in Western Europe who had lost contact following Germany's invasion of Poland and Russia. Supplying their isolated contacts with much-needed money and wireless sets capable of reaching Moscow meant that the Soviet Union could receive important military, political, and economic information that would help them in their war effort. It would also allow them to send back further instructions. For the SOE, the Pickaxe operations presented an opportunity to establish contact with the intelligence services of their Communist ally, to learn more about the individuals who ran it, and their political, military and economic intentions.

Politically, the Pickaxe operations emphasised the prevailing attitude of mistrust between the Soviet Union and the Britain. O'Sullivan quoted Winston Churchill's comment that 'if Hitler invaded Hell [he] would at least make a favourable reference to the Devil in the House of Commons'. The fight against the Nazis meant that Britain's intelligence services had to embrace their former adversary, the Soviet Union.

The NKVD's intention of infiltrating nearly 200 Soviet agents was thwarted by the Foreign Office and SOE's refusal, prevarication, and deliberate delaying tactics. Only twenty-eight Pickaxes were sent. Unwilling to send large numbers of communists into Allied countries whose governments-in-exile were unaware of Churchill's secret agreement with Stalin, the upper echelons of the War Office were worried about the long-term political implications of strengthening Communist influence in occupied Europe.

Some in the SOE were keen to infiltrate Soviet agents in the hope that they too could light fires to help keep Europe ablaze. At the signing of the agreement, the SOE expected the Pickaxes to orchestrate sabotage operations and encourage Communist groups in Western Europe to take action against the Nazi occupiers. The SOE could only surmise what the Communists' political intentions were during and after the war.

The many problems that plagued the whole enterprise from the start made it impossible for the SOE to assess the activities or success of the Pickaxes they had infiltrated. They were unable to keep track of the agents; it was only from captured Gestapo and other German personnel that they learned what happened to many of them.

The majority of the Pickaxes did not survive the war. Several were returned to the Soviet Union for medical reasons; four were returned for refusing to follow instruction; a few committed suicide when they were caught in the field; many were captured and executed, with some being forced to send German-inspired messages back to Moscow. Some, like the Pickaxe sent to Italy, we still know nothing about.

An underlying feeling of mistrust between the British and Soviet intelligence agencies hamstrung the Pickaxe operation from the start. It did not have a significant impact on the outcome of the War. Both the NKVD and the SOE were disbanded soon after the War, and it was not long before the new intelligence agencies of both countries started working against each other during the Cold War. The intelligence gathered by the SAM mission in Moscow and the DPR mission in London during the Pickaxe operation was naturally exploited by both sides; this is the greatest legacy of the Pickaxe operation.

APPENDICES

A. Translation of Willi Kruyt's (Burgundy) diary, from his arrival in Britain to his departure, (May to June 1942).

10 May

4½ scotch trawler six aircraft, 11 gave up. arrived Gourock 6 o'clock reception and parting from ship. Tea in the evening slept in camp bed.

13 May

Breakfast at home met Russian chief. Sorted out clothes. 4 for lunch. Visit to Belgian Specialty [?] after dinner Hyde Park and dutchmen.

14 May

Up at 9 breakfast together. 10.30 to 1 Belgian bulletins two news papers. Lunch at Lyons complet outfit. Dinner at large Lyons. Speech Hyde Park. To Westminster after supper. To bed at one o'clock.

16 May

Nick at Breakfast; sleeping at home. News papers taken back ... [illegible] Bought Dutch books and magazines. Three of us to news film and tea in the evening. Home at 1.30.

17 May

Breakfast, read papers in Hyde Park. Dinner at Czech restaurant. 6.30 French ... [illegible]. English film ... Turkish restaurant.

18 May

Three men in evening to Marylebone Town Hall. Large chief ... Read a lot in the evening.

19 May

French cigarettes. Bought outfit. Teeth seen to. Nick to Doctor. Revolver practice, worked at home in the evening, then walked together.

20 May

Breakfast in tea room. Nick radio test. I to St. Pauls ... 6 to 9 film then walk Tower St Pauls etc.

21 May
Lunch at Paddington. Shooting practice. Film and Madame Tussauds. Landing in Holland pointless [?] Late supper at Scotts.

22 May
Changed clothes at Michelis. The Belgians handed in laundry.

23 May
Shooting at 11. one o'clock lunch with Gaskell. 2.30 Belgians ... Supper Turkish restaurant.

24 May
Breakfast together prepared for journey. Lunch with Walsh. 5 o'clock Euston. 7.45 arrived by bus. Supper, walk and bath.

25 May
Strong south east wind, so scheme at home and compass theory. Jumping tests in ...

26 May
Landing theory and burying practice. Wind too strong for jumping. In the evening film to pass the time, early to bed as jumping early.

27 May
Wind too strong. Revolver practice. A day of waiting ... in the evening.

28 May
Telephone to London. 1.30 took Nick and ... To Manchester Art Gallery and tea, back by bus and Major's car. Wind calm in evening, what tomorrow?

29 May
Strong wind. 1.15 saying good-bye and left. Arrived Euston 6.25. KOLAI and MORRIS at home. Got into contact with Russians.

30 May
10.30 discussions, first Nick and then me. Shooting practice 2.40 ... [five words illegible] In the afternoon I mend socks, Nick coat. Evening film, Les Gens de Voyage. Polish restaurant.

31 May
Visit by chief and simple lunch. Together St Pauls, Westminster Abbey and Cathedral. Dinner alone at Cumberland.

1 June
11 Shooting practice. Hunted on foot for wallet and purse. 5 to Euston. No fellow travellers! Back home again dinner in Italian restaurant.

2 June
10.5. left Euston arrived 2.25. Nick jumped from plane I from balloon ... [illegible] early to bed.

3 June
10.55 depart, dining car arrived Euston 4. Walsh congratulations! Reassured by these.

4 June

12 to 1 shooting practice. Three of us for lunch together. Hunting for books. 4.30 wireless lesson. I to Italian restaurant in the evening talk with Darton.

5 June

9 o'clock sundry purchases. 10 o'clock car trip to Cambridge walk and lunch. Arrived at Rochford. Tea Nick ... Swimming bath dinner. Nick to swimming bath and bed.

6 June

8.30 Nick swimming bath, breakfast. Cypher practice and work in garden. 12 o'clock swimming together. 12.30 lunch, siesta tea gardening, Nick swam again and I walked through village.

7 June

9 breakfast, church service, Church of England. After lunch, cigarettes coffee liqueurs. Afternoon walk together early to bed.

9 June

Gardening, swimming and gardening again. Table in room.

9 June

Worked at table in the morning. Lunch. To Hertford to see film 'Next of Kin'. More gardening. 9.30 to bed.

10 June

8.30 up, together on foot to Hertford, return by bus. Weeded rose bed.

11 June

Lunch together eight of us for supper. Rose bed finished.

12 June

9.30 to London with Morris. Lunch with Darton and Gaskell. Went home. Nick went to Hertford.

13 June

Gardening.

14 June

Did not go to Church. Walk to Bayford.

15 June

Together to Hertford. Gardening. Nick did not go swimming.

16 June

Together to St Albans and Hatfield. 2.45 lunch, weeding roses after tea. Nearly ready.

17 June

Together set out to Hoddesdon. Morris on bike. Twice police [?] 1 lunch. 2.50 left Hatfield after saying good-bye. 3 home, met Gaskill and Darton.

18 June

After breakfast visit to ... [illegible]. Received new landing map. 2.30 saw boring film together. Wrote a letter to Herman and Els.

19 June

All sorts of preparations. Talk with Thompson and Cameron. Very fine parting lunch with two Majors. Once again to the film Les gens de Voyage.

20 June

A few more purchases. Tomorrow possibly off. Last part drink.

21 June

9 o'clock breakfast with Gaskell. 10.30 message Nick gone today. Went to lunch together at Lyons. 3 parting. 6.30 supper alone at Lyons. Darton came home. Sewed belt. To bed at 1.30.

22 June

... [illegible] Darton rang and told me Nick left at 11.30 and landed safely. To Kew with Morris. 7 ... Listen to wireless. Hear 7th symphony Sostokowitsch.

23 June

Message leaving today. 12.30 not leaving today. Lunch with ... [illegible] Wimbledon. Dinner Hungarian restaurant, film 'One day in U.S.S.R.' Final talk with Dalton.

24 June

Departure today.[1]

B. A memorandum from Colonel Sheridan to George Taylor, director of SOE's overseas groups and missions, dated 27 September 1943, discussing the future of the SOE/NKVD Agreement.

Recent telegrams received from Moscow and a long conversation I have had with D/P.101 [Hill] show that the future of our Russian Mission is nearing a crisis. This is a matter of concern, not merely to S.O.E. but also to ZP [The Foreign Office], S.I.S, and H.M.G. as a whole.

A decision is necessary, and I feel that in view of its importance, any decision taken should be discussed and approved by the Council.

In my view while the Russians continue to believe that we are not giving them the full assistance we could give, there is a risk that they will close down our Mission in Moscow completely.

How great this risk is, is of course a matter of opinion.

I note that in your AD/751 of 23rd September to C.D. [Sir Charles Hambro] you say, in referring to such a possibility: -

'I cannot myself take these fears so seriously. The Russians have got substantial benefits out of this liaison; they have given us nothing. I do not, therefore, think it likely that, even if they suspect us of delaying tactics, they will want to cut off their nose to spite their face.'

I also note that C.D. has pencilled against this paragraph the words 'I agree'.

The facts are that since October 1941 we have been asked to introduce fifty-seven specific Russian agents into various countries. The number so far introduced alive (four have been killed) is seventeen, and these have been transported only after they have been in this country for a very long time – delays of three to six months are common, and twelve months has been recorded....

D/P.101 told me that it was his considered view that the Russians would close his Mission if better results were not obtained.

In this connection I refer to telegram 1227 from Moscow on 19th September in which it was stated that last winter Colonel Ossipov was not in favour of continuing collaboration unless the scope of our work could be enlarged, and that unless there were an improvement there would be no reprieve when the situation was next reviewed.

Today here is another telegram from Moscow (no.1235) which records that D/PR.2 [Colonel Graur] has protested at the 'interminable delay in carrying out Pickaxe operations', and has expressed himself as thoroughly dissatisfied.

D/PR.2 said he could not understand why Pickaxes, who form a relatively small proportion of all our operations, should have to remain in London month after month. The same attitude is taken by D/PR.1 [Chichaev] in London with his conversations with D/P [the Russian Section].

D.PR.1 has access to Station 61 [Gaynes Hall], for the efficiency of which he has a great admiration; and it is very difficult, after he has been told at 61 – as he has been on several occasions – that we have had a record moon and have dropped great numbers of agents and supplies, to convince him that failure to drop Russian agents is due to weather or shortage of aircraft. The conviction is growing in his mind that Russian agents are given very low priority.

As already reported, D/P thinks the danger of our being closed down in Moscow is a very real one.

It would seem therefore that while you and C.D. are confident that the continuance of our Mission in Moscow is assured, those who are [in] touch with our Russian Colleagues, D/P.101 in Moscow and D/P in London – cannot share that confidence.

If S.O.E. were alone interested in this matter it would not assume on my mind the importance that it does. It is fully admitted that the work of our Russian Mission for S.O.E. is at the moment of little advantage to this organisations, but other people are interested in the work of the Mission.

Firstly there is S.O. [Special Operations Section] who, as you will recall, has given an instruction that he is to be consulted about the new Treaty that is is proposed to negotiate with the N.K.V.D. and has ordered that nothing is to be settle finally until he has considered it.

Secondly there is YP [?], who I understand greatly appreciates the contacts that our Mission has and the information which it gathers.

Thirdly there is ZP [the Foreign Office], which, whatever its point of view, is I think interested in giving its YP the support he requires, and also finds the information produced from time to time by our Mission of interest.

Fourthly there is S.I.S., which has, I am advised, only the most tenuous contacts in Soviet Russia and, as we know, is glad to avail itself of Sam's contacts, and sends to him requests for information through our channels.

Finally there is H.M.G. as a whole. It is well-known that H.M.G.'s contacts with the Soviet are limited, and it is reasonable to suppose that it does not wish them diminished.

It should be remembered that the influence of N.K.V.D. on all forms of life in Soviet Russia – save possible the ten people at the top – is, to put it at its lowest, considerable.

It should also be remembered that S.O.E. is the only British organisation which will be recognised by the N.K.V.D., or with which it will have any dealings whatever.

In twenty-five months D/P.101 and his staff have – again to put it at its lowest – got their foot in the door. It is useless to pretend that if our Russian Mission is ejected another Mission from some other British organisation can take its place. The foot is personal; certainly to S.O.E., and to a very large extent personal to D/P.101, who has access, among others, to Molotov and has been called in by Molotov in moments of crisis to assist in translation and interpreting.

It is, of course, true that certain Country Sections or Regions within S.O.E., notably French and Polish, are hostile (purely in the course of business since personalities are not concerned) to our Russian Mission, and are opposed to S.O.E. giving any assistance to the Russians in the countries which concern them, but I suggest the matter must be viewed as one of high policy for S.O.E. and not from a Country Section level.

To sum up, I believe from the information given to me that unless we can do better for the Pickaxes in the future than we have done in the past our Mission in Moscow will probably be closed.

We should, I think, consult S.O. ZP and S.I.S., inform them fully of the risk and get a definite statement as to whether they are willing to run the risk, whether they really want the Mission to continue.

If the answer is that they are indifferent, then of course we can continue our present policy of delaying tactics, feeble excuses and prevarication as long as the Russians will allow us to do so.

If on the other hand the answer is that we must take all reasonable steps we can to prevent the Mission being wound up, then it is clear that we cannot continue as we are now doing.

We must take a stronger line with Allied Governments, and in some cases of need ZP must come to our assistance.

Internally Country Sections must be informed by C.D. that they must be less rigid in their opposition to the introduction of Pickaxes; and finally once a departure of Pickaxes has been approved, instructions should be given to the Air Despatch people that they are to have reasonable priority.[2]

C. A memorandum of situation regarding NKVD request for infiltration of Soviet agents into Northern France, dated 1 November 1943.

The following is a resume of facts connected with this request :

The N.K.V.D. requested our assistance to drop thee agents in France, in March, 1943.

On 8th April at a meeting at the Foreign Office, it was decided that owing to uncertainty of situation resulting from discussions between Generals Giraud and de Gaulle, S.O.E. Moscow should be instructed to stall.

On 12th June, owing to N.K.V.D. insistence, the matter was again referred to Sir Alexander Cadogan by C.D. and in his reply of 22nd June, Sir Alexander stated that, in his opinion, the agents could not be accepted without the permission of the appropriate Allied French authority and permission of the appropriate Allied French authority and requested that the matter be further postponed for a week or ten days.

On 5th July, the N.K.V.D. again reverted to the request and asked that these agents proceed on 8th July. S.O.E. replied that no approval had as yet come from the French authority and that they could not therefore accept them.

On 6 July, Colonel CHICHAEV produced a letter signed by General COCHET giving French agreement to the operation. This letter was considered by the S.O.E. Council, who decided that General COCHET's signature was not sufficient and that authority must be obtained from a competent member of the French Committee of Liberation. General GUBBINS had a conference with M. MASSIGLI on 19th July at which MASSIGLI expressed great surprise and said that the matter was so important that he would have to refer it to Algiers at one. This decision was communicated immediately to Colonel CHICHAEV who expressed annoyance and stated that he had already produced the authority for which he had been asked and that he could not understand why S.O.E. had changed its mind.

Subsequently CHICHAEV asked if D'ASTIER's signature would suffice and he was informed that he must obtain the authority of M. André PHILIP or that of someone authorised to act for him. He pointed out that PHILIP was in Algiers and that considerable delay would be entailed if he was forced to obtain this signature, and on the 13th September, he produced a letter signed by M. Georges BORIS and written under the heading of the French Committee of Liberation, stating that 'I have been in touch with M. André PHILIP and am authorised to inform you that in answer to the question put by M. CHICHAEV that we have no objection to the forwarding of agents of whom we are assured by an Allied Government that they are to do military work for our common cause.' This letter was submitted to C.D. who, on 18th September, wrote 'We must have a warrant signed by PHILIP on behalf of the Committee of National Liberation. Without that, the men cannot come and should not be accepted.

On the arrival in this country of Colonel Hill on 22nd September, he at once raised the question and pointed out the unfortunate situation caused in Moscow by this procrastination, and C.D. then authorised us to apply for André PHILIP's authority through the Algier's Office.

On 7th October, Algiers cabled that André PHILIP considered the matter too delicate to decide without reference to BORIS and that he intended to discuss this on his return to London.

This information was conveyed to CHICHAEV who was advised to get into touch with André PHILIP direct, and on subsequent enquiry, he implied by his answer that he had seen PHILIP and that he was expecting him to give his approval direct to S.O.E. Such notification has not yet reached us.

Since then, no further result of the conversation has been forthcoming.

Moscow telegram 1174 of 26th October, 1943, brings the matter to a head and, viewed purely from the angle of S.O.E. agreement with the N.K.V.D., it is fair to say that the N/K.V.D. have definite grounds upon which to base a complaint. According to Article 8 of the Charter, S.O.E. undertakes to assist in the introduction of Soviet agents into occupied territory. This article was somewhat modified in C.D.'s letter, CD/3861 of 2nd December, 1943, [sic] and addressed to Sir Alexander Cadogan, in which he stated that in the case of occupied France, each case would be judged on its merits but that in general, S.O.E. could not agree to introducing N.K.V.D. agents without consulting the Fighting French.

When the original request for introduction of these agents was made, there was no French authority other than the Fighting French Committee and the question of the National Committee had not yet arisen. It was in these circumstances that Colonel CHICHAEV was requested to obtain the authority of the Fighting French, which request, he submits, was complied with in the letter signed by General COCHET on behalf of the Fighting French. Subsequent changes in our policy were dictated by the political discussions in Algiers but it is a matter for argument as to whether a decision already taken on the old set-up should have been reversed as the result of a situation which arose later. There seems little doubt that N.K.V.D.'s request has been subjected to a policy of vacillation and in all fairness to them it would appear that they are justified in reading into our actions a desire to obstruct.

The Foreign Office is of the opinion that a solution of this problem would have to be based on the solution of two main possibilities:

That of S.O.E. being forced to give up the entire control of these operations to France and thereby leaving themselves completely in the dark as to Soviet policy.

That of S.O.E. acting merely as travel agents for an unspecified and possibly large number of Soviet agents for France.

S.O.E. policy in respect of Pickaxe operations has always been to accept these operations within the limits of the Charter and without question, but this policy has had to be modified with the march of events which has imposed political qualifications on the interpretation of the various articles. This policy of acceptance has been based upon S.O.E.'s desire to retain control of Pickaxe operations in Western Europe and to have a proper knowledge of the identities of Soviet agents put into the field. For this reason it is obvious that S.O.E. policy would reject an arrangement whereby entire control was passed to the French, and would prefer the alternative of acting, as heretofore, as travel agents.

S.O.E. has repeatedly stressed the lack of reciprocity resulting from the Charter, but in the matter of the Pickaxe operations this fact has no real bearing on the case, since S.O.E. has so far not made any concrete demands of N.K.V.D. for the introduction of British agents, and it would seem not unreasonable to presume that, failing these counter-proposals, they should carry out to the best of their ability the conditions imposed upon them in respect of the introduction of agent. Whilst it is undoubtedly true to say that S.O.E. has itself received no specific dividend from the collaboration, at the same time it is difficult to explain the long delay in the implementation of commitments already accepted, and whilst a general charge of non-cooperation might be made against the N.K.V.D., this would not, in itself, support a defence of S.O.E. failure in regard to specific clauses.

(N.B. Since writing the above memorandum, notification has been received from the N.K.V.D. that they desire to terminate collaboration in respect of those clauses which relate to the infiltration of agents, which may be taken in general to presage a total breakdown of S.O.E./N.K.V.D. collaboration.)[3]

D. George Hill's report on the USSR's 'moral leadership' in the 'new Europe', 28 January 1944.

SECRET

I have the honour to bring to your attention a factor in the present struggle against Nazi Germany which is constantly obtruding itself and has an important bearing on the relations between the Soviet Union and the other united nations. This factor is the efforts of the peoples of the occupied territories to free themselves of Nazi tyranny.

In some respects the resistance of the people in occupied territory is assuming the same characteristics as the uprising of the people of Europe against Napoleon 130 years ago. It is another illustration of the much closer resemblance of this war to the Napoleonic wars than to the war of 1914-18, a circumstance yet to be grasped by our military leaders. In the Napoleonic wars little progress was made against Napoleon so long as the war was regarded as a matter chiefly of concern to the Crown Heads of Europe and their Military Staffs. After the retreat from Moscow the peoples of Europe took matters into their own hands, rose up against French tyranny and a decisive battle of Leipzig was the result.

In this war we have had at the head of the Governments of both the United Kingdom and the United States two men whose careers have been closely identified with the armed services. This has made them superb war leaders and has brought about a close harmony between the political and military direction of the war. It has had the effect, however, of giving the armed services a decisive voice in the conduct of the war and explains why so little weight has been attached to a purely non-military factor such as the resistance of the peoples of Occupied Territory. Moreover, we have had in the Foreign Offices of the two principal Western Powers men whose careers were formed during the period when political stability in Europe was threatened by subversive movements. To them future peace and stability in Europe depends upon the restoration of the regimes threatened before the war by these subversive means. This attitude of mind coincides closely with that of the Armed Services who are serious that their task of maintaining order in Europe after the conclusion of hostilities will not be complicated by civil strife. This combination is perfect for supporting those determined to protect the vested interest of privileged groups. It is natural that these vested interests should be represented in the refugee governments who have continued to represent the peoples of occupied countries and to be their mouthpiece in relations with the governments of the United Kingdom and the United States.

Under these circumstances it is not surprising that a blind eye has been turned in London and Washington to the military possibilities of the resistance movements. In Moscow the situation is exactly the reverse. The Soviet Government itself at one time was actively identified with promoting the very subversive movements which created uneasiness in the other capitals. The Soviet leaders came to power as revolutionaries and are very much alive to the possibilities of the active resistance of whole peoples. Thus we find the Moscow radio blazoning forth appeals for armed revolt against the Germans. In contrast the radios controlled by the official representatives of the peoples suffering from Nazi tyranny have been broadcasting the slogans 'be patient', 'the hour of deliverance is at hand'; 'passive resistance'; 'sabotage'. In one occupied country after another leaders of active armed resistance have arisen who have rallied around them the support, either passive or active, of the majority of the oppressed people. The picture has been different in each country according to the local conditions, but in every case it has always been the Soviet Government that has been the first great power to give encouragement and moral support to the proponents of active resistance.

London and Washington on the contrary have seemed to lag behind and only accept the inevitable when it is clear that the movement encouraged by Moscow is gaining overwhelming popular support of the peoples affected. This situation in different aspects has been duplicated in France, in Poland, in Yugoslavia, and is now shaping up in Greece.

All this means what I have endeavoured to point out in previous despatches that the moral leadership of the new Europe has passed to the Soviet Union in much the same manner as England had the moral leadership in the nineteenth century when Liberal movements were astir in Europe. The day has passed when this new movement should be considered in terms of ideologies. It is no longer a matter of communism versus capitalism or even socialism versus capitalism. It is rather a struggle of the peoples of Europe to free themselves of some of the vested interests of the past. These vested interests have been throttling the efforts of the peoples to attain that degree of political and economic security they feel will put an end to the miseries which have vitiated the lives of a whole generation. The peoples have been looking to the leadership of one of the great powers and in this way they have been finding it in the Soviet Union. It is up to the real democracies of the West not to lag behind but to keep in step with the progressive movements now preparing the way to a brighter future for the oppressed people of Europe. It is my hope that in the real democracies a powerful mind will emerge to throw a searchlight beam through the fog that is now beclouding the basic issues of this war.

To come down from the Olympian heights to the immediate business in hand – that of winning the war, we have only to point to the experience in Corsica after the armistice with Italy to illustrate the number of British, American and Canadian lives that can be saved if only our strategies can be brought to realise the military value of the active armed resistance of the people of occupied territory. Marshall Stalin is the only allied leader who is under no illusion on this score. Experience has taught him that while it takes a uniform to make a soldier it is the spirit within that makes a fighter.[4]

E. Conclusion to George Hill's report to SOE about the Soviet Union's post-war intentions, 9 March 1944.

The Soviet leaders are immensely gratified at the place the Soviet Union had attained as one of the great powers. They realise and want to make use, in co-operation with the other great powers, of the great influence which this gives them on world affairs. They have commenced to act with that sense of responsibility which consciousness of great power usually confers. More than people outside, they are very much aware of the economic weaknesses of the Soviet Union. They know that the future is theirs if they only have the time and the freedom from threats of war to build up the country and to make its strength, measured in terms of national income, commensurate with its resources. They probably also believe that as they are able to confer on the peoples of the Soviet Union the blessings of a plentiful supply of consumers' goods, of a higher standard of living and of marked economic development, the power of attraction to the Union amongst the neighbouring peoples to the West, but more particularly to the South and to the East, may become so strong that they will be able to add to their already huge expanses of territory without provoking the same degree of armed resistance which would now result from any attempts at territorial expansion. Moreover, apart from the old yearning for outlets to the sea, the Soviet Union will have all the territory she needs and the development of the resources of this territory will provide full scope for the energies of the Soviet peoples for many years to come. The little principality of Moscow, when it threw off the Tartar yoke, embarked on a career of expansion, the end of which may not yet be in sight, but for the immediate future a breathing spell appears to be very necessary.[5]

ENDNOTES

The Historical Background

1. www.historylearningsite.co.uk/operation_barbarossa.htm
2. http://greatspeeches.wordpress.com/2008/09/29/winston-churchill-germany-invades-russian-june-22-1941
3. Foot, M. R. D. (1999), op.cit.

The SOE and the NKVD

1. Chamberlain, N. Official paper, 19 July 1940.
2. Smith, G. (1999), *Cambridgeshire airfields in the Second World War*, Countryside
3. Letter by Minister Hugh Dalton to Foreign Minister Halifax on July 2, 1940. Quoted in M. R. D. Foot, (1984), *An outline history of the Special Operations Executive 1940-1946*, London: British Broadcasting Cooperation, p.19.
4. Hue, A. and Southby-Tailyour, E, (2004), *The Next Moon*, Michael Joseph
5. www.our-secret-war.org/interviewees
6. Manderstam, L. & Heron, R. (1985), *From the Red Army to SOE*, William Kimber, London, p. 58
7. The National Archives (TNA) CAB 102/650; Mackenzie, W. M. *The Special Operations Executive History*, pp. 602-3
8. O'Sullivan, D. 'Dealing With the Devil: The Anglo-Soviet Parachute Agents' (Operation 'Pickaxe'), *Journal of Intelligence History* , Volume 4, Number 2, Winter 2004, p. 38
9. O'Sullivan, D. (2004), op.cit. p. 39
10. Hill, G. (1968), op.cit. p. 126
11. TNA HS 7/728, p. 4
12. TNA HS 2/2827 in O'Sullivan, D. (2010), p. 265
13. Granovsky, A. (1962), *I was an NKVD Agent*, The Devin-Adair Company, New York, pp. 155-176
14. McLoughlin, B. 'Proletarian cadres on route: Austrian agents in Britain 1941-43, published in *Labour History Review*, (1997). p. 299; O'Sullivan, D. (2004), op.cit. p. 52-53
15. TNA CAB 120/650
16. TNA KV 2/2827; Foot, M. R. D. op.cit. p. 209
17. Hill, G. (1932), *Go Spy the Land: Being the Adventure of IK 8 of the British Secret Service*, Cassel and Company, London; Hill, G. (1936), *Dreaded Hour*, Cassel and Company, London; Hill, G.A. (1968), *Reminiscences of Four Years with the N.K.V.D.* Hoover Institution Archives, p. 34
18. Hill, G. (1968), op.cit. p. 2
19. Ibid, pp. 4-13
20. Hill, G. (1968), op.cit. p. 13
21. Philby, H. A. R. (1968), *My Secret War*, MacGibbon & Kee, London; Kemp, T. (1983), *Caviar and Commissars: The Experiences of a U.S. Naval Officer in Stalin's Russia*, Naval Institute Press, p. 196; Cunningham, C. (1997), *Beaulieu: Finishing School for Secret Agents*, Pen and Sword

RAF Tempsford

1. Verity, H. (1978), *We Landed By Moonlight*, Ian Allan Ltd, Surrey; revised edition (1995)
2. Fish, R. (1990), *They Flew By Night: Memories of the 801st/492nd Bombardment Group, p. 46*

The SOE and NKVD Agreement

1. TNA CAB 120/650
2. Wheeler, M. (2006), 'Resistance from Abroad: Anglo-Soviet efforts to co-ordinate Yugoslav resistance, 1941-42', *Special Operations Executive: A New Instrument of War*, edited by Mark Seaman, Routledge, Abingdon, p. 107
3. O'Sullivan, D. (2010), *Dealing With the Devil: Anglo Soviet Intelligence During the Second World War*, Peter Lang Publishing, New York, p. 27; Unknown at the time, Kim Philby, Donald Maclean, Anthony Blunt, Guy Burgess and John Cairncross were working in British Intelligence as Soviet 'moles'.
4. O'Sullivan, D. (2010), op.cit. p. 32
5. Ibud, pp. 40-45
6. TNA HS 4/329, 17 September 1941, quoted in O'Sullivan, D. (2004). p. 43
7. Kitchen, M. 'SOE's Man in Moscow', *Intelligence Studies: National Security*, 1997, Vol. 12, July, p. 97
8. TNA CAB 102/650, p. 604
9. TNA HS 4/334
10. O'Sullivan, D. (2004), op.cit. p. 44
11. TNA HS 4/327, quoted in O'Sullivan, D. op.cit. p. 45
12. Hill, G. (1968), op.cit. pp. 14-15
13. Ibid, p. 20
14. Ibid, p. 23
15. Philby, op.cit. p. 8
16. Kemp, T. op.cit. p. 196
17. Hill, G. (1968), op.cit. pp. 33-34
18. TNA HS 4/273, 25 June 1941, S.O.2 (sabotage) service for the U.S.S.R. Quoted in O'Sullivan, D. (2010), p. 17-18; OGPU was the *Ob'edinennoe Gosudarstvennoye Politicheskoya Upravienie* – the USSR's security and political police before the KGB
19. TNA HS 4/327, quoted in O'Sullivan, D. op.cit. pp. 40-41
20. O'Sullivan, D. op.cit. pp. 48-51
21. Ibid
22. Ibid. p. 73
23. Ibid. p. 103
24. TNA KV 2/2827
25. Hill, G. op.cit. pp. 148,153
26. Kitchen, op.cit; Philby, op.cit.
27. Hill, G. (1968), op.cit. pp. 121-2
28. Ibid. p. 147, 162
29. Foot, M. R. D. op.cit. p. 209
30. Hill, G. (1968), op.cit. p. 145
31. O'Sullivan, D. (2004), op.cit. pp. 37-8
32. TNA KV 2/2827, Notes on the Russian Section of S.O.E.
33. TNA KV 2/2827, Notes on the Russian Section of S.O.E. Their codes for Chichaev were D/PR.1, Toropchenko D/PR.2 until Graur took over as second in command when he took over Suvorov's post as D/PR.3 and Captain Yeshin D/PR.4. Major K. Krassowski, D/PR.5, acted as the Soviet Liaison officer until early-1944

Operations Pickaxe I and Pickaxe II

1. http://socialistalternative.org/literature/trotsky/assassination.html
2. TNA K2/2827
3. TNA HS 4/336, 25 November 1941
4. Ibid, 5 December 1942
5. Ibid
6. Ibid
7. Ibid
8. TNA HS 4/340
9. Ibid
10. Ibid
11. Ibid
12. Ibid
13. Ibid
14. Ibid

15. TNA HS 4/340; Richards, B. (1996), *Secret Flotillas*, HMSO, London, pp. 120-22; Foot, M. R. D. op.cit. p. 397
16. Ibid
17. Ibid
18. Author's communication with Steven Kippax and Robert Pearson; Tolstoy, N. (1977), '*Victims of Yalta'*, Hodder and Stoughton, London, p. 67
19. Ibid
20. Ibid, 13 December 1942
21. Ibid (translation)
22. O'Sullivan, D. (2004), op.cit. pp. 54-5
23. TNA KV 2/2827
24. Ibid
25. TNA HS 4/341. Similar forms were found in other Pickaxe mission files.
26. Ibid
27. Ibid
28. Stafford, D. (1983), *Britain and European Resistance 1940-1945, A History of the Special Operations Executive*, Macmillan, with Documents. London
29. O'Sullivan, D. (2004), op.cit. p. 551
30. TNA HS 4/341
31. Ibid
32. Ibid
33. Clark, op.cit. pp. 32, 303; http://www.rafinfo.org.uk/BCWW2Losses/1941.htm
34. TNA HS 4/336
35. Ibid

Operation Coffee

1. McLoughlin, op.cit. pp. 304-5
2. Ibid. p. 305-6
3. TNA HS 2/2827
4. Ibid. p. 306
5. Ibid. p. 307
6. TNA HS 4/347, 31 January 1942
7. Ibid
8. TNA HS 4/336
9. McLoughlin, op.cit. p. 310
10. TNA HS 4/347, 7 May 1942
11. Ibid
12. TNA HS 4/347, 29 August 1942
13. McLoughlin, op.cit. p. 307
14. Ibid
15. McLoughlin, op.cit. p. 307
16. TNA HS 4/347 1 September 1942
17. Ibid
18. Ibid
19. Ibid
20. Kitchen, op.cit. p. 102
21. McLoughlin pp. 308-9
22. TNA HS 4/347
23. Ibid, 7 April 1943
24. TNA HS 4/347 Gustav Story, 20-28 March 1942
25. Ibid, 2, 8 and 16 April 1943
26. TNA HS 4/347
27. TNA KV 2/2827
28. TNA HS 4/347, 14 April 1943
29. Ibid, 17 April 1943
30. Ibid, 20 April 1943
31. Ibid
32. TNA KV 2/2827
33. TNA HS 4/347, 17 April 1943
34. TNA HS 4/337, 19 August 1943
35. Sweet-Escott, *Baker Street Irregular,* p. 117
36. McLoughlin. op.cit. p. 309; http://de.doew.braintrust.at/b225.html

Operation Rum

1. Kitchen, op.cit. p. 100
2. Kitchen, op.cit. p. 100; Hill (1968), op.cit. p. 125
3. TNA HS 4/342, 15 December 1941
4. TNA HS 4/336, 19 February 1942
5. TNA HS 4/342
6. Ibid
7. Ibid
8. Ibid; KV 2/2827
9. TNA HS 4/342
10. Ibid
11. Ibid
12. Clark, op.cit. p. 47
13. TNA KV 2/2827, Philby was secretly working for the NKVD
14. Ibid, 23 April 1945
15. O'Sullivan, D. (2010), pp. 75-6
16. TNA HS 4/336
17. TNA HS 4/379, 15 April 1942; Kitchen, op.cit. p. 100
18. O'Sullivan, D. (2010), p. 83
19. Kitchen, op.cit. p. 100
20. TNA HS 7/278, p. 6
21. TNA HS 7/278, p. 51

Operation Whiskey

1. TNA HS 4/342
2. O'Sullivan, D. op.cit. p. 47
3. TNA HS 4/342
4. Ibid
5. Ibid
6. Sweet-Escott, op.cit.
7. Clark, op.cit. p. 51
8. TNA HS 4/342
9. Clark, op.cit. p. 59
10. McCall, (1981), *Flight Most Secret: Air Missions for SOE and SIS*, William Kimber, London
11. Sweet-Escott, op.cit. pp. 117-18
12. Verity, op.cit.
13. TNA HS 4/342, 22 April 1942
14. Author's communication with Michael Heim, 2001
15. Ibid
16. Chorley, W. R. (1998), *Bomber Command Losses*, Vol. 3, Midland Publishing
17. Bomber Command Losses, Vol. 3, p. 74; www.roll-of-honour.com/Bedfordshire/
TempsfordAircrewLost1942.html; O'Sullivan, D. (2010), p. 77; www.nachkriegsjustiz.at/
vgew/1110_simmeringerhauptstrasse.php

'Die Rote Kapelle'

1. www.permanentrevolution.net/entry/1009; www.spartacus.schoolnet.co.uk/RUStrepper.htm; http://
www.spiritus-temporis.com/red-orchestra/the-trepper-group.html; O'Sullivan, D. (2010), pp. 22-25
2. Ibid
3. O'Sullivan, D. (2010), pp. 89, 136
4. O'Sullivan, D. (2004), op.cit. p. 51
5. Schranfranek, op.cit. p. 41; O'Sullivan, D. (2004), pp. 60, 257-8
6. O'Sullivan, D. (2010), pp. 255; Schranfranek, pp. 33-4

Operations Barsac and Burgundy

1. TNA HS 4/343
2. TNA KV 2/2827, 'Notes of the Russian Section of S.O.E'
3. TNA HS 4/343, 14 May 1942
4. TNA HS 4/336
5. TNA HS 4/343, 24 May 1942
6. Ibid, 30 May 1942

7. Ibid
8. TNA HS 4/343
9. Ibid
10. O'Sullivan, D. (2010), p. 71
11. Clark, op.cit. p. 73
12. TNA HS 4.343
13. Ibid
14. Clark, op.cit. p. 73
15. TNA HS 4/343
16. TNA HS 4/336, 3 August 1943
17. Ibid, 8 August 1943
18. Warmbrunn, W. (1963), *The Dutch under German Occupation 1940-1945*, Stanford University Press, Stanford
19. Ibid
20. Cornelissen, I. (1998), *The Rote Kapelle*, pp. 61, 71; O'Sullivan, D. (2010), pp. 136-7
21. Deacon, R. (1989), *The Greatest Treason. The Bizarre Story of Hollis, Liddell and Mountbatten*, London, p. 123
22. TNA HS 4/338, 31 May 1944
23. Ibid
24. TNA KV 2/2827, 28 January 1947
25. O'Sullivan, D. (2010), pp. 141-2
26. Foot, M. R. D. (2001), *The SOE in the Low Countries*, St Ermin's Press, p. 28
27. Clark, op.cit. p. 75
28. Clark, op.cit. p. 75
29. Clark, op.cit. p. 75
30. www.iisg.nl/bwsa/bios/kruyt.html; O'Sullivan, D. (2010), pp. 127-8
31. O'Sullivan, D. (2010), p. 128
32. www.nisa-intelligence.nl/PDF-bestanden/KluitersDAG2foto.pdf
33. Quoted in O'Sullivan, D. (2010), p. 132
34. Nollau, G. and Zindel, L. (1977), *Gestapo ruft Moskau,Sowjetische Fallschirmagenten in Zweiten Weltkrieg*, Blanvalet, München, pp. 33-35; O'Sullivan, D. (2010), pp. 118-119
35. TNA HS 4/343, 3 July, 1942

Operation Sauterne

1. O'Sullivan, D. (2010), p. 72
2. TNA HS 4/341; 6 February 1942
3. Ibid
4. Ibid
5. Ibid
6. Ibid
7. TNA HS 7/278
8. Ibid, 20 October 1942
9. TNA HS 4/341; Clark, op.cit. p. 114
10. Cornelissen, *Vrij Nederland*, 19 November 1998
11. O'Sullivan, D. (2004), op.cit. pp. 50-51
12. TNA HS 4/341
13. Ibid
14. Ibid
15. Ibid
16. Ibid
17. Marks, L. (2000), *Between Silk and Cyanide*, Harper Collins, London; Foot, M. R. D. op.cit. p. 175; O'Connor, B. (2009), *Return to Holland*, p. 19
18. Ibid
19. Cornelissen, op.cit.
20. http://de.wikipedia.org/wiki/Bruno_K%C3%BChn; O'Sullivan, D. (2004), op.cit. p. 55-6; (2010), p. 154, 158
21. O'Sullivian, (2010), p. 147-8
22. Ibid

Infiltrations and Prevarications

1. O'Sullivan, D. (2010, p. 72
2. O'Sullivan, D. (2004), op.cit. p. 60

3. Ibid
4. TNA HS KV/2/1500 Kopkow's post-war testimony July 1946 in O'Sullivan, D. (2010), p. 79
5. Schafranek, H. & Tuchel, J. (2004), *Krieg im ther. Widerstand und Spionage im Zweien Weltkrieg*, Wien, Picus, p. 41; quoted in O'Sullivan, D. (2010)
6. O'Sullivan, D. (2004), op.cit. p. 52
7. www.ravensbrueckblaetter.de/.../120/9_120.html; http://de.academic.ru/dic.nsf/dewiki/1385746)
8. O'Sullivan, D. (2010), p. 268
9. Oliver, D. (2005), *Airborne Espionage*, Sutton Publishing, p. 99
10. O'Sullivan, D. (2010), p. 78; quoting *Essays on the History of Russian Foreign Intelligence*, p. 389
11. Ibid
12. TNA HS 4/345, 8 August 1942
13. Hill, G. op.cit. p. 208
14. Ibid, pp. 210, 219
15. TNA HS 4/226, 10 November 1942
16. Ibid
17. Ibid
18. Ibid, 24 November 1942
19. TNA HS 7/278, 8 December 1942
20. TNA HS 4/226, 13 December 1942

Operations Tonic and Sodawater

1. TNA HS 4/344
2. TNA HS 7/278, p. 10
3. TNA HS 4/344
4. TNA HS 4/336
5. www.naval.history.net/WW2Memoir-RussianConvoyCoxwain06.htm
6. TNA HS 4/344
7. TNA HS 7/278, p. 17
8. Ibid, p. 18; O'Sullivan, D. (2010), p. 85
9. TNA HS 4/344, 3 November 1942
10. Ibid
11. TNA HS 7/278, p. 21
12. Ibid, p. 22
13. TNA HS 7/278, p. 31
14. Ibid, pp. 32-34
15. Ibid, p. 22
16. Clark, op.cit. p.133-4
17. TNA HS 4/344
18. Ibid
19. Clark, op.cit. p. 134
20. TNA HS 4/344
21. Clark, op.cit. p. 137-8; TNA HS 4/344
22. Ibid, 20 February 1943
23. TNA HS 4/328, 19 February 1943; Kitchen, op.cit. p. 101
24. Clark, op.cit. p. 138
25. TNA HS 4/344
26. Kajetan Bieniecki, (2005), Polish garrisons over Europe 1942-1945. *Poles in Special Operations*, Warsaw pp. 43-44
27. Clark, op.cit. p. 134
28. TNA HS 4/344
29. Ibid
30. TNA HS 7/278, p. 34
31. TNA HS 4/344
32. O'Sullivan, D. (2004), op.cit. p. 58
33. TNA HS 4/344
34. Ibid
35. O'Sullivan, D. (2010), p. 87
36. TNA KV 3/137, 17 January 1947
37. Ibid
38. Ibid
39. TNA KV 2/2827
40. http://en.doew.braintrust.at/db_gestapo_4446.html
41. http://www.klahrgesellschaft.at/KaempferInnen/Koehler.html

42. TNA KV 2/2827
43. O'Sullivan, D. (2010), pp. 89-90

Operations Ararat and Etna

1. Clark, op.cit. p. 159; Nollau, G. and Zindel, L. (1977), op.cit. pp. 161-5; TNA HS 4/337, 20 August 1943
2. TNA KS 2/2827
3. TNA HS 4/337
4. TNA HS 7/278, p. 7
5. TNA HS 6/800, 11 January 1943
6. Ibid
7. TNA HS 7/278, p. 27
8. TNA HS 3/65
9. Ibid
10. TNA HS 3/65, 13 March 1943
11. Ibid
12. Ibid
13. Ibid
14. Ibid
15. Ibid
16. Ibid
17. Ibid
18. Ibid, 21 April 1943
19. Ibid
20. Ibid
21. Ibid
22. Ibid
23. TNA HS 4/337, telegram dated 26 May 1943
24. Ibid, 28 May 1943
25. Ibid
26. Ibid, 4 June 1943
27. Manderstam, L. & Heron, R. (1985), *From the Red Army to SOE*, William Kimber, London, p. 110
28. TNA HS 4/337
29. Ibid
30. Ibid
31. Ibid
32. TNA HS 7/278, p. 27
33. TNA HS 4/337
34. Ibid, 9 August 1943; X = NKVD, Y = Russia, Z = Occupied Allied Countries

Operation Orange

1. TNA HS 7/278, p. 18; TNA KS 2/2827
2. TNA KS 2/2827; Nollau, G. and Zindel, L. op.cit. pp. 161-5
3. TNA HS 4/337
4. Ibid, 18 July 1943
5. Ibid
6. Ibid, 16 September 1943
7. Ibid

Operations Rigi and Jungfrau

1. TNA KS 2/2827; Nollau, G. and Zindel, L. op.cit. pp. 161-5
2. TNA HS 4/337
3. Ibid, 24 August 1943
4. Ibid, 25 September 1943
5. TNA KS 2/2827; HS 7/278, p. 31; O'Sullivan, D. (2010), pp. 97-98
6. Clark, op.cit. pp. 201-2
7. TNA HS 4/337, 18 November 1943
8. Ibid, 11December 1943
9. Ibid, 16 December 1943. Subsequent correspondence showed that some in SOE used the term YMCA (Young Men's Christian Association) instead of NKVD

10. TNA HS 4/337
11. Clark, op.cit. p. 211
12. Nollau, G. and Zindel, L. op,cit. p. 165
13. TNA HS9 566/8, 9 November 1943

Operation Everest

1. TNA HS 3/345
2. Ibid
3. Ibid
4. Ibid, 16 March 1943
5. Ibid
6. Ibid
7. TNA HS 7/278, p. 27
8. TNA HS 3/345
9. Ibid
10. McLoughlin, p. 311
11. Ibid
12. Ibid
13. Ibid
14. TNA HS 4/337
15. TNA HS 4/345
16. Ibid
17. Manderstam, op.cit. p. 113
18. TNA HS 4/337, Telegram 17 November 1943
19. Ibid, 19 November 1943
20. Ibid
21. Ibid
22. Clark, op.cit. p. 212
23. TNA HS 4/337, 10 January 1944
24. TNA KV2/2827
25. Nollau G. and Zindel, L. op.cit. pp. 76-77
26. TNA KV 2/2827
27. TNA HS 7/278
28. O'Sullivan, D. (2010), p. 262-3, 269

Operation Eiger

1. TNA HS 4/337
2. Ibid; TNA HS 7/278, p. 71
3. TNA HS 4/346
4. Ibid
5. Ibid
6. Ibid, 8 January 1944
7. TNA HS 4/228
8. TNA HS 4/338, 14 January 1944
9. O'Sullivan, D. (2010), pp. 100-101
10. Ibid
11. Ibid. p. 100; Nollau, G. and Zindel, L. op.cit. p.54
12. TNA HS 4/346
13. Ibid
14. Ibid
15. Ibid
16. Ibid
17. Ibid, 3 July1944
18. TNA HS 4/331
19. Ibid
20. Ibid
21. TNA KV 2/2827
22. Ibid

The Rising Tension of 1943

1. TNA HS 7/278, p. 47

2. TNA HS 4/337, 17 August 1943 signed with large red X
3. Ibid, 17 August 1943
4. Ibid, 17 August 1943
5. Ibid, 18 August 1943
6. Ibid
7. Ibid
8. Ibid, 20 August 1943
9. Ibid
10. Ibid
11. Ibid
12. Ibid
13. Ibid, telegram dated 29 Sept. 1943; 19 October 1943
14. Ibid
15. TNA HS 4/331, 27 September 1943. The rest of the memorandum can be found in the Appendix B.
16. TNA HS 4/337, 28 September 1943
17. Ibid
18. Ibid
19. TNA HS 4/331
20. Ibid
21. TNA HS 4/337, 1 November 1943
22. Ibid, 1 November 1943
23. Hill, G. *Reminiscences of Four Years with the N.K.V.D.*, p. 189
24. TNA HS 4/337, 1 November 1943
25. Ibid, 2 November 1943
26. Ibid
27. TNA HS 4/331
28. Ibid
29. TNA HS 7/278, p. 67
30. TNA HS 4/337, 27 November 1943
31. Ibid
32. Ibid, 7 December 1943

The End of the Pickaxe Operations

1. TNA HS 4/337, 5 February 1944
2. Clark, op.cit. p. 223
3. TNA KV 2/2827; HS 7/278, p. 85; O'Sullivan, D. (2010), p. 84
4. TNA KV 2/2827, 27 July 1944
5. **Ibid**
6. TNA HS 4/338
7. Ibid, 5 February 1944
8. TNA HS 4/331, 21 January 1944
9. Ibid
10. TNA HS 4/338, 11/12 February 1944
11. TNA HS 7/278, p. 97
12. TNA HS 4/331; HS 4/338
13. TNA HS 4/338, 19 February 1944
14. Ibid
15. Ibid
16. TNA HS 4/331, 12 April 1944
17. Ibid; HS 4/338
18. TNA HS 7/278, p. 89
19. TNA HS 4/350, 24 April 1944
20. TNA HS 7/278, pp. 113-4
21. TNA HS 4/338, 14 May 1944
22. Ibid, 15 May 1944

Major Manderstam's Endeavours

1. Tolstoy, N. op.cit. p. 65
2. Manderstam, L. & Heron, R. (1985), op.cit. pp. 129-30
3. Ibid; Richard, L. (2005), *Black Propaganda: Operation Periwig*, http://www.psywar.org/periwig.
   php
4. Manderstam, op.cit; Marks, L. op.cit.

5. Ibid, pp. 130-31
6. Howe, E. (1982), *The Black Game: British Subversive Operations against the Germans during the Second World War,* Michael Joseph, London
7. Manderstam, op.cit. p. 131-2
8. Ibid, pp. 146-7
9. Ibid, pp. 150-51
10. Ibid
11. Quoted in O'Sullivan, D. (2010), p. 231
12. TNA HS 4/339, 28 September 1944; quoted in O'Sullivan, D. (2010), p. 230

The Yalta Conference and the End of the SOE/NKVD Agreement

1. Manderstam, op.cit. p. 153. Benham managed about eight months in Moscow and died shortly after returning to London
2. TNA KV 2/2827, Notes on the Russian Section of S.O.E.
3. Hill,   G. op.cit. p. 250
4. *Essays on the History of Russian Foreign Intelligence*, p. 397; quoted in O'Sullivan, D. (2010), p. 245
5. Hill, G. p. 253; quoted in O'Sullivan, D. (2010), p. 246
6. O'Sullivan, D. (2010), p. 67
7. TNA KV 2/2827, 'Notes on the Russian Section of S.O.E.'
8. Foot, M. R. D. op.cit. p. 209
9. Manderstam, op.cit. p. 152
10. O'Sullivan, D. (2010), p. 49
11. TNA KV 2/2827
12. TNA HS 4/338
13. HS 7/187, p. 9; HS7/287, p. 39
14. HS 7/278, p. 74; O'Sullivan, D. (2010), pp. 278-9
15. Manderstam, op.cit. pp. 150-51

The Legacy of the SAM Mission

1. **Foot, M. R. D.** (1999), *SOE : The Special Operations Executive 1940-46*, Pimlico, London, p. 204
2. Author's communication with Bill Streifer, OSS Society
3. O'Sullivan, D. (2004), op.cit. p. 314; TNA HS 4/328; HS 4/334, Schedule 'A', Autumn 1944
4. Hill, G. op.cit. pp. 160-61
5. TNA HS 4/338, 9 March 1944, included in Appendix E
6. Ibid
7. O'Sullivan, D. (2010), pp. 58-61; TNA HS 4/339, 10 October 1944
8. Kitchen, op.cit. p. 103
9. TNA HS 4/328, 3 September 1945; quoted in O'Sullivan, D. (2010), p. 247

Conclusion

1. TNA KV 2/2827, 12 November 1946
2. TNA HS 4/334.22; O'Sullivan, D. (2004), p. 53
3. West, N. (2005), *The Guy Liddell diaries: 1939-42*, Routledge, vol.1.p.289, 14 August 1942
4. O'Sullivan, D. (2010), p. 103; Schafranek, op.cit. p. 21
5. O'Sullivan, D. (2010), p. 267
6. O'Sullivan, D. (2004), p. 54
7. TNA KV 2/2827, 'Notes on the Russian Section of S.O.E.'
8. TNA CAB 102/650, p. 604; Mackenzie, W. M., Section V, *SOE History of Polish Minorities*, TNA KV 2/378
9. TNA CAB 102/650, p. 604
10. Stafford, D. op.cit. p. 70
11. www.nationalarchives.gov.uk/catalogue/DisplayCatalogueDetails.asp?CATID=4138&CATLN=4& FullDetails=True&j=1

Appendices

1. TNA HS 4/343, May to June1942
2. TNA HS 4/337, 27 September 1943
3. TNA HS 4/331, 1 November 1943
4. TNA HS 4/338, 28 January 1944
5. Ibid, 9 March 1944

BIBLIOGRAPHY

Books and Periodicals

Chorley, W. R. (1998), *Bomber Command Losses*, Vol.3, Midland Publishing

Deacon, R. (1989), *The Greatest Treason. The Bizarre Story of Hollis, Liddell and Mountbatten*, London

Clark, F. (1999), *Agents by Moonlight*, Tempus Publishing, Stroud

Cunningham, C. (1997), *Beaulieu: Finishing School for Secret Agents*, Pen and Sword, Barnsley

Essays on the History of Russian Foreign Intelligence, Moscow, Mezhdunaraodnaya Otnosheniia, 1999

Fish, R. (1990), *They Flew By Night: Memories of the 801st/492nd Bombardment Group*

Foot, M. R. D. (1999), *The Special Operations Executive 1940-1946*, Pimlico, London

Granovsky, A. (1962), *I was an NKVD Agent*, The Devin-Adair Company, New York

Hill, G. (1932), *Go Spy the Land: Being the Adventure of IK 8 of the British Secret Service*, Cassel and Company, London

Hill, G. (1936), *Dreaded Hour*, Cassel and Company, London

Hill, G. (1968), *Reminiscences of Four Years with the N.K.V.D.* Private publication, Hoover Institution Archives

Hue, A. and Southby-Tailyour, E. (2004), *The Next Moon*, Michael Joseph

Kajetan Bieniecki, (2005), 'Polish Garrisons over Europe 1942-1945', *Poles in Special Operations*, Warsaw

Kemp, T. (1983), *Caviar and Commissars: The Experiences of a U.S. Naval Officer in Stalin's Russia*, Naval Institute Press

Kitchen, M. 'SOE's Man in Moscow', *Intelligence Studies: National Security*, 1997, Vol. 12, July, pp. 95-109

MacKenzie, W. (2002), *The Secret History of S.O.E.: Special Operations Executive 1940-1945*, St Ermin's Press

Manderstam, L. & Heron, R. (1985), *From the Red Army to SOE*, Kimber

Marks, L. (2000), *Between Silk and Cyanide*, Harper Collins, London

McCall, (1981), *Flight Most Secret: Air Missions for SOE and SIS*, William Kimber, London

McLoughlin, B. 'Proletarian Cadres en Route. Austrian Agents in Britain 1941-43', *Labour History Review*, 62.3 (1997), pp. 296-317

Merrick, K. A. (1989), *Flights of the Forgotten; Special Duties Operations in World War Two. Arms and Armour*, pp. 55-56

Nollau, G. and Zindel, L. (1977), *Gestapo ruft Moskau, Sowjetische Fallschirmagenten in Zweiten Weltkrieg*, Blanvalet, München

O'Sullivan, D. (1997), 'Dealing With the Devil: The Anglo-Soviet Parachute Agents (Operation 'Pickaxe')', *Journal of Intelligence History*, Volume 4, Number 2, Winter 2004, pp. 33-65

O'Sullivan, D. (2010), *Dealing With the Devil: Anglo Soviet Intelligence During the Second World War*, Peter Lang Publishing, New York

Philby, H. A. R. (1968), *My Secret War*, MacGibbon & Kee, London

Schafranek, H. & Tuchel, J. (2004), *Krieg im ther. Widerstand und Spionage im Zweien Weltkrieg*, Wien, Picus,

Seaman, M. (2006), *Special Operations Executive: A New Instrument of War*, Routledge, Abingdon

Stafford, D. (1983), *Britain and European Resistance 1940-1945, A History of the Special Operations Executive*, Macmillan, London

Stafford, D. (1997) *Churchill and the Secret Service*, John Murray, London

Verity, H. (1978), *We Landed By Moonlight*, Ian Allan Ltd, Surrey; revised edition (1995)

Warmbrunn, W. (1963), *The Dutch under German Occupation 1940-1945*, Stanford University Press, Stanford

West, N. (2005), *The Guy Liddell Diaries: 1939-42*, Routledge, Vol.1

Wheeler, M. (2006), 'Resistance from Abroad: Anglo-Soviet efforts to co-ordinate Yugoslav resistance, 1941-42', *Special Operations Executive: A New Instrument of War*, edited by Mark Seaman, Routledge, Abingdon

Websites

http://en.doew.braintrust.at/db_gestapo_4446.html

http://www.harringtonmuseum.org.uk/Aircraft%20lost%20on%20Allied%20Forces%20Special%20Duty%20Operations.pdf

http://www.historylearningsite.co.uk/operation_barbarossa.htm

http://www.iisg.nl/bwsa/bios/kruyt.html

http://www.intelligence-history.org/jih/osullivan.html

http://www.klahrgesellschaft.at/KaempferInnen/Koehler.html

https://www.mi5.gov.uk/output/intelligence-operations-and-cases.html

http://www.nachkriegsjustiz.at/vgew/1110_simmeringerhauptstrasse.php http://www.nationalarchives.gov.uk/catalogue/DisplayCatalogueDetails.asp?CATID=4138&CATLN=4&FullDetails=True&=1

http://www.naval.history.net/WW2Memoir-RussianConvoyCoxwain06.htm

http://www.nisa-intelligence.nl/PDF-bestanden/KluitersDAGversie2.pdf

http://www.our-secret-war.org/interviewees

http://www.permanentrevolution.net/entry/1009

http://www.psywar.org/periwig.php (Richard, L. (2005), *Black Propaganda: Operation Periwig)*

http://www.rafcommands.com/cgi-bin/dcforum/dcboard.cgi?az=printer_format&om=274&forum=DCForumID6

http://www.rafinfo.org.uk/BCWW2Losses/1941.htm

http://www.roll-of-honour.com/Bedfordshire/TempsfordAircrewLost1942.html

http://socialistalternative.org/literature/trotsky/assassination.html

http://www.spartacus.schoolnet.co.uk/RUStrepper.htm

http://www.spiritus-temporis.com/red-orchestra/the-trepper-group.html

http://www.tempsford.20m.com/v9976.html

http://www.tempsford-squadrons.info/Newsletter%20files/Newsletter%20Jan%202005v3.pdf

http://www.roll-of-honour.com/Bedfordshire/TempsfordAircrewLost1942.html

Documents at The National Archives (TNA)

HS 3/65 Etna

HS 4/329 Cabinet policy on contacts with Russian Intelligence Service

HS 4/331 Pickaxe NKVD Liaison; operations Rigi, Jungfrau, Eiger, Everest; Russia 1943-1945

HS 4/336 Pickaxe projects

HS 4/337 Pickaxe Projects

HS 4/338 Pickaxe Projects

HS 4/340 Pickaxe I, Anna Ouspenskaya 1941-43

HS 4/341 Pickaxe II, Sauterne (Pavel Koubitsky; Pavel Kousnetsov)

HS 4/342 Whiskey, Rum

HS 4/343 Burgundy, Barsac

HS 4/344 Tonic, Sodawater, Russia

HS 4/345 Pickaxe operations Everest

HS 4/346 Eiger 1943-45

HS 4/347 Coffee

HS 4/358 Soviet agents in Holland 1944

HS 6/799 Pickaxe SOE/Soviet/NKVD relations 1944 in Italy

HS 6/800 Etna

KV 2/2827 SOE and NKVD agreements

KV 2/1500 Kopkow's postwar testimony